A commitment to campaign

WITHDRAWN

A commitment to campaign

A sociological study of CND

John Mattausch

Manchester University Press
Manchester and New York
Distributed exclusively in the USA and Canada by St Martin's Press

Copyright © John Mattausch 1989

Published by Manchester University Press
Oxford Road, Manchester M13 9PL, UK

and Room 400, 175 Fifth Avenue,
New York, NY 10010, USA

*Distributed exclusively in the USA and Canada
by* St. Martin's Press, Inc.,
175 Fifth Avenue, New York, NY 10010, USA

British Library cataloguing in publication data
Mattausch, John
  A commitment to campaign: a sociological study
  of CND.
  1. Great Britain.   Nuclear disarmament movements.
  Campaign for Nuclear Disarmament.   Social aspects
  I. Title
  327.1'74'0941

Library of Congress cataloging in publication data
Mattausch, John.
  A commitment to campaign.
  Revision of author's doctoral thesis (Edinburgh
  University).
  Bibliography: p.
  Includes index.
  1. Antinuclear movement——Great Britain.   2. Campaign
  for Nuclear Disarmament.   I. Title.
  JX1974.7.M334   1989   327.1'74'0941   88–32592

ISBN 0–7190–2908–2 *hardback*

Photoset in Linotron Sabon
by Northern Phototypesetting Co, Bolton

Printed in Great Britain
by Biddles Ltd., Guildford and King's Lynn

Contents

Preface

It is my own belief that nuclear 'deterrence' is a dangerous fallacy and that the threat of nuclear holocaust grows day by day with the unceasing accumulation and proliferation of nuclear weaponry. Faced with this threat, a large international nuclear disarmament movement has arisen. In Britain, the most significant component of this movement has been the Campaign for Nuclear Disarmament (CND) which was founded in 1958, waned in the Sixties, and revived dramatically in late 1979, early 1980. CND is comprised of a wide variety of individuals who wish to lessen the nuclear peril. I have never met an insincere member of CND.

The support for CND comes, however, from only a minority of the population and the membership of the Campaign is not socially representative of the British public: in its ten years of existence as a mass social movement, the revived Campaign has been unable to muster the volume of support which it requires in order to effect its disarmament objectives. In *A commitment to campaign*, I try to explain why CND proves attractive to only a socially specific section of the British population and I consider the structural features of British political life that impede CND and the peace movement in general.

The book takes the following form: Chapters One and Two are largely concerned with theory and method. Readers who dislike theoretical discussions may wish to skip the first chapter and begin at Chapter Two. I should, however, stress that the theory which is developed in the first chapter informs the rest of the work. Chapters Three to Seven are comprised of my analyses of interviews with samples of Campaigners drawn from two local CND groups. The eighth chapter compares my work with other studies of the revived

Campaign and the ninth and final chapter addresses the wider political and sociological implications of my study; in particular, the problems facing CND in the future, problems which emanate from the character of the contemporary British state.

J.M.

Acknowledgements

This book is based upon doctoral research carried out at Edinburgh University between 1982 and 1986 which was partly funded by the Economic and Social Research Council. The research would have been impossible without the kind co-operation I received from the members of New Town and Scots City CNDs and the help and support of my two supervisors, Frank Bechhofer and Dr Donald Mackenzie. Dr Richard Smith and Professor Peter Worsley made useful comments on the study and my long-suffering students at Royal Holloway and Bedford New College helped me clarify my ideas. My sister, Edith Mattausch, did her best to improve my poor English, and Tony Dennis generously helped me with the preparation and editing of the manuscript, which was expertly typed by Diana Pritchard. My family gave me love and support. Naturally, the opinions and judgements expressed in this book are my own, as are any errors and shortcomings. This book is dedicated to my wife, Dipti Mattausch.

1

Middle-class radicals?

Introduction

Between late 1979 and early 1980, the British Campaign for Nuclear Disarmament was reborn as a mass social movement.[1] Although CND is one of the largest mass movements in recent British history, the support which it enjoys is still only drawn from a minority of the population. Moreover, the social base of support for the present Campaign is not drawn equally from all walks of life and the available evidence strongly suggests that this was also true for the original Movement.

In this study, I discuss and analyse interviews which I conducted with systematically selected samples of Campaigners, both activists and lay members, drawn from two CND groups located in markedly different towns. My intention is to show how social factors play a part in the interviewees' decisions to join the Campaign and in the expression of their protest against nuclear weapons. I try to shed some light upon the following questions. First, why it is that CND appears to be peculiarly attractive to a particular minority of the British population? Second, why is opposition to nuclear weapons expressed in a particular way? Third, what relationship does CND have to other facets of British society? In addition, I try to convey to the reader a sense of how the CND members whom I interviewed saw the social world and their place within it. CND, like any other social movement, is largely the product of the members' actions and orientations; if CNDers were to stop campaigning the Movement would, once again, become history. In order to understand the character of CND one must, therefore, examine the sociological characteristics of the Campaign's membership.

In this first chapter, prior to beginning my own analysis, I critically discuss the work of two of the major writers on CND: Frank Parkin

and Richard Taylor. I have concentrated upon these particular
works because they are important contributions to our understanding of peace movements and because, unlike most other academic
studies of CND, these writers drew upon original research data, data
which I wish to use for comparative purposes in this study. (Other
writings on the Campaign are considered in Chapter Eight.) This
critical discussion is a necessary prelude to my own analysis for it
permits me to identify the strengths and insights of these authors
whilst at the same time uncovering potential theoretical pitfalls
which can thus be avoided.

Frank Parkin's 'middle-class radicals'

Any social analyst interested in CND must begin with an appreciation of Frank Parkin's classic study of the original Movement.
Published in 1968, Parkin's *Middle-Class Radicalism* has become
widely known and has the distinction of being the only major study
in which the research was contemporaneous with the first Campaign; the title has entered into the sociologists' lexicon. The
research data and the many useful insights contained within the
study constitute a valuable resource for analysts of the revived
nuclear disarmament movement.

Parkin's study drew upon an analysis of 445 mail questionnaires
completed by youth supporters contacted at the 1965 annual Easter
CND march, 358 mail questionnaires completed by adult activitists
from CND branches throughout the country, and interviews with
branch secretaries and local supporters drawn mainly from London,
Yorkshire and North-West regions. In the Introductory Preface, the
book is presented as 'a study of the social bases of support for a
political mass movement'. Parkin is not concerned with the Campaign's 'general aims and strategies', nor does he intend to give 'an
historical narrative'. Instead, 'the political movement which resulted
is examined here for the light it throws on certain problems of
current interest in the sociology of politics' (p. 1). Moreover, '. . . it is
not CND itself which is of primary interest so much as the theoretical
issues it helps to illuminate. For certain of these issues, but not all,
some other movement might have served my purposes equally well'
(p. 1).

The main theoretical issues in the sociology of politics which
Parkin hoped to illuminate in his study are as follows. First, noting

the studies already done on working-class conservatives, Parkin wished to redress the imbalance of research by considering the 'analogous case of that small minority of the middle class which endorses left wing political and social views' (p. 2). Second, he intended to give 'a consideration to CND supporters' perception of the social structure and their place within it' (p. 3). Third, Parkin believed that 'CND also provides a useful test case for current propositions in political sociology concerning the sources of recruitment to mass movements' and, allied with this, the 'relationship between alienation and recruitment to mass politics will be considered in some detail . . .' (p. 4). Fourth, 'CND also provides a useful laboratory for investigating one other set of problems of interest to the political sociologist – namely the involvement of youth in radical politics' (p. 5).

The foregoing are, then, the main issues and themes with which the author was engaged and, in summary, Parkin presents us with the following portrayal of CND and CND members. In his study, CND is characterised as an exemplar of an 'expressive' mass political movement from which the Campaigners accrue emotional and psychological rewards. The social basis of support for the Movement derives from the highly educated stratum of the middle class and Parkin argues that the members' class location and experiences of higher education have caused them to reject 'certain dominant' societal values; in this sense, they are held to be alienated and likely to engage in a 'deviance syndrome' wherein they have a 'propensity to endorse minority or deviant standpoints'. Their choice of employment reflects their already formed political stance in that they opt for those areas of work, the 'welfare and creative' fields, in which they are least likely to have to compromise their radical ideals. Religious and political members of the Campaign are said to be motivated more by a wish to further their religious-political goals than by any 'rational' assessment of nuclear disarmament. The youth supporters of CND are portrayed as incipient middle-class radicals, attracted to the Campaign by its anti-establishment appeal.

Problems in Parkin's analysis

The primary strength of Parkin's study is his recognition of the need to examine the social base of support for the Campaign – the recognition that social factors shape the character of CND and can be seen to play a part in the recruitment of individuals to the Movement. Furthermore, Parkin draws attention to the socially specific constituency from which the Campaign draws its support and hints at an important distinction between different class forms of politics. However, *Middle-Class Radicalism* is the product of a particular intellectual milieu: in the twenty years since the book was published the discipline of sociology, and the social sciences in general, have witnessed important and profound theoretical developments which call into question the viability of Parkin's theoretical paradigm. Parkin's characterisation of CND and CND members stems directly from the thrust of this theoretical paradigm.

Since the publication of Parkin's study, the contributions of ethnomethodologists, conversation analysts, and the insights of philosophers of language (particularly the writings of the 'later' Wittgenstein) have encouraged sociologists to treat social phenomena as the products of social activity. The recognition of the generative importance of context has pervaded sociological analysis, with the result that many modern theorists, especially ethnomethodogists and conversation analysts, stress the interplay between 'context' and 'agency'.[2] Crudely expressed, social phenomena such as CND are nowadays seen by many sociologists as expressions of continuous accomplishment. This paradigmatic shift means that today's social theorists can operate with a set of conceptions and assumptions which are in marked contrast to the relatively simple approach favoured in the earlier stages of the discipline's history.

Parkin's approach to CND is reflected in his choice of methodology and language (for example, CND would be 'a useful test case', 'a useful laboratory'). His analysis attempted to employ CND as a test case for certain, then current, propositions and arguments in political sociology, and the parameters of these theories and the 'social scientist' stance he adopted inform his whole analysis; they are the limits of his work. In the following discussion, I identify the main consequences of this theoretical paradigm and argue that there are major weaknesses in Parkin's analysis and characterisation of CND and CNDers. The identification of these weaknesses is the necessary prelude to building constructively upon the strengths and insights of Parkin's work.

At the outset, Parkin *a priori* classified CND as a mass *political* movement, and chose not to discuss the Campaign's 'general aims and strategies', (p. 1); an exclusion which is of course related to his intellectual concerns – CND served Parkin as an example with which to explore theoretical issues in political sociology. However, there are two severe drawbacks to this strategy: first, de-emphasising CND's aims and strategies, treating it as one of several 'similar' movements, may lead to an analytical undervaluing of features of the Campaign which are unique; second, it virtually forces upon Parkin a methodological decision (albeit one he might in any case have wished to take), in that he cannot permit the members' own motives to be accorded the status of causes for their actions and must abandon the conscious expectations and desires which would have to be bound up in their aims and which would have to be included in such casual explanations.[3] Abandoning 'aims' in this fashion also involved jettisoning 'beliefs', a serious step in the distancing of the CNDers' experience from Parkin's analytic construct.

This *a priori* classification of CND, and the ignoring of the members' aims, leads Parkin, in the words of Day and Robbins (1987, p. 219), to show a 'consistent unwillingness to take CNDers' motivations on their own terms'. Instead, he assumed that his analysis would reveal the respondents' more profound motives. For example, when considering the question of recruitment to the Campaign, Parkin couched his explanation solely in terms of theories of alienation and completely ignored the members' own reasons in respect of a 'rational' consideration of the merits of nuclear disarmament. Having plumped for explanation in terms of alienation, Parkin then proceeded to adduce evidence to show that his respondents were indeed suffering from this psychological state. However, the answers which the author obtained from his adult sample actually only reveal whether they agreed with certain statements relating to the monarchy, to nationalisation and to their religious beliefs. There is nothing in these answers which, as they stand, tell us why they agreed/disagreed, or why they considered themselves religious. Rather, these responses are interpreted within the framework of the explanatory paradigm of alienation as evidence for a cause of recruitment to the Movement; that is, the meaning of the responses is derived not from anything intrinsic to the answers themselves but from the implications of Parkin's chosen theoretical paradigm.

It was initially assumed that the concept of alienation would allow us to explain recruitment to CND and evidence of such alienation was then sought. Is it reasonable to interpret the respondents' answers in this manner? The responses are taken as evidence of a state of mind which the respondents make no claim to possess and which is presented as affecting all the members in a *similar,* uniform fashion. Could not 'alientation' be experienced in different ways by different people? And what is the formal relation between disagreeing with a statement and being alienated from a value? The respondents were asked whether 'the monarchy is an institution we should be justly proud of?' Cannot one, for example, still value the institution of the monarchy and yet not feel justly proud of it? How many ways are there to feel 'justly proud'? In his analysis of alienation Parkin is trying to discover a *common* attribute which all CNDers share. This adherence to an 'essentialist perspective'[4] squares well with Parkin's 'scientific' stance; all the hallmarks of the classic explanation are in evidence – the search for causal factors, the refusal to be content with appearances and the identification of formative essences which the members are supposed to share.

Parkin's social-scientist approach, coupled with his essentialist position and unwillingness to take the respondents' accounts of their behaviour seriously, has, I feel, the effect of depriving the reader of a sense of the rich creative nature of social enterprise. In particular, we are not given any theoretical space in which to locate an understanding of ethical social behaviour. According to Parkin, such behaviour is to be accounted for by 'alienation' and the 'deviance syndrome' (which also override any 'rational' considerations of nuclear defence policy). The members' consciousness is subsumed to the requirements of Parkin's causal explanation.

In his analysis Parkin characterised middle-class radicalism as an example of 'expressive' politics from which the Campaigners derived emotional/psychological rewards. This *political* classification is used to account for the *moral* nature of middle-class radicalism. The fact that many CNDers saw their actions as a moral response to a moral problem is accepted by Parkin and used in the crucial distinction between instrumental/expressive politics. However, his *a priori* classification of CND as a political movement, and his unwillingness to take the CNDers' account of their reasons seriously, means that moral aims and desires cannot be accorded the status of sufficient motives for campaigning.

Parkin's use of the term 'moral' is somewhat analytically misleading. It is not at all clear that those political aims which Parkin locates within his 'instrumental' category are primarily non-moral. For example, surely it is reasonable to think that the Chartists (cited by Parkin as an instance of a working-class instrumental movement, p. 40) were, at times, primarily orientated to ethical aims such as justice. Material goals may be a means of securing moral ends such as a fair wage. Although Parkin admits that the non-moral instrumental and moral expressive dichotomy is rarely found in a pure form in the real world, he nevertheless employs this pure distinction in his own analysis, inferential conclusions and characterisation of the Campaign.

For Parkin, the term 'moral', a distinguishing feature of expressive politics, is seemingly unproblematic and applicable to a large number of activities; the only attempt at definition is by negative comparison (that is, it is not applicable to those forms of political activity which are addressed to bread-and-butter issues). But Parkin, locked in his theoretical paradigm, forgets that issues are not automatically moral or otherwise. If the first wave of CND activity took on a moral character, it was because the CND supporters *made it moral*; CND was created, and the moral nature of the Campaign was not axiomatic. There is nothing about disarmament or the Bomb which forces them to be moral issues; issues are made by people. Nor were the sort of morals that came to concern CND supporters exactly the same as those which pertain in other social movements. It may seem that instances of moral campaigns all possess a common quality which legitimises the use of the word 'moral' when speaking of them. This view is, however, fundamentally mistaken and is spawned by a misunderstanding of the ways in which linguistic categorisation is accomplished (this point is taken up and developed in later chapters throughout this study).

When Parkin employs the word 'moral' in his analysis, he makes it appear as though all moral ventures can be happily grouped together and simply contrasted with non-moral enterprises (instrumental politics). One important consequence of this procedure is that it robs us of any understanding of the unique nature of CND ethics. Parkin could not, therefore, relate this important aspect of the Campaign to any other facet of British society and he is, thus, unable to develop an adequate sociology of CND. I believe this to be a most serious weakness of Parkin's work, a deficiency which I hope to repair in this study.

Significantly, Parkin chose to discuss the importance of the class and occupational locations of his (male) adult sample in the final chapter of his study. Parkin argues that CNDers initially enter into the job market equipped with a political orientation which is out of accord with the ethos of commercial, capitalist employment. Consequently, they opt for work in the 'welfare and creative' fields, wherein they experience the minimum of conflict between their radicalism and their work; 'the welfare professions provide the kind of milieux most amenable to their political orientations'. Thus, they are held to be *already radicalised* before entering into their chosen professions and their political outlook is 'to be explained not as a result of individuals adopting the humanistic values generated within the professions . . .' (p. 185).

There are three main imbricated flaws in this argument. First, it presupposes a sharp distinction between higher *academic* education and the respondents' world of work. For many of these welfare professions a further qualification (for example, a State Registered Nursing Certificate) is often necessary and in-work training is usual.[5] Parkin does not consider the possibility of his respondents' view developing in the course of their experiences at work (even through eleven per cent of the sample had been to teacher training college – the only category of professional training which is specified in his questionnaire). For Parkin, these respondents already possess a radical political orientation which, presumably, does not alter for the rest of their lives. This *supposition* is not explored or justified by his research. Second, in accord with his essentialist and 'social-scientist' outlook, Parkin *presumes* that all of his respondents will share a single common reason for entering their *chosen* fields of employment. In reality, there are a variety of reasons why people can be found in particular jobs and their reasons share similarities and differences. The evidence which would support Parkin's presumption could only be found by taking the respondents' accounts of their motives seriously; this, of course, is outside the scope of Parkin's analysis. Third, because Parkin does not engage analytically with the members' own perceptions of their world, there can be no attempt to relate their occupations with their radical views. These views must, therefore, remain divorced from the social context in which they were expressed and the distinctive occupational location of CNDers must be explained in terms of an already existing common proclivity.

This prior orientation is, seemingly, to be accounted for by the middle-class CNDers' class position and educational experiences. Parkin argues that, freed from the ideological constraints of deriving their status and life chances from property ownership and imbued with a disrespect for certain dominant social values by their education, the middle-class CNDers' are 'freer' in their choice of political allegiance and will favour 'minority or deviant' issues. This is a problematic argument which could only be supported by a consideration of the members' educational biographies. If the highly educated CND members are 'freer' in their choice of political allegiance, why do they favour 'left-wing' politics? Presumably, they are just as free to support 'right-wing' organisations? And why do they opt to join CND? Clearly, this argument, which rests upon the unproved classification of CND as a political campaign, is the product of Parkin's theoretical paradigm.

Although Parkin has identified an important correlation between occupation, education and membership of CND, he lacks the analytical tools with which to convert this correlation into either a causal statement or a useful heuristic. The development of this heuristic requires an appreciation of the formative relationship existing between context and meaning; this appreciation is absent from Parkin's analysis.

Middle-class radicals?

In conclusion, I have argued that Parkin's analysis and characterisations of CND and CND members, in common with any other study, can be read as a reflection of theoretical perspectives which, although respectable at the time when the book was written, are now superseded by subsequent developments within the discipline of sociology. Parkin's general theoretical stance and essentialist perspective served to produce a picture of the Campaign which must now be seen as inadequate. His analysis divorces meaning from context and does not shed any light upon the unique social creativity which constituted the first Movement. The main arguments and inferences in the study – that CND members are alienated, caught within a deviance syndrome and are already radical prior to entering their occupations, and that CND is a political movement captured by the concept of expressive politics – lack credible theoretical foundation. Parkin's interpretation of his empirical findings is only viable in terms of his theoretical paradigm; there is nothing intrinsic in his data which would support his analytical findings.

Parkin's theoretical perspective led him to devalue and subsume

the members' own motives and perspectives and excluded an appreciation of the ethical protest which was a distinctive feature of the
first Campaign. In his study, CND appears as an autonomous entity
analytically divorced from the activities of its supporters. In turn, the
views and opinions of the members are divorced from the context of
their expression. In order to gain a heuristical purchase upon the
creative enterprise of CND, a radically different approach is called
for: a paradigm whose occupational foundations do not rest upon an
essentialist theory of categorisation and one which relates the
members' account of their campaigning to their social contexts.

A failed Movement?

In the Preface to their retrospective study of CND activities, *The
Protest Makers* (1980), Taylor and Pritchard state:

> . . . this study is not intended as a *history* of the British nuclear disarmament
> movement. Our aim is two-fold: to explore the political and ideological
> dimensions of the Movement and the problems which its experience has
> posed for achieving radical change in modern Britain, and to analyse the
> current attitudes and activities of Movement supporters some twenty years
> later. On the basis of a questionnaire completed by over 400 'core activists',
> and in-depth interviews with leading figures in the Movement, we try to
> analyse and discuss these themes and draw some conclusions about the
> nature, purpose and significant of the Movement. The focus is thus political
> and sociological rather than historical. (p. vii, Preface)

Although this focus may appear somewhat similar to Parkin's, the
actual flavour of the two books is markedly different for the following reasons. First, Taylor and Pritchard's research was mainly
carried out in 1977 and 1978 and, consequently, their analysis is a
retrospective study of an historical phenomenon; equally impor-
tantly, their research was conducted before the recent resurgence of
CND activity. Second, despite the disclaimer in the Preface, the
authors are concerned to locate the original Campaign within its
specific historical context and are very knowledgeable about the
development of CND and its various ideologies. Third, the book is
not an isolated study but is, at least in part, an extension of research
carried out by Richard Taylor for his impressive Ph.D. thesis (revealingly entitled 'The British Disarmament Movement of 1958/65 and
its legacy to the Left').[6] Fourth, the authors have a clear allegiance to
both socialist politics and the disarmament cause.

Before beginning my discussion of the book, two general observations need to be made. First, it is well-presented and informative and includes much interesting and useful historical information concerning the Movement and the Movement's leadership. Second, the authors are clearly well acquainted with their material and are aware of the historical origins of the Campaign. These are virtues which are not affected by the theoretical value of their analysis.

Taylor and Pritchard's study is essentially an analysis of what the authors took to be a *failed* social movement and much of their work is concerned to show that, because of the internal conflicting ideological components contained within the Movement, CND was unable to develop an adequate *political* strategy with which to secure disarmament objectives. It is the author's contention that none of the various ideological factions within the Campaign was able to formulate a strategy which could effect the necessary *political* changes. Neither the advocates of Direct Action, nor the New Left (as it was then), nor the Labour Party supporters within the Movement were able to overcome the inherently middle-class nature and moralistic character of the Campaign in order to build a Movement involving working-class support which appreciated the need for economic realities to be incorporated within disarmament strategies. CND failed because it could not find a viable socialist articulation; 'The great moral and emotive spasm which gave rise to the Movement in 1958 did not find adequate political expression' (p. 131). This portrayal of CND as a failed social movement is rather less credible in the light of the dramatic resurgence of both interest and activity since late 1979. However, it should be remembered that Taylor and Pritchard carried out the bulk of their research between 1977 and 1978 and they therefore felt able to state that:

With the election of the first Wilson Government in 1964 CND rapidly disappeared from the public scene: the Aldermaston March, and other mass rallies, continued to be organized throughout the late 1960s – and CND became one of the constituent organisations of the Anti-Vietnam War Movement – but its days as a *mass movement* had ended by 1964/5. (p. 137)

Nevertheless, such unfortunate statements are not solely the consequence of ill luck; in part, they are a logical product of the author's theoretical and political perspectives.

Taylor and Pritchard argue that the impetus for the rise of CND came not only from a greater appreciation of the nuclear threat, but also because in the late Fifties certain political and social events had left a gap within British political life. The failure of the Labour Party radically to restructure Britain in a socialist mould, the 1956 Hungarian uprising and the Suez fiasco had produced 'an increased scepticism and mistrust of the old ideologies and the old institutions' combined with 'a heightened political atmosphere' (p. 3). Thus, historically specific events engendered a distrust of existing politics and an increased political consciousness. In addition, the authors also cite two other related historical factors which may be seen as contributory: 'the growth of a new and unique youth culture' and the publication of the Sandys White Paper on British 'defence' policy (which 'affirmed vigorously the need for an *independent* British nuclear deterrent' whilst publicly recognising the inability of the government to defend the British population from nuclear attack) (p. 5). So 'By 1956 the time was indeed ripe for a "new kind of politics" to rekindle the idealism and commitment of the radical strata in British society' (p. 2).

These events of the late Fifties created a political vacuum, 'a vacuum which CND was shortly to fill' (p. 5). Taylor and Pritchard go on to cite four episodes which occurred in the aumtumn of 1957 and which acted as catalysts to the formation of the Campaign: first, the launching of the Russian Sputnik; second, Professor G. F. Kennan's Reith Lectures in which he argued against the 'hard-line' Cold-War orientation of Dulles' American policy'; third, Aneurin Bevan's denouncement of unilateralist policy at the 1957 Labour Party Annual Conference and, fourth, J. B. Priestley's moral 'call to arms' in the *New Statesman*[7] which led to the famous meeting of concerned intellectuals at Canon Collin's home on 16 January 1958 and the subsequent, surprisingly successful, inaugural meeting of CND at Central Hall on 17 February 1958.

Taylor and Pritchard's theoretical perspective on the ¬ise of CND can be characterised as a 'how-possibly' rather than a 'why-necessarily'[8] explanation, in that all the authors attempt is an identification of the historical factors which permitted the Campaign to develop, and it should be noted that whilst the radicalism of some sections of the middle class is taken for granted, the motives of the members are not impugned within this paradigm. However, in order to account for what they see as the failure of the Movement, Taylor and Pritchard are obliged to introduce a *teleological* element into their analysis.

It is instructive to learn that some respondents 'strongly disagreed' with the statement from the questionnaire: 'I believe that the disarmament movement failed in its major objectives between 1958 and 1965 because . . .' Indeed, some respondents objected so strongly to this question that they refused to complete the questionnaire. It is only within the authors' work that the achievements of CND assume such importance; if you are a 'protest-maker' you may be as interested in the quality of *making* a protest as in the *effects* of such protest. If one protests well, but without effect, this does not make one's protest a failure. By orientating themselves to the achievements of the Campaign, Taylor and Pritchard, in common with Parkin, have distanced the reader from the CNDers' own motives.

Although Taylor and Pritchard recognise that, for the majority of the protestors, CND was a moral issue, and although they recognise that the Movement had an undeniable moral character, they are not prepared to treat it as a moral phenomenon. The authors seem to suggest that whereas ethics may be acceptable stimuli for social movements, they will inevitably prove to be an insufficient basis for actual achievements; nuclear disarmament is only obtainable by the recasting of CND in a New-Left mould. Regardless of the validity of this belief, it is clear that this analytical premise will not yield any understanding of the distinctive moral behaviour which is being studied. CND, for the majority of its members, was not a political movement (this is repeatedly acknowledged by Taylor and Pritchard). An act of moral protest can be complete in itself and predicating one's analysis upon the effects of such protest will not further our understanding of the form which disarmament campaigning took in the first wave of CND activity.

For Taylor and Pritchard, the moral character of the original CND is to be explained by an appreciation of the intrinsic character of the nuclear threat as 'a qualitative moral change as a result of this massive quantitative increase in destructive potential' (p. 53), and by the Campaign leaders' reluctance to sully their aims in political waters.[9] However, accepting these arguments, an explanatory lacuna becomes evident for it is still unclear why it was that the moral form of the Campaign should have proved so attractive to a *particular minority* of the population, that minority who were to become CNDers and whose social behaviour constituted the Campaign. In Taylor and Pritchard's analysis, this attraction would have to be explained by reference to the '*political* vacuum' which had been formed in the mid-Fifties – once again, in the authors' theoretical paradigm, there can be no analytical purchase upon the Campaigners' ethical form of protest. In this study, I show that this attraction can be accounted for by the members' social location and that, rather than presuming an already-formed radicalism, this social location can be seen as the generative context of their commitment to campaign.

Conclusion

The studies of Parkin, and Taylor and Pritchard, constitute valuable resourses for analysts of the peace movement and radical British politics in general. Both works contain useful insights and the authors draws our attention to the socially specific basis of support for the Campaign and the ethical manner in which disarmament was expressed. However, these analyses are couched within the parameters of political sociology, employing questionable theoretical suppositions and perspectives. In particular, these analyses tend to take the radicalism of the middle-class members of CND as a given fact or a prior predilection. Their work obscures the creative nature of the Campaign and does not further our understanding of the particular moral form which disarmament campaigning took. Consequently, these authors cannot adequately relate their conception of the Campaign to other aspects of British society; a sociology of CND has not been fully developed and questions surrounding the recruitment of individuals to the Campaign remain unanswered.

In this study, in contrast to the positivistic perspective of Parkin, I shall be considering and analysing CND as a 'form of social life'. I seek to illuminate the creative nature of the Campaign and the ways in which the biographic experiences of the members, whom I interviewed, rendered them peculiarly susceptible to joining the Campaign and expressing their concern about nuclear weapons in a particular form. In this way, the relationship between the social context of the members and the expression of their protest will be clarified without recourse to *a priori* judgements regarding the character and origins of their views and political orientations. Furthermore, I show that the Campaign's social base of support has a significance which was not fully realised in either Parkin's or Taylor and Pritchard's studies.

2

Similarities and differences

In the studies of Parkin, Taylor and Pritchard, the members' own understanding and accounts of their campaigning tend to become subsumed to the implications of the authors' theoretical perspectives. As I have already indicated in the first chapter, in Parkin's work in particular, an essentialist theory of categorisation underpins the analysis and the questions in political sociology which his study addresses. This covert epistemological position generates analyses wherein it is assumed that there will be common, uniform characteristics which, for example, all campaigners share and which licenses them for inclusion into the 'CNDer' category. Although both authors acknowledged that the original Campaign embraced different ideological factions, and recognised this diversity within their analyses, each sub-set of the category (for instance, the Labour Party supporters) is still considered in essentialist terms.

This commitment to essentialism gives rise to conclusions which are plausible only within sociological analyses which are themselves grounded in this theory of categorisation. For example, the form of Parkin's explanation regarding the occupational location of his adult male sample – that welfare and creative professions provide a comfortable sanctuary for the already radical middle class – does not jar the reader when presented as a conclusion to his study. Nevertheless, reflection upon the varied and diverse reasons individuals give for entering particular jobs brings into question the viability of this Procrustean explanation. Why should we presume that only one uniform motive was shared by Parkin's respondents? Such a presumption would be a reflection of the analytical thrust of an essentialist methodology.

All sociological inquiries are informed by a theory of categorisation, although the theory is rarely made explicit. Fortunately, an alternative to essentialism is available to sociologists and social scientists in general. In this study, I will be employing the 'family resemblance' theory of categorisation and the related concept of 'lebensformen' in order to study the revived Campaign. Both of these philosophical arguments are taken from the writings of the 'later' Wittgenstein, writings which helped effect a paradigmatic shift in Western philosophical thought. The influence of this paradigmatic shift has made its mark on sociological theory and it is in part this shift which has rendered obsolete the 'positivistic' approach which prevailed at the time when Parkin embarked upon his study. In particular, 'ethnomethodology', its sibling 'conversation analysis'[10] and the sociological study of science clearly reflect the impact of Wittgenstein's arguments and the development of 'ordinary language' philosophy. These modern schools of analysis have sensitised sociologists to the importance of studying the social world as an accomplishment, a continuous process whereby meaning is continually ratified in specific contexts.

The major spur to Wittgenstein's mature philosophical enterprise came from his realisation that, in his important earlier work, he had been 'bewitched' by language and had misunderstood its character and its relation to the world. Wittgenstein sought to highlight the traps which words and grammar set for us and attempted to point the way out of our language-induced confusions. In so doing, he outlined a profound sociological philosophy.

The 'family resemblance' model of categorisation and the notion of 'lebensformen' are two key linchpins for Wittenstein's later philosophy. It is not my intention, in this short discussion, to elaborate upon the whole of this complex achievement; such an exposition falls far outside the scope and needs of this study. Instead, I shall be utilising the philosopher's work in the spirit in which it was intended: as a corrective to the confusions which result from the 'deceptive pointing' of language. Wittgenstein saw his own work as a 'therapy', as a cure for the ills which he thought beset academic philosophers and it is in his sense that I make use of his ideas.

In the first chapter I drew attention to Parkin's analytical quest for the reasons why individuals became members of CND and for their engagement in what he termed 'expressive' politics. He explained their behaviour by arguing that they were all alienated from dominant social norms, partook in a (uniform) 'deviance syndrome' and accrued 'emotional and psychological' rewards from their political activity. These factors were not acknowledged by the activists themselves; rather, they were deduced by Parkin with the aid of his analytical paradigm. In this paradigm, there lurks the presumption that there will be a *common* explanation for the activists' behaviour and, by implication, this explanation will be valid even if the members themselves are unaware of its existence. Why should we accept the internal logic of this paradigm?

The bedrock of this approach can be found in Parkin's presentation and use of terms such as 'CND' and 'Movement'. In his study these terms appear as the *name* for a *something*. Similarly, 'campaigner', 'supporter', etc. are used as the name for a particular sort of individual. Consequently, Parkin can ask: 'Why is it that people become members of CND?' And yet, CND does not have an existence comparable to, say, a building. I can ask, why do people go to X Hotel? But where do people go to when they join CND? CND is a social activity and not an entity; I cannot bring you a piece of CND. Joining CND is a matter of completing a subscription form, being moved by a speaker, having a commitment, etc., etc.

Nevertheless, it is not meaningless to talk of 'CND' or of 'the Campaign' – but the definition and understanding of such categories bedevils sociology. Whole books have been devoted to the ways in which a 'social movement' may be defined and the adoption of a particular definition and theory of categorisation has a marked effect upon the resultant analysis. It is at this fundamental level that the ideas of Wittgenstein are both pertinent and fruitful, allowing sociologists to escape from their self-induced perplexity.

Wittgenstein's solution to the problem of categorisation is most clearly understood by examining his famous treatment of the example of 'games' which he gave in his most important mature work, *Philosophical Investigations Part 1*:[11]

Consider for example the proceedings that we call 'games'. I mean board-games, card-games, ball-games, Olympic games and so on. What is common to them all? – Don't say: 'There *must* be something common, or they would not be called 'games' – but *look and see* whether there is anything common to all. For if you look at them you will not see something that is common to *all*, but similarities, relationships, and a whole series of them at that. To repeat: don't think, but look! – Look for example at board-games, with their multifarious relationships. Now pass to card-games; here you may find many correspondences with the first group, but many features drop out, and others appear. When we pass next to ball games, much that is common is

retained, but much is lost. – Are they all 'amusing'? Compare chess with
noughts and crosses. Or is there always winning and losing, or competition
between players? Think of patience. In ball-games there is winning and
losing; but when a child throws a ball against a wall and catches it again, this
feature has disappeared. Look at the parts played by skill and luck; and the
differences between skill in chess and skill in tennis. Think now of games like
ring-a-ring-a-roses; here is the element of amusement, but how many other
characteristic features have disappeared! And we can go through the many,
many, other groups of games in the same way; we can see how similarities
crop up and disappear.

And the result of this examimation is: we see a complicated network of
similarities overlapping and criss-crossing; sometimes overall similarities,
sometimes similarities of detail.

I can think of no better expression to characterise these similarities than
'family resemblance'; for the various resemblances between members of a
family: build, features, colour of eyes, gait, temperament, etc., etc., overlap
and criss-cross in the same way. – And I shall say: 'games' form a family.

And for instance the kinds of number form a family in the same way. Why
do we call something a 'number'? Well, perhaps because it has a – direct –
relationship with several things that have hitherto been called number; and
this can be said to give it an indirect relationship to other things we call the
same name. And we extend our concept of number as in spinning a thread we
twist fibre on fibre. And the strength of the thread does not reside in the fact
that one fibre runs through its whole length, but in the overlapping of many
fibres.

But if someone wished to say: 'There is something common to all these
constructions – namely the disjunction of all their common properties' – and
I should reply: 'Something runs through the whole thread – namely the
overlapping of many fibres'.

One can summarise the main arguments in these well-known pas-
sages as follows: first, words do not get their sense by being predicated upon a defining 'essence'; second, a practice does not qualify
for inclusion in a category (such as 'game') by virtue of it sharing a
single common quality with the other practices included in this
category; third, the relation between practices with a common name
is best understood as a complex and subtle question of differences as
well as similarities. These arguments are cornerstones of Wittgenstein's philosophical stance with, one would have thought, exciting
promise for sociological analysis. This promise is substantiated by
the philosopher's other main arguments relating to linguistic accomplishment.

If it is not through the apprehension of essences that we understand words, how is meaning achieved? Basically, Wittgenstein
argues that language gains meaning through usage in particular

lebensformen. This German expression is always given the literal English translation of 'forms of life', a convention which I follow in this book. However, a more sympathetic translation would be '*way of life*'.[12] This rendering brings out the sense of people using language as a tool for social accomplishment in their day-to-day affairs, whereas the phrase 'form of life' tempts one to think of 'form' as a somehow independent entity. Regardless, Wittgenstein's argument is that particular forms of life are the homes of the grammar of 'language games'; words and language are tools for doing things with, and they gain their meaning in the social context which they help create.

These remarks on Wittgenstein's philosophical position are not intended as a summary of his extensive and complex arguments, but, rather, as a prelude to a reconsideration of the most beneficial way in which to understand terms such as the 'Campaign'. I hope that it will be appreciated from the brief foregoing discussion that it is not at all clear that an essentialist definition of the practices which we call CND is possible; the onus is upon those who favour this approach to present us with the essence of the Movement. Nor is it clear that CND is the name of an 'anything', or that all the middle-class members of CND would possess a uniform defining quality or state or mind which impels them to join the Campaign. The only way analysts such as Parkin can justify this perspective is by inventing unacknowledged criteria such as 'alienation'. Again, what are we to understand by such terms – yet more problematic essences?

In this study, CND will be considered as a form of life and it will not be assumed *a priori* that CNDers possess a common characteristic. Instead, similarities and *differences* are stressed and any commonalities will be understood as a question of non-essentialist 'family resemblances'. Furthermore, CND will be shown to consist of a composite of only partially complementary ideologies, commitments, practices, etc. However, the CND form of life is not discrete; it is part of the wider British society. To make the Campaign sociologically intelligible requires an appreciation of the ways in which the CND form of life is imbricated within other prevalent social practices.

The research design and methodology

The methodology and design of the original research component of this study reflects the theoretical concerns and approach which I have outlined above. The interviews which I shall be analysing and discussing in subsequent chapters were carried out between April and September 1984 and the samples of members were drawn from two groups, New Town and Scots City CNDs. Prior to interviewing, I had attended meetings of various Scots City groups – specialised groups, locally-based groups and the group on which I eventually decided to focus. In the case of each new group to whose meetings I went, I first wrote to the Secretary asking for permission to attend, explaining that I was a student researching the peace movement and that I wished to understand how the group organised itself. In all cases, permission was willingly granted and I would sit, usually at the back of the room, taking rather poor field notes. In this way, I gained at least an initial impression of the various memberships and how the groups conducted their campaigning affairs. In addition, I read extensively on the historical development of CND, nuclear weapons and nuclear weapons policy. This proved invaluable when it came to talking, especially with members who had belonged to the original Campaign.

At this time, there were three types of CND group active in Scots City: first, groups based in one locality from which the majority of their membership was drawn; second, specialised groups comprised mainly of members drawn from a particular profession or religion; third, the Scots City campaign. This latter group was the largest (350 members), with supporters living in different parts of the city. After some deliberation, I decided for various reasons to concentrate solely upon Scots City CND. I needed a sample of CNDers which could be compared with Parkin's adult male sample, with another 'control' group, and with the available survey data on the Campaign's membership. This requirement ruled out the specialist groups. And, as I have said, Scots City was the largest group and the one with the highest public profile.

Scots City CND has elected officials (a Secretary, Membership Secretary, Treasurer, Chairperson) and speakers, trade-union liaising officers, and various specialist sections. A publicity group produces a monthly Newsletter which is distributed free to all of the members and is sold at outlets such as radical bookshops. A Steering Committee, which meets once a month, co-ordinates and plans the group's activities. General Meetings are also held monthly with an average attendance of about twenty-five, including all the elected officials. In a sense, Scots City CND is an anachronism as it predates the formation of the local groups and, consequently, is in something of a competition with them for new members. The group carries out the normal campaigning activities: leafleting, marches, group out-ings to Scottish and national demonstrations, etc. and liaises with the local, Scottish and national Movement. In addition, they maintain close links with the city's trade-unions.

My second sample of CNDers was drawn from a group in the South of England. This sample was intended to serve as a 'control', a comparative sample chosen from a town markedly different from Scots City; New Town stands in the greatest conceivable contrast to the Scottish city. In common with the Scottish group, New Town CND has elected officers, a Steering Committee and monthly General Meetings (at which the attendance averages about twenty). At the time when this research was carried out, the group boasted approximately 250 members and carried out campaigning activities similar to its Scottish counterpart.

My decision to conduct tape-recorded, semi-structured interviews was a choice of methodology determined by three major factors. First, as a lone researcher, the size of the samples had, of necessity, to be reasonably small if the interviews were to be in-depth. Second, and following on from my critique of Parkin, I was concerned to reflect in my study the members' own perspectives and views rather than interpreting their responses by reference to a supposedly superior epistemology derived from some 'social science' paradigm. Third, because of my own theoretical stance, I was not attempting to quantify values or opinions. However, I did wish to be able to compare easily the quantifiable characteristics, such as age, gender, educational achievements, with Parkin's study and with the other available data on CND members. With these considerations in mind, semi-structured interviews seemed to be the best available methodo-logical option.

Having chosen which CND groups I would study, I then set about obtaining the two samples of members. For both groups the same approach was employed, an approach which developed out of my attendance at Steering and General Committee meetings of the Scots City group. Having attended this group's meetings for about two months, I asked the Secretary if it would be possible to interview a sample of his group's members. He replied that my request would have to be put to a meeting of the Steering Committee which met later that month (and I attended). At this meeting the only objection to my request was made on the grounds of confidentiality. I was able to reassure them that the research would be written in such a way as to preserve the anonymity of those interviewed. Fortunately, one of the members at the meeting suggested that the names of the members to be contacted could be selected from the membership file by the Membership Secretary and that my 'contact letter' to them could be posted by the group. In this way, the confidentiality of the membership file would be respected.

To obtain, the New Town sample, I attended one of the group's General Meetings (having sought permission to do so from the Secretary). At the end of the meeting, in the 'any other business' slot on the agenda, I introduced myself, explained what I was hoping to achieve by my research, and suggested the method of obtaining the sample which had been agreed upon by the Scots City campaign. After answering questions from the members present, a vote was taken which approved my research project by a large majority. Unfortunately, some members of the New Town group were clearly unhappy with this decision, which, I learnt later, was occasioned by personal hostility from one or two members who were prejudiced against sociological research (having, so they alleged, been misrepresented in a past study of the town), and by the perplexing rumour, spread by one of the older members, that I was covertly working for the Government.

In the case of both groups, the Membership Secretary selected every fifth name from their membership records. These members were then sent my letter, asking them whether they would be prepared to help me by being interviewed and asking what date would be convenient (a copy of this letter is reproduced in Appendix A), and a reply-paid envelope. Seventy letters were sent out by the Scots City group (one-fifth of 350) and fifty of the New Town group (one-fifth of 250) of which forty from the former group and fifteen from the latter agreed to be interviewed. In addition, all the elected officials from both the groups agreed to be interviewed. I felt this was necessary as I had learnt from my attendance of various meetings how important these officials were in shaping the character and strategies of the campaigns.

The interviews were conducted either in my university office or in the interviewee's own home or place of work, depending on the respondent's preference. The interviews lasted on average an hour and a copy of the semi-structured interview schedule is reproduced in Appendix B. The schedule was initially 'piloted' on friends, colleagues and postgraduate students pursuing a diploma course in social work. In the light of my theoretical approach, I was concerned in the interviews to examine the biographies of the CNDers in order to gain insight into their social world. In the interviews the members' idiosyncratic politicisations and campaigning perspectives are related to their social context. In this way, their opinions and commitments become sociologically intelligible. Any commonality existing between the members is treated as a question of similarities and differences, as subtle 'family resemblances'.

Unlike Parkin or Taylor and Pritchard, I interviewed both activists and lay members and in the discussion of the interviews I have grouped together respondents in terms of their occupational locations. Upon first reading Parkin, and having subsequently reanalysed the available data on peace movement supporters (see Appendix C), I was struck by the large number of CNDers who were employed in *welfare state* professions: this observation seemed to offer a heuristical purchase upon the correlation between membership and occupation which was highlighted, but unsatisfactorily accounted for, in Parkin's study. Consequently, I have separated the welfare-state interviewees (teachers, doctors, social workers, etc). from those in other forms of employment. The viability of this distinction is borne out by the analysis and, as will become clear, this approach yields a stronger sociology of CND than alternative classification of the members utilised in other studies.

For the sake of confidentiality, all names in this study are pseudonyms and I have omitted or slightly altered personal interviewees details which I felt might prejudice anonymity. Furthermore, I have deliberately not provided any details concerning either Scots City or New Town which, in the analyses, I occasionally abbreviate to 'SC' and 'NT' respectively. The effect of local characteristics upon campaigning practices are brought out, where applicable, in the context of the interview discussions. The interview material has, for the sake of brevity, been slightly abridged from the original research. All quotes are, as far as possible, verbatim, any clarifications which I have added are placed in square brackets, i.e. [. . .], and when referring to CND I use a capital letter, i.e. Campaign, Movement. At first reading, some of the quotations in the discussions of the interviews may appear somewhat disjointed with repetitions and unfinished clauses in the sentences. However, in naturally produced talk, speakers will often start a sentence afresh as they search for an appropriate word or phrase. This striving for expression conveys a sense of intention to the listener and I have considered it worth preserving in the text.

A tacit commitment

I have attended numerous CND and peace group meetings, been on national demonstrations, and have had many lengthy informal conversations with peace campaigners, but I have never heard anyone ask, 'Why did you join CND?' Even when new and unknown individuals attend meetings for the first time they are not asked this question. It would seem, from my experience, that this is not a question that CNDers ask each other – the answer seems too obvious, the question has no place in the CND culture. This is not to suggest that they would not have an answer if asked, nor is it to suggest that it is not a question which they have not asked themselves. Rather, their interest is in the reasons why other people *do not* join the Movement. Once someone has joined, or has come along to a meeting, it is presumed that they share a common reason for belonging, a presumption on the part of the other CNDers. When initially gaining access to the campaigns which I studied, my major licence for entrance into the group was my own avowed concern with the nuclear issue. What was required from me was a sincere commitment to the CND cause; an insincere campaigner is an inadmissable contradiction. And yet, nobody wished to know *exactly* what I was concerned or frightened about – for instance, whether I was motivated by terror of an all-out holocaust or whether I was opposed merely to some particular weapons system such as Trident.

Of course, this tacit sense of common concern and point of view is not unique to CND (although what is presumed in the Campaign is distinctive). For those who attend meetings, what is not said, the opinions which are not voiced, confirm the members' sense of sharing values and aims. And indeed, it seems to be the case that there is a general consensus on social and political issues; for example, an opposition to the policies of the present Government and a belief in the possibility of greater social justice (of my two samples, only one or two respondents expressed any support for any of Mrs Thatcher's administration politics).

Most of the members of the two groups which I studied were not activists, they did not attend meetings and did not regularly take part in campaigning activities. In the case of both groups, most of the campaigning work was undertaken by a small minority of the members. For the majority, the presumption of a shared point of view was not ratified by campaigning experience and, as I will show in the analysis of the interviews, there is a suprising divergence of opinions on questions of disarmament and the nature of the Campaign. However, there is a real sense of commonality, a real sense in which the members all belong to a recognisable form of life. It will be argued in this study that one way to understand how it is that CND attracts individuals capable of creating a sense of shared aims is by examining their wider societal relations, the members' position in the British social structure. Such an approach will shed some light upon the unasked question of why they joined CND and why it is that only a particular minority of the British population develop a commitment to the campaign.

CND has always embraced a very diverse group of individuals and ideologies. As Stuart Hall (1963, p. 225), writing of the first Campaign asked:

Can a political shape be imposed upon or rise from a movement which contains within its ranks such garden varieties as anarchists, non-violent revolutionaries, proto-Trotskyists, New Left socialists, soft shoe communists, constituency Labour Party members, renegade liberals, pacifist old-timers, beatniks and vegetarians, *Peace News, Sanity, Solidarity, Anarchy* and *War and Peace*. By any book, the answer should be 'No'. No single flag, no slogan, no ideology can command so motley an army of the good.

My own impression of the revived 'motley army' is that they are at least as heterogeneous as their predecessors. Certainly, those members I interviewed were distinct individuals. This diversity is as important as any similarities which they shared and should not be neglected for the sake of supposed analytical convenience. As I have remarked, my respondents voiced markedly different views and opinions – even on fundamental matters such as the possibility of achieving nuclear disarmament. Their answers to such seemingly basic questions reflected their idiosyncratic social histories and cannot legitimately be abstracted from these generative contexts. This is important in an analysis of CND, because there is little disagreement about who joins the Campaign. It is widely (even if sometimes implicitly) agreed that, in the words of Chris Rootes (1984, p. 5), CND appears to be especially attractive to 'the highly educated practitioners of the service, welfare and creative professions of the non-market sector of the economy'. The crucial question, however, is *why* should the Campaign prove so attractive to this section of society? To answer this question, I believe that I have as far as possible to let my respondents speak for themselves, and to take their accounts of their biographies seriously.

3

The teachers' commitment

Introduction

All the studies of the peace movement have commented upon the fact that the members tend to be highly educated and that teachers, lecturers and students have a high profile in the Campaign (see Appendix C). Certainly, my own two samples of CND members contained a large number of teacher members, and higher education in some form was the norm rather than the exception for the majority of my interviewees. And yet, there exists no necessary correlation between higher education and CND membership; the majority of the highly educated population do not belong to CND or to any other peace group. How, then, can we account for this tendency?

The teachers' commitment

Geoff Koelbach is a 28-year-old languages teacher who has been unemployed for the past two years. The son of continental immigrants, he has lived in New Town all his life except for a period when he was an undergraduate, a few months when he was employed as a student-teacher and three years spent abroad. His father works as a labourer in one of the light engineering firms in the town and his mother is a housewife. For Geoff, the single most important influence in his life so far has been his experience of university which has, he believes, completely changed his views on society and his place within it, including his opinion of his New Town contemporaries.

At a large Midlands university, Geoff read for a languages degree. Whilst a student, he came into contact with a 'left-wing' lecturer, a man who, according to Geoff, was largely responsible for his change in attitudes. This lecturer started Geoff 'questioning things' and encouraged his capacity for critical thought. Geoff considers the dialogues he had with the lecturer as the stimulus to his own political awakening: 'I suddenly realised that a lot of things were as they were, but I didn't believe they should be . . . they were wrong.' Following on from this, he began to take an interest in politics and chose to study the rise of the German National Socialist Party as a special option. By the time he left university he considered himself a Marxist.

A year studying for the Postgraduate Certificate of Education (PGCE) was followed by a temporary job in a hospital which he enjoyed for its 'charitable' character and for the personal contact and involvement which the work afforded. Geoff left the hospital to take up a teaching post in a large Midlands school, but he soon resigned because of his distaste for the corporal punishment meted out by the other teachers. He then decided to work in Europe, both to gain experience of teaching English and to take the opportunity to travel.

Upon returning to this country, Geoff settled in a small terraced house in New Town with his wife, also a languages teacher, and their two young children. On the morning when I arrived for the interview it was raining heavily and Geoff, who was babysitting, seemed pleased to talk with me. He has been unemployed for the past year and is now reluctantly thinking of returning to teaching children; although he would prefer to teach adults, he has been unable to find any teaching positions in the local colleges of further education. Geoff now considers himself a 'socialist' rather than Marxist as he has come to believe that Marxism is impractical and outdated; a change of view he attributes to his disillusionment with his fellow human beings. He does not belong to a trade-union but intends to join when he starts working again. Nor does Geoff belong to any political party; he has thought of joining the Labour Party but was put off by what he sees as the unnecessarily large amount of bureaucracy and by the likelihood that he could not make enough of a personal contribution, that he would not be able to make his voice heard in the Party. In CND, however, he feels that he will be effective and that he will be listened to.

Geoff and his wife joined New Town CND a year before I conducted the interview. However, his interest in nuclear disarmament dates from the time he spent abroad as an English language teacher which coincided with the outbreak of the Falklands War. As a Briton living abroad, he felt 'horrified' by his country's actions, but unable to protest because he was not doing, and had not done, anything to try to change British political policies. Shortly after returning to New Town Geoff joined his local CND. With two young children and a working wife, his campaigning activities are necessarily restricted to attending the group's monthly General Meetings as often as he can.

Geoff sees nuclear disarmament as the most important issue at the present time. He thinks that the majority of the population do not support CND mainly because they have been brainwashed by an anti-CND media (in particular, television) and also because the British, as a nation, are more conservative than other Europeans. This latter point of view is based on his experiences and observations whilst living abroad as a teacher. The former reason is directly related to his experiences as an undergraduate and teacher.

Geoff is acutely aware of the changes wrought in him by university and it affects how he sees his contemporaries and former friends in New Town: 'It really has moulded my life. When I see other people [whom he knows] who haven't been to university, I think they haven't moved on at all, they're no different.' He sees other people in New Town who have not been to university as unwitting dupes of the media, a media controlled by the capitalist class, and feels that he was lucky in escaping their fate:

I became politically aware when I went to university. Before that I was just like one of the other sheep. I do feel that so many people are just like sheep in the way that they think and I left the pen when I went to university and began to think for myself. Well, basically, I was taught to think for myself. And CND was just a logical conclusion of that, I feel.

Geoff does not believe that the membership of New Town CND is drawn equally from all social classes: 'Certain people aren't represented. It does tend to be people from a more middle-class background, although there are a few trade-unionists there. There are a lot of old people, not very many young people actually.' He thinks that the predominance of older members can be explained by the fact that New Town has 'no sense of community' and that most of the young people are 'alienated, they don't really belong anywhere' and because of this they are 'much more materialistically motivated, it's very materialistic in New Town and very selfish. I don't really like New Town.' In addition, New Town 'is very, very much a young people's town and very working-class in general. And I think the young working-class adult just doesn't relate to CND. I think very few of them have anything in common with the ideas of CND.'

Luckily for Geoff, he no longer counts himself as one of these alienated, media-duped, young working-class adults; although unemployed, he has had the advantages of going to university. As he says, 'It wasn't until going to university that I knew what the [CND] symbol meant.'

Geoff found it difficult to answer my question on his attitude to non-violent disarmament protesting as he thinks it is hard to distinguish between force and violence. He is opposed to violence and claims that he would be a conscientious objector in the advent of a (conventional) war for he does not see himself as an 'aggressive' person. Geoff thinks the main reason we have an arms race is because:

basically the human being is not as intelligent as I had originally thought him to be. I had a lot more faith in human beings, people, before but I've quickly come to realise that they're a lot more stupid than I originally thought, and people just want for themselves and for their own and they don't really care for other people. They're all sort of personally motivated, and I think that's the reason there's total deadlock and there's no progress ever made [in arms negotiations]. Nobody is ever prepared to back down, and I don't think it's ever really going to change.

In addition, Geoff believes there is a tendency for males to be more aggressive than females, a point of view he supports by citing evidence of male aggression which he 'saw' exhibited by young schoolboys at the Midlands school where he worked for a short time. Such male aggression is particularly pronounced, he feels, amongst the British and he is prepared to give some credence to the idea of a link between nuclear armaments and male behaviour.

As a socialist, and a Labour Party voter, Geoff does not agree with any of the policies of Mrs Thatcher's Government. He thinks that the 'cuts in social services and education are tragic' and he opposes privatisation and praises the welfare state. When I asked him whether he thought that CND's stance of not being aligned to any one political party was a good policy, he replied that he thought it was, as CND 'should appeal to as many people as possible' although, again, he believes that, because of political indoctrination through the media, the Campaign cannot effectively voice that appeal. Moreover, his undergraduate studies of Brecht and The Popular Front Against Fascism in the Thirties in Germany have convinced him that CND's present party neutrality is best from 'an organisational point of view', if the Campaign is to secure mass support. Nevertheless, he thinks that nuclear disarmament is 'primarily a political issue'. He recognises that there are moral dimensions to the Movement but, for him, there are secondary considerations. He described himself as an atheist and clearly dislikes religion for 'its hypocrisy'. Too young to remember the first Campaign, his impression of his predecessors is, rather scathingly, of people led by the Church who went on demonstrations 'to have a nice day out, and that's all there was to it'. With his lack of faith in the human race, Geoff does not think that nuclear disarmament is in fact achievable, 'but it doesn't stop me doing what I think is right'.

At first reading, Geoff may appear to be an archetypal 'middle-class radical'; certainly, his profession is 'middle-class'. He voices opposition to what he sees as society's norms and, as there seem to be no tangible rewards for his campaigning activities, presumably he derives purely 'emotional or psychological' gratification from being a CNDer. Such a portrayal is misleading. It is not the case that Geoff is simply 'alienated' in Parkin's definition of the word; rather, he is opposed to what he sees as his contemporaries' materialism and he believes that his values are preferable.

In Britain, education had become the responsibility of the *state* and the majority of teachers are employed by local authorities. Similarly, the training of teachers has fallen into the province of the state. When Geoff decided to become a teacher he had to undergo a period of higher state-administered education and a state-run post-graduate teaching course before he could work in a state school which the children are compelled to attend by legal injunction. In his own sixth-form, Geoff had intended to study geography but a careers visit to a local school convinced him that he would prefer to study to be a teacher and consequently he read languages (for which his family background gave him an advantage), with the intention of becoming a languages teacher. In so doing, Geoff committed himself to a type of state-run apprenticeship and eventually qualified to become a legitimate member of the state; that is to say, he learnt to create properly and legitimately the social relations of the state of which he himself became a part. Not surprisingly, this process has changed his attitudes and perceptions.

At university, Geoff was encouraged to adopt a critical perspective to existing social institutions and ways of living. In addition, through his training as a teacher, he was made to feel responsible for his work, for state policy. This process of internalising state social relations transformed Geoff's life. When he sees his contemporaries, he sees benighted individuals, 'sheep', without his capacity for critical thought, deluded by the media. Geoff believes he has a duty to campaign and to protest and to try to effect political change. In common with most of the members I interviewed, Geoff sees people who do not join CND as unenlightened; the idea that they might have sound reasons for not joining the Movement does not enter into his calculations.

In addition to the personal effects which university wrought, Geoff also received more concrete benefits, for example, the opportunity to travel and the avoidance of the working-class jobs in which most New Town men are employed. Nevertheless, these advantages and opportunities were experienced by Geoff through the phenomenological social relations of a 'student' or a 'teacher' and when he compares himself with his New Town contemporaries he castigates (though does not blame) them for their unthinking materialism, an outlook which he feels himself to have transcended. His contemporaries have 'dominant norms' which he believes are shallow compared with his own.

Of course, Geoff is not a 'typical' teacher. Part of the reason university and teacher training made such a big impression on him can be laid at the door of the class contrast between his New Town upbringing and his teacher status. Like many children of immigrants, Geoff sees education as especially valuable, 'something they can't take away from you', and university permitted him to mix with students from different class backgrounds and with different social perspectives. His views on CND policy reflect his early family socialisation, for example, his reluctance to break the law in the pursuit of disarmament goals. Nonetheless, upon returning to New Town, he no longer felt himself to be typical New Towner; he had become a teacher, a state professional with a set of values different from those of his contemporaries. These values include the belief that although disarmament may not be achievable, it is still the right thing to be a CNDer and to protest.

When asked about his attitude to Mrs Thatcher's Government and its policies, Geoff's first and primary objection was to the cuts in the financing of education and the social services ('tragic'). When considering the Government's handling of the economy, he denounced what he saw as Thatcher's policy of privatising nationalised industries for the benefit of an already wealthy minority. For Geoff,

Thatcher's politics represent an attack on the welfare state which he believes should be cherished rather than sold – especially the educational services, which should be 'planning twenty years ahead for the education of children to their future role . . .' In a real sense, Thatcher's attack on the structure and ideology of the welfare state is an attack against Geoff.

A similar self-awareness of the effects of being a student and entering the teaching profession was shown in an interview I held with Malcolm R., a lecturer in a large college in Scots City. The son of a mining under-manager, Malcolm left school and worked for four years as a mining engineer apprentice in the Northern mining community where his family lived. During this time he took an Ordinary National Certificate (ONC) by day-release and shortly afterwards went to work for a large electrical engineering concern. As a mature student, he attended Runcharge College for a year before becoming an undergraduate at a large Midlands university. Upon completing his first degree, Malcolm undertook an MA in industrial relations and, after carrying out research on health workers, moved to Scots City where he now has a permanent job as a lecturer at Cranmeer College. Thirty-seven years old, Malcolm is married to a senior health worker in a local hospital. An articulate and politically sophisticated lecturer, Malcolm agreed to be interviewed at his college where we sat in a deserted classroom.

Two years ago Malcolm had joined Scots City CND, 'partly over Cruise and partly because my wife joined'. He has never attended any of the group's General Meeings and has only been on one demonstration; his only activity is to take part in the group's 'telephone tree'. He believes that the political élites in the Soviet Union and the United States perpetuate the threat of nuclear war but that such threats are in reality only bluffs designed to sustain these countries' leaders. Non-violent protesting is, he thinks, a highly desirable policy because it encourages others to join the Movement. In addition, if one starts to use violence, 'you throw away an enormous moral advantage'.

A little too young to have been a member of the first Campaign, Malcolm only remembers feeling frightened at the time when his predecessors were marching. However, he had recently seen a television showing of Lindsay Anderson's film[13] about the first CND and he had been struck by, and felt admiration for, the 'disciplined' nature of the Fifties' marches. Furthermore, he felt that, on seeing the film, 'Britain had qualitatively gone down since then', and that he would like to see today's Campaigners acting in a similarly disciplined fashion. When questioned about the social background of CND members, he replied, 'My impression, from Scots City, is of an élite middle-class group, a middle-class group with a reasonable amount of education experience and things like that. I hope they're not, but that's the feeling I get.' He thinks the majority of the population do not belong to CND because 'there's a barrier on joining organisations' and that the British, as a nation, are 'a mass of people who are open to fairly simplistic explanations of what's going on, who don't tend to join groups and are regionally fragmented'. In common with Geoff, Malcolm does not credit the British public with the capacity for forming reasonable views which are opposed to his own.

Malcolm thinks defence 'is far too important' to be left to the government. An ex-Territorial-Army volunteer, he does not consider himself a pacifist and believes it would be necessary to retain a residual conventional force in the event of British nuclear disarmament. He agrees with CND's policy of not aligning itself to any one political party because, 'given that you want to attract as large a number as possible at an early stage, it's a good idea to spread yourself as wide as possible'. Describing himself as 'right-wing Labour' ('I'm right-wing in my economics because I'm a technocrat'), Malcolm has been a member of the Labour Party since he was eighteen years old and has been a member of a trade-union since he started work. The 'extension of home ownership' is the only one of Mrs Thatcher's policies which he thinks is desirable because it 'increases people's stake in their homes' and because he thinks this policy is popular with the electorate. Every other one of her policies he opposes. He criticises Mrs Thatcher for:

cutting for dogmatic reasons, right across the board, when we have got a chance to qualitatively improve our higher education, destroying the state system, for what? To produce a whole lot of people from these élite public schools who we've got chapter and verse research to show that these are the very people in our public service who've understood nothing about technology, nothing about manufacturing and nothing about social policy.

He thinks that Thatcher is a shrewd but not admirable politician, whose popularity rests on her ability to appeal to chauvinistic tendencies in the British; a national failing which he believes was clearly in evidence during the Falklands War.

In contrast to Geoff, Malcolm's experience of higher education has not effected a political awakening; rather, it has been part of his maturing process. He sees himself as upwardly socially mobile and thinks that his years as a student 'made me smoother, more middle-class', giving him the time to study and reflect and the opportunity to mix with people from different backgrounds. Everyone, he argues, has an aggressive side to their character and goes through stages of maturity. He feels that he has now learnt to be less aggressive and would no longer be part of the Territorial Army (although he has no regrets at having been a volunteer when he was younger). Admiring the courage of the Greenham Common peace campers, he bemoans the lack of television coverage they receive. Malcolm's political views were formed at an early age; he was a Labour man before going to university 'and wouldn't vote for anyone else in any circumstances'.

Malcolm is proud of his mining background and his knowledge of engineering which makes him more credible, he believes, in the eyes of the students he teaches on a 'Science and Society' course. Malcolm thinks that 'science and technology have got to be considered quite thoroughly'. Part of this thorough consideration involves the moral aspects and social dimensions of technology. He takes this role as teacher very seriously and endeavours to help his students resolve their moral dilemmas; for example, giving advice to a student who was worried that entering the army catering corps might imply a condonation of killing: 'He knew that'd been in the Reserve Army for years and he came to me for advice. I have to play the role of liberal teacher.'

Interestingly, when I asked Malcolm about the extent of his campaigning activities he referred to his role as a teacher:

I'm also a teacher, I teach a lot of technologists and scientists. I make a point, and I think that's quite a powerful situation to be in. I teach about technology as much as anything . . . one of the lectures I look at is war and the economy and I've actually been accused by the students of putting a particular perspective across! As a liberal, I immediately put another perspective across.

He considers these opportunities to influence the attitudes of future generations of technologists and scientists as being very important and his own role as one necessarily involving moral responsibility.

Unlike Geoff, Malcolm sees CND as being primarily a moral movement: 'I think that's probably its greatest strength, CND has got to make that [moral] point again and again.' For he believes that everybody has got a moral side to their character which will respond to such an ethical appeal. Furthermore:

I think that, as a bargaining tactic, the sort of stand for nuclear disarmament gives us an enormous moral authority which we're pretty short of in Britain. I mean, we haven't got any moral authority as far as I can make out, and it's getting worse internationally, that could give us some moral authority, but I think it was suicidal tactics during the last election [the 1983 General Election; Malcolm is referring to the Labour Party's support for unilateral disarmament].

These views of Malcolm's, that unilateral disarmament gives Britain moral authority, that the moral case is the Campaign's greatest strategic strength and that Britain is in a state of ethical decline, find definite resonance in the ideology of the first Movement and I will be discussing them more fully in later chapters.

I was fortunate to have an ex-student from Malcolm's college in my Scots City sample. Brian P. is twenty-three years old, works for the local authority and is, in common with many others, a nominal member of Scots City CND. He had never been to any of the group's meetings, nor been on any demonstration or any other campaigning activity.

Brian left school and went to work for the local authority where he served his apprenticeship as a fitter, an apprenticeship which included a day-release course at Cranmeer College. Whilst at Cranmeer, he:

met people with diverse views. I come from Brackmoor which is a fairly small village outside Scots City. I'd never heard of CND, well in the papers like, but when you go to college you get interested in things like that because everybody's got an attitude like that. One of the instructors was a member of CND, peace badges and that white dove, and I was curious at the time and I didn't understand anything about it or know anything about it which is why I joined CND. The instructor brought the magazine [Scots City CND Newsletter] and it had the address in and I filled it out.

In comparison with either Geoff or Malcolm, Brian's experience of state education was relatively short-lived and does not appear to have significantly altered his views. He admits to knowing very little about the nuclear issue and thinks this means that he 'dunnae have the same interest I should have . . . it's lack of knowledge I think'. Not a member of any political party, which he thinks are all a 'hotch-potch', he does not have a voting preference and has no interest in politics except for the issue of law and order on which he strongly agrees with the Conservative Party's stance and for which he thinks William Whitelaw is a good spokesman. Although not a pacifist, he is opposed to violence and favours the Campaign's stance of not aligning themselves to any one political party because 'if they stuck to any one party and the party changed its policy, CND would have to change its policy'. This non-aligned stance, he thinks, encourages people from all walks of life to join the Movement. Brian believes the reason the majority of the population do not belong to CND is because of the Campaign's poor public image: 'The image of CND is linked with Greenham Common, student types and y'know lassies in long frocks.' Brian does not think unilateral disarmament is possible but he still considers it worthwhile to protest: 'if you do make a protest at least someone knows you're there and trying; if you make no protest at all you deserve all that's coming to you, it just means you're accepting it. Just making an effort, that's the idea.'

Brian had given in his notice to the local authority the day before the interview and I asked him why. It seemed that he was shocked by, as he saw it, the immorality of his fellow-workers and managers who indulged in minor infringements of the company rules. Unwilling to be part of such unethical behaviour, Brian left his job to become a salesman.[14]

Brian's account of how he became a CNDer is not, I think, uncommon. Simply, his ONC course permitted him to enter into a social environment, the college, where 'everybody's got an attitude like that', an attitude embracing social and political causes including CND and one not found in his home town. For many students, who comprise a large percentage of the Campaign (see Appendix C), joining CND is an opportunity afforded to them by a Freshers' Week stall, and for many the commitment is fairly short-lived.[15] Brian's case is somewhat similar to this: by entering into the social role of a student he was exposed to the extra-curricular attitude of CNDing promulgated by his lecturer. However, Brian's involvement with CND is nominal and he sees it largely as the individual's responsibility to join the Movement, otherwise 'you deserve all that's coming to you . . .' Malcolm, on the other hand, has come to feel that he has a duty because of his role as a lecturer at least to bring the issue to the attention of his students. This is not surprising, for part of being a teacher entails adopting the ideology of the profession and having a sense of duty: in common with other welfare state professions, the internalisation of a sense of duty can turn a job into a vocation.

This notion of a duty to campaign and protest was evident in many of the interviews with teacher members in both of my samples. Donald G. is a 38-year-old teacher, married to a teacher, with parents who are also both teachers. Donald read for an English degree and, after a short period abroad spent doing voluntary work, came to teach in a school in Scots City. Donald's interest in CND is predated by an earlier interest in the anti-nuclear-power cause. He joined Scots City CND after attending a teachers' meeting at his school which 'turned out to be a subgroup of Scots City CND trying to widen interest' in the Campaign.

Whilst an undergraduate, Donald had joined his university's religious society and, although he gradually lost his religious faith, these activities inculcated in him a desire to undertake 'social service'. When I asked him whether being a student had changed his views, he told me that, after joining the religious society: 'I decided my major interest was really social service and I got to the point where I thought, "Why are we doing anything else? Doesn't that matter most?" It was then I started getting involved in summer camps and overseas in Europe, working with physically handicapped children.'

Donald continues to have an interest in social service, subscribing to, and working for, Oxfam on a local basis. He supports non-violent direct action and agrees with CND's non-party-alignment policy 'as most people within CND probably do share widely differing views' and because he does not wish to see nuclear disarmament linked with other issues. He has only attended two of his group's General Meetings, partly because he 'didn't feel part of it' and partly because he is short of time; most of Donald's free time is currently taken up with extensively rebuilding his house.

Donald belongs to a professional teaching association (although not an active member), but he has never belonged to any political party. He would vote Labour at a General Election and describes his politics as 'certainly left'. He deplores the present government's 'general and undiscriminating policy of cut-backs' on funding for the social services. This policy will, he feels, result in a sharp increase in social problems. The only good word he had to say for the present Government's policies was a grudging admiration for their success in bringing down the rate of inflation.

The membership of CND is, Donald thinks, drawn from all walks of life, and he blames the existence of the arms race on a 'sinister

conspiracy' of arms manufacturers who are motivated by the drive
for profit. Unilateral disarmament is 'possible within Britain. I don't
see why a government shouldn't embark on it.' However, he thinks
the British unilateral effort might be subverted by the Central Intelli-
gence Agency or some other similar American organisation.

Donald thinks that schools and teachers in Britain are losing their
former respect and status, a decline which he feels 'is the cause of
many of our problems'. Governments have, especially in recent
years, only 'paid lip-service to the needs of education, not really
recognising their [the teachers'] central place in the values of society'.
Greater government recognition of the importance of education
would mean not only attracting higher-calibre applicants to the
profession and an increase in funds, but, also, a reconsideration of
the dimensions of education; the government should 'enlarge the
scope of education, bringing peace studies into the curricula . . .' as
Donald has attempted to do (in the face of strong opposition from
some parents and teachers) at his own school. Indeed, when I asked
him what he thought was the best way to protest against nuclear
weapons he replied, 'Being in education, I suppose I would say
education.'

For Donald, teaching is not a 'sanctuary' (Parkin's phrase) from
the harsh reality of private enterprise where his social and political
values would place him at a disadvantage. Instead, it is an occupation which best allows him to fulfil his desire for social service; he has
thought of taking other jobs but none appear to offer him the
contact, 'the real contact', with people. For Donald, morality and
politics are part of the human experience and should not be separated, and thus he thinks that CND is 'a moral thing of course, but
political as well . . .' He believes that the majority of people do not
support the Campaign because 'they don't belong *en masse* to any
movement at all'; all populations 'are too ready to pass on their
responsibility to others'. For Donald, such an abdication of responsibility is unacceptable. Both as a teacher and as a CNDer, he feels that
he has a duty to live out his values, values nutured in his undergraduate years and practised through voluntary work and state
employment as a teacher. Rather than a sanctuary from personal
disadvantage, teaching is where Donald feels he can be of most social
service.

Of course, such a growth and consistency of values and perspectives, from undergraduate days through to one's state profession, is

by no means the one and only way in which an individual can be affected by his or her experiences of coming into contact with state training and employment. For example, Mrs Janet Frierley, a 39-year-old married woman, decided, after spending eight years as a housewife bringing up her two children, not to return to office work (she had previously been employed as a copy-typist). Instead, she decided to read for a Bachelor of Education degree, specialised in primary-school education, and has been an infant teacher for the past two years. She finds her new career very satisfying despite the long hours and low pay; as she herself says, 'I wouldn't have gone into teaching for the money!'

Janet joined Scots City CND about three and a half years ago at the same time as she joined the Labour Party: 'I just wakened up to the real seriousness of it.' Her only campaigning activity to date has been attending one demonstration and she has never been to any of the group's meetings. In common with many of the women I interviewed, Janet's home and family commitments do not leave her as much time as she would like for her outside interests. Being an activist, of the kind focused upon by Parkin, and Taylor and Pritchard, is conditional upon having a fair amount of free time to devote to CND. But it does not necessarily follow that those who are not particularly active are any less committed to the disarmament cause.

Janet thinks 'people should stand up and say they're opposed' to nuclear weapons and does not believe that non-violent protesting is realistic as 'inevitably, there will always be conflicts . . .' To support this view, she drew a parallel with the current miners' strike, arguing that if one attempted to disrupt the existing *status quo,* the powerful would inevitably move against you. She disagrees with the Campaign's non-party alignment: 'I'd prefer them to be aligned to the Labour Party'. In fact, she sees CND as properly part of the Party although she admits to not having thought through the implications and effects of such an alignment on the Movement's membership.

Although she is opposed to all nuclear weapons, Janet does not consider herself a pacifist as she believes in 'defence up to a point'. She thinks that Britain could disarm unilaterally and cites the Dutch resistance to the siting of Cruise missiles as an encouraging example of what can be achieved by small countries. For her, the arms race results from 'fear between nations and it's tied in with the capitalist system. I see it very much as tied in with the capitalist system.' Although old enough to have been a member, the first Campaign did not make much of an impression on Janet. She thinks that people then 'were still in a state of lack of knowledge' about nuclear weapons but that today the general public is better informed and the present Campaign leaders are more hard-headed, in contrast to their predecessors who indulged in 'Sunday demonstrations'. Furthermore, today's Campaign has a 'membership which seems to be a more fairer representation. I think it's increasingly so, but I wouldn't be surprised to find that there's not so many working-class people involved in CND.'

A member of her teachers' union and the Labour Party, and a staunch Labour voter, Janet describes herself as 'a humanist Labour Party person' on the left of the Party. She sees capitalism as a 'doomed' system and deplores Mrs Thatcher's championing of individualistic self-sufficiency and 'Victorian values'. For Janet, society should be 'a community of people' and she sees individuals, in a rather Rousseauesque fashion, as the products of their socialisation: '. . . I teach children, see children; they've all got good characters. What happens to them along the way is a different thing.'

Whilst admiring the Greenham Common women, she does not like to attach the blame for the arms race to men and does not believe that girls are naturally more passive than boys, a point of view substantiated by her observations at work: 'I teach both boys and girls and I wouldn't say there's much of a difference.' For Janet, gender differences are more a question of social upbringing which in this country, so she believes, is also responsible for the apathy and lack of commitment which characterises the majority of people who do not belong to CND:

I see that very much as the way young people are brought up, particularly in this country, a lack of education. Most of them leave school in ignorance of even their own political system, how it works, how councils work. How can people make choices if they don't have the education? And I think that leads on to the fact that they don't become political and don't get commitment; they see people and they think 'Oh well, they go in for that sort of thing, they take that upon themselves'.

Janet has become one of the people who 'take things upon themselves', who thinks we have to protest (despite the siting of Cruise). She sponsors a child through Action Aid and sees this as 'part and parcel of the same thing . . .', the same commitment. And yet, her commitment is of quite recent origin; it came about when she decided to undertake a teaching degree. This experience deeply changed her views of herself and of others:

Teaching seems to suit me very well. In some ways it surprises me because I didn't think, hmm [she pauses], I think a lot of people who haven't been through the higher education system when they were young, I think confidence comes into it a lot, and if someone had said to me years ago the position I'd be in now I'd have just thought it was not on because I think people who are not in the higher education system see those who are as being people who have different qualities and it's not until you look back on it that you see with amazement, 'Well, you could do that', and so could just about everyone else you know [she laughs] and the myth sort of dissolves.

Many mature students who have worked for a number of years are able to identify strongly with Janet's experience of higher education. One of the most profound personal effects of university for many mature students and also for many working-class undergraduates is the realisation that the commonly-held belief that those with degrees are more intelligent or gifted than you is, in Janet's phrase, largely a 'myth'. And this realisation does change the way you see them and yourself; in Janet's words:

The world opened up, and I've heard other mature students who had not been in the higher education say the same thing. Suddenly you realise there are not whole areas of society closed to you, that you've almost oh, sunk into that way of thinking, and I think the people I meet, either in higher education, or the professions, you realise the people you know who've had no higher education who are every bit as intelligent and have certain qualities which make them good at this and that – especially teaching – there's people who have a very good way with people, and yet because they haven't been through the higher education system are not in these positions.

Fortunately, Janet did manage to get her teaching degree and part of the hidden curriculum of her education was the dissolution of the élitist myth and the growth of a new-found confidence in her own views and capabilities. Her contact with the state acted as a catalyst to personal change and development, whereby she could see herself as one of the people who 'take that upon themselves'.

Being a teacher can also have other unsought effects which help promote attitudes conducive to joining CND. I interviewed Jenny Armlong at her own home where she was looking after her two children. Divorced, Jenny, in common with Janet, does not have as much time as she would wish for CND and her other activities. She has only been able to attend a couple of local marches and has never been to any of the group's meetings. She joined Scots City CND about three years ago after seeing a showing of *The War Game* and hearing a talk given by the well known peace campaigner, Helen Caldicott. Her joining the group took place shortly after her divorce, a time in her life when she had resolved to 'do things. I'm not just going to sit and vegetate, although in fact I didn't do very much, and it was particularly when the media was saying there wasn't very much popular support for disarmament and I wanted, if nothing else, just to be a statistic, someone who showed they did support this.'

Jenny saw *The War Game* and heard Dr Caldicott speak 'as a mother' and her concern for her children's future prompted her to send her subscription to Scots City CND. She favours non-violent campaigning and the non-party-alignment policy and thinks marches and demonstrations are the best way to protest because 'they raise public consciousness'. We have a nuclear arms race, she believes, because of 'suspicion and fear of other people, and not wanting anybody else to have more weapons than you have and feeling secure in that way'. Jenny thinks that the majority of people do not support CND because the Campaign has a bad image, that it is seen as unpatriotic and suspect. When I asked her whether she thought that the members were drawn from all walks of life, she replied, 'Well, I think people who join CND tend to be younger and perhaps on the left politically, but I'm always really pleased to see people like Joan Ruddock putting forward such a nice middle-class, middle-aged image. I think she's a good spokesperson and that will attract people.' She is also pleased to see Bruce Kent and Church spokespeople on the Campaign's platform as she thinks they counter the Movement's left-wing image, an image which could deter would-be members, and 'the broader the appeal the better'.

Jenny is quite active in her teachers' union, has always voted Labour is the only party to which she feels she could give her support. politicians and feels that, as a breed, they are all liars. Even so, Labour is the only part to which she feels she could give her support. For Jenny, nuclear disarmament is secondary in importance to the current problem of unemployment. Jenny sees herself as somebody who has not 'advanced beyond the Sixties'. Whilst an undergraduate, she 'was very apolitical' and, although she wore CND badges and 'long baggy jumpers', she 'didn't know what it meant'. Jenny attended a university with a strong right-wing reputation, read for an English and Philosophy degree and then enrolled at a teacher training college in Scots City to do a PGCE course. After a year spent abroad teaching English as a foreign language, she returned to Scots City to become a teacher in a secondary school.

In the course of her career as a teacher, Jenny stopped being an apolitical person. Her work engendered a political awakening: 'I began to think about things more after I grew up I suppose, and when I started teaching I became more interested in everything.' Working as an English and remedial teacher, she 'became more aware of the injustices in society and I saw the way that some families live and the way that some kids lived, and I became struck by the unfairness and the inequality of it all.' Subsequently, she joined her teachers' union and CND.

I am not arguing that the cause of Jenny joining CND was solely the result of this political awakening. Clearly, in the interview Jenny saw herself as a Sixties person who had matured, and her concern for her children's future was a major factor in her decision to become a CNDer. Rather, I am suggesting that her experience of being part of the state, a teacher, inadvertently opened her eyes to the class inequalities in British society from which she had previously been shielded by her privileged background. Her experiences of being part of the state had, inadvertently, acted as a catalyst in the gestation of her political and social perspectives. (Jenny is unusual in that, unlike the other teacher members I interviewed, she no longer wishes to be a teacher: 'I don't like being a teacher, I'd rather be more directly involved with helping people.')

Jenny's experiences of teaching produced unsought changes in her social and political perspectives. The same was true, although in a different fashion, for Bill Racmullan who chose to be interviewed in my office in the early evening after he had finished teaching at a Scots City secondary school. Looking like everyone's idea of a 38-year-old teacher, Bill actually had chalk dust on his jacket collar. Bill considers himself an open-minded man who weighs up the pros and cons of an argument and then makes an informed judgement. He joined Scots City CND a year ago having, in characteristic fashion, bought some literature from the group's bookstall and assessed their arguments which 'convinced me I should be doing something more than just sitting on the sidelines'.

Bill thinks that any form of protesting which gains publicity is invaluable although he believes that, in Britain, disarmament protesting must stay within the bounds of the law. The non-party-alignment policy of CND is, for Bill, sound, for he fears that alignment would lead to the Campaign being controlled by a particular party. He sees the arms race as simply a consequence of people wanting to make money and he is optimistic about the chances of Britain achieving unilateral disarmament. Bill is reluctant to call nuclear disarmament the most important contemporary priority. As he explains:

Well, I wouldn't want to put anything in an order of priority as such. I think nuclear weapons is an important issue, I think getting rid of chemical and biological weapons is important, I think the problem of racism is important, and the distribution of world resources; they're all interdependent. I think that if we start off with nuclear weapons first we can go on to get rid of chemical and biological weapons using the [campaigning] techniques we've learnt.

Bill believes that the majority of the British public do not support CND because of our history as a great imperial power which has left a legacy of pride for our armed forces. In addition, he believes that the British are a naturally aggressive nation. When I asked him whether he thought members of CND were drawn from all walks of life, he replied, 'I don't classify people. When I go into a meeting I try not to classify people. So, I don't make judgements as to the membership or where it's drawn from.' Similarly, he refused to answer my questions on whether he thought there was a connection between nuclear weapons and male attitudes as he regarded any answer as a classifying judgement.

The non-classifying attitude to people is linked to his own belief in his capacity to think 'reasonably', which I referred to earlier. Bill spent his undergraduate years as a home student (that is, living at home with his family) and he read for a chemistry degree with a language option. As an undergraduate, he did not feel part of the university's student culture and he certainly did not belong to the first Campaign. At that time, he thought the dropping of the Bomb on Hiroshima and Nagasaki had helped foreshorten the war. Furthermore, he 'thought old Bertie [Russell] was round the twist and the people who were following him were being influenced by this once great thinker who had gone into senility'.

Bill now realises his assessment of the first Campaign was wrong. Leaving university was a disillusioning experience: 'I used to think Highbrough University Chemistry Department was God's gift to the universe, but when I left I realised the lecturers all wanted to go to Oxford or Cambridge because that's where the really good people are.' This idea of the brilliant and profound academic is very precious for Bill:

I'm always attracted to the idea of the medieval scholar who would walk hundreds of miles to sit at the feet of a great teacher. And I asked my wife [who is taking a teaching diploma] how far she'd walk to see her lecturers [he laughs]. I wouldn't have walked very far to see any of mine. They just hadn't got the quality, the intellectual rigour to be great men you could go and converse with and learn really deeply from.

Disillusioned with his lecturers, and having decided that he did not wish to be an academic researcher, Bill decided to capitalise on his language option and take a PGCE course. He tries to live up to his ideal of the 'great teacher' and strives to emulate what he imagines is their way of thinking – the questioning, non-classifying approach. He told me that he thinks 'teaching is a magnificent job. Their [the pupils'] minds are opening up to things and you have the opportunity to get them to think about things, to teach them about some of the more important issues in the world.'

During the course of the interview he told a revealing anecdote about a holiday he had been on with other teachers from his school, superintending the school-children. In the evenings, the teachers had sat around debating and arguing over various issues. Bill had deliberately taken contradictory debating positions on different days, a process which, he proudly assured me, had puzzled his colleagues. Bill, however, thinks that such practices sharpen the mind, permitting one to assess properly the merits of your opponents' arguments. After carefully weighing up the arguments, Bill has now decided that nuclear disarmament is, for him, one of these 'more important issues'.

Bill's experience of university and of teaching are, I feel, particularly interesting and stand in marked contrast to those of Janet whose politicisation involved the dissolution of the myth which Bill cherishes. His answers to my questions, the form his answers took, clearly reflected his admiration for the chimera of the 'great teacher'. His whole attitude, and many of his views, are the result of his internalising and cherishing the ideology of his profession.

Indeed, it would be extraordinary if CND members like Bill were not influenced and affected by their careers and their careers' ideologies. In most of the interviews with state-employed professionals, the interviewees referenced their opinions and views to their career experiences.

Nor does the internalisation of such attitudes cease when the individual is no longer in employment. Mrs Belinda Oumlann is a retired and widowed ex-teacher living by herself in a small New Town flat. In consideration of her age (Mrs Oumlann is eighty-three) the interview was truncated. Belinda, like many older people, tended to wander from the point and, furthermore, I did not wish to overtire her with my questions. However, Belinda was pleased to talk with me, for she feels that those in higher education should be studying issues relating to war and peace.

For Belinda, nuclear disarmament is part and parcel of the wider issue of peace, a goal which she feels is best achieved through the correct education of children. Her concern with peace dates from 1924 when, after finishing at teacher training college, she 'went abroad with a friend to a [student] conference given by the Fellowship of Reconciliation in Denmark, all nationalities present, and the theme was "No More War!" we believed in it, it was 1924', and Mrs Oumlann was twenty-three. At the conference she met her husband-to-be, an English student of law who, after the conference went to do famine relief work in Russia for a year. She described him as 'touched by pacifism'.

Mrs Oumlann eventually married the pacifist English lawyer and settled in this country where she first went to work at Bertrand Russell's progressive school until the birth of her children. When her own children were old enough to attend a nearby pacifist school, Mrs Oumlann began to take in 'problem' children whom the local authorities were having trouble placing. From what she told me, these would seem to be, typically, aggressive, overactive children and Mrs Oumlann's technique would be to have them as guests for a period of some months in her large country house on the outskirts of what is now New Town, where they could enjoy the country environment and benefit from the approach to education which Belinda had learnt at Russell's school. (The motto and theme of Russell's school was, Belinda told me, 'Teach them anything as long as they're interested.') Seemingly, Belinda was very successful at helping her charges; she proudly showed me photographs and letters from some of her former pupils, many of whom still keep in touch, though they have long since grown up.

Too old to attend meetings or actively to campaign, Belinda passively supports New Town CND, which she joined two years ago. For her, this commitment is an extension of her long-standing concern with peace. Not surprisingly, she is in favour of non-violent protesting ('To me, that's a principle, it's not done by violence.') and she agrees with the Campaign's non-party-alignment policy, which she feels helps to increase the membership. Having been a communist in the Thirties, 'it was either communism or fascism', and a Labour Party and Fabian member in the past, she would now vote for the Social Democratic Party (SDP)/Liberal Alliance because she feels that the internal conflicts in the Labour Party are splitting the liberal opposition to the Conservatives. Mrs Oumlann strongly dislikes Mrs Thatcher: 'I can't see how she's justified to do what she does and how she gets her support. She supports the wrong things; she should be supporting the arts, the schools, the hospitals.'

Mrs Oumlann is a little uneasy over the way in which CND members campaign: 'I'm not fully in agreement with them. They should discuss it at meetings' rather than going on demonstrations 'where they have to be dragged away [by the police]'. This reservation is based on her rejection of violence of any sort, for any end. She is puzzled by the fact that the majority do not support CND and by the fact that so many people seem to have aggressive tendencies. She feels that television is partly to blame and thinks that academics should be doing research to find the roots of human aggression. Because of her own experiences and beliefs, she thinks that education is the key to a peaceful future. When I asked her whether nuclear disarmament was the most important issue for her at the present time, she replied, 'No. It's education, education from the family. If a child has a good family life without violence, then they grow up non-violent', an argument which she supported by citing the peaceful nature of her own children and the beneficial effects of her Russell-inspired treatment of maladjusted children. Although retired for over twenty years, this remarkable CND member thinks of nuclear disarmament and peace as inseparably linked in with the philosophy of education which she has practised for the greater part of her life.

Of course, not all teachers or students are as deeply affected by the world of education and its ideologies. As I have already remarked, some student members, whom I have spoken to, seemingly drift into CND as part of their more general and temporary way of life. Furthermore, I am *not* suggesting that all teachers are compelled to join the Campaign solely by virtue of their experiences of higher education (a crudely deterministic view of social behaviour which is at variance with the theoretical position advanced in this study).

Such experiences need to be related to the Campaigners' personal biographies which, as I have tried to show, affect their views on CND and politics and may be just as important an incentive to join the Movement, as this final interview, with a teacher member, clearly demonstrates.

Ellen Bauchline joined New Town CND about nine months ago. The October national rally had brought the Campaign to her attention and she felt (this was at the time of the Falklands War) that 'the way this Government goes, I just *had* to take a stand'. A Quaker and an Oxfam and World Wildlife Fund supporter with an interest in ecological issues, Ellen does not have much time left over to attend her group's meetings and has, in the relatively short time she has been a member, only been on one local march. She believes that disarmament campaigning must be 'absolutely' non-violent, would refuse to break the law in the pursuit of disarmament and agrees with the Campaign's non-party-alignment policy as she feels that the Movement needs the widest possible base of support. She does not agree with any of the policies of Mrs Thatcher's administration and deplores the government's cuts in public expenditure. Ellen thinks that 'the government is supposed to be us' and that the people who think that matters of defence are best left to the government 'deserve to get a bomb on their head'.

Ellen emigrated to Britain from Germany in 1965. Being an arts student in a large German city did not provoke a political awakening in Ellen, nor did it affect her in the ways which the other interviewees in this chapter have described. Her arts school was, she told me, intensively competitive and non-political. Ellen dislikes political labels and has not joined a British political party; she is unhappy with what she perceives as Labour's anti-European stance and with the SDP's defence policy. 'Reluctantly', she would vote Labour at the next General Election. Ellen is not, however, an apolitical person and she has perhaps more reason than most to be concerned about European and defence issues, for her childhood was overshadowed by the Second World War and her parents were persecuted for their left-wing political activities. As she says, 'I was born and bred on politics.'

Ellen thinks that the majority of the public do not support CND because 'an awful lot of people like fighting', and she points to the 'nasty euphoria through the Falklands campaign' as evidence of this unpleasant human tendency. The membership of New Town CND is not, she is sure, drawn from all walks of life, 'sixty to seventy per cent are teachers, possibly more than that', and they are 'the same little crowd' who are involved in the town's other political, social and charitable groups; indeed, 'half the CND members I know as friends, we're that sort of school'.

I interviewed Ellen in her own home in New Town. Clearly, Ellen did not wish to discuss her past with me and I felt it would be both tactless and impertinent to probe for details. In addition, her mother was present in the room during the interview. Nonetheless, from the tone of her voice, and by the tacit assumptions she expected me to make when she referred to her past, I was in no doubt that it was her experiences of the war that had been the most profound factor in the formation of her views. My inclusion of Ellen in this discussion of teacher members is, I hope, a stark illustration of the fact that CNDers who share a common profession can and do have very important and different formative episodes in their personal lives which can act as elective spurs to their joining the Campaign and which can profoundly shape and colour their social and political perspectives.

Conclusion: similarities and differences

At the beginning of this chapter I posed the question, 'How are we to account for the fact that CND members tend to be highly educated and that teachers, lecturers and students have such a high profile in the Campaign?' Clearly, this is a tendency rather than a strict unyielding causal relation, otherwise all people who are teachers would be members of the Campaign, which they are not. Nor does it seem to be the teachers and students from just one particular discipline who feel compelled to join the Movement. Although impressionistic evidence and the history of the first Campaign would suggest that the arts and social sciences[16] are the most fertile breeding ground of CNDers, this is by no means an exclusive academic proclivity, as the involvement of many eminent natural scientists in both the original and revived Campaigns show.[17] Nor is it simply the case that greater knowledge or learning generates a pro-CND attitude; none of the teachers, lecturers or students I interviewed had been persuaded to join CND solely by virtue of a study of nuclear weaponry. Rather, I will argue, there is an affinity between becoming a teacher/lecturer and being a CNDer, that being a part of the welfare state renders teachers able to become, and susceptible to becoming, members of the Campaign.

In my discussion of these interviews I have tried to show that the teacher members in my two samples are individuals with different personalities and idiosyncratic biographies and that their views on CND and politics in general need to be related to their own histories; that, for example, whilst Geoff (the unemployed languages teacher) and Ellen may both be CNDers, the significance of the Campaign is markedly different for each of them. For some, disarmament is achievable, for others not. For some it is a political campaign, for others it is a single issue movement. Some are pacifists, some not, etc., etc. There is *no one common consensus* of views on what CND is or should be. However, for all those I interviewed in this chapter, CND is imbricated within their experiences of (higher) state education and employment.

CND is a created phenomenon; it has literally to be made and without the members' creative endeavours the Campaign would be history, as the first Movement has become. The same is true of the world of education. What is the relation between these two spheres of creative social activity? In the interviews, certain themes can be identified, for example, the teachers' feeling of a duty to protest, a moral concern with social and political issues etc. Furthermore, the interviewees' adoption of these views and attitudes clearly shows the influence of their experiences of higher education. Such experiences either directly generated, helped nurture or were conducive to ways of thinking and behaving which find expression in the interviewees' perspectives on disarmament campaigning.

This is not to suggest that these CNDers do not sincerely wish to achieve nuclear disarmament. I had no reason to think that any of the members I interviewed were anything less than completely sincere in their desire for nuclear disarmament. However, millions of people sincerely wish that nuclear weapons could be abolished and yet they do not join CND or any other peace group. To be a CNDer requires more than sincere concern, it requires the individual to feel that joining the Campaign is appropriate and worthwhile. It is unlikely that this is simply a question of non-joiners disagreeing with the strategies of CND (I am thinking here particularly of unilateralism), as there are many other peace groups with different strategies and campaigning emphases and, alternatively, there is nothing to stop the formation of new disarmament groups with new strategies. In addition, the membership of CND is not drawn from all walks of life; it displays an overrepresentation of well-educated welfare state employees. It seems to be the case that CND is particularly appealing to those who work is a welfare state vocation. This sense of vocation runs deep in the consciousness of welfare state employees and can on occasion inhibit their political actions, as in the case of teachers and nurses who are reluctant to strike at the expense of their pupils or patients; they have an unwillingness to put their own interests before their sense of social duty.

There is no one common quality, or set of qualities, that CNDers necessarily share that impel them to join the Movement. Instead, I suggest that they live within a category of social activity and concomitant attitudes. An understanding of the nature of this category, and an analytical purchase upon it, can be achieved by approaching it through Wittgenstein's 'family resemblance' theory which I discussed in the second chapter of this study.

Let us assign letters to some of the teachers' attitudes to which I have drawn attention. Thus, for example, a duty to protest = A; a responsibility to call the issue to the attention of one's students = B; desire to do social service = C; confidence inspired by becoming a teacher = D; mixing with pro-CND teachers = E, etc. We could then represent the first teacher as:

1. A B C D E

The next hypothetical teacher, although similar to the first, does not feel a duty to bring the issue to the attention of his students, but he does feel the Campaign to be a moral movement which we will call F. Consequently, he is represented as:

2. A   C D E F

The third example is of a Christian student CNDer without attitudes A, B, D or E but with the belief that CND is a moral movement and with a desire to do social service:

3.   C   F

The final example is of a politically-inspired teacher who feels that she has a duty to bring the issues to the attention of her students but that disarmament is only a vain protest against inevitable holocaust (G), and the Campaign is part of a struggle for a better world (H):

4.   B   G H

If we now compare all four hypothetical examples:

1. A B C D E
2. A   C D E F

3.   C   F
4.   B   G H

It will be seen that none of the four CNDers have *all* the attributes in common, and that numbers 3 and 4 have *none* in common.[18] Even so, they all fit within the one category.[19] Seen in this way, it should be clear why it is the case that individuals with different views on disarmament and CND can feel themselves part of a Campaign whose members share the same aims, and why it is the case that questions of specific strategy can provoke disagreement.

Nevertheless, such views and attitudes which underpin the CNDers' form of life are not the unique product of isolated individuals. These are social attitudes, ways of creating the world which arise from wider social practices – in the case of teacher CNDers, largely from the creation of the educational dimension of the welfare state. The vocational aspect of teaching, the internalisation of a sense of duty which spills over into other areas of the teachers' lives, can also be found, with differences as well as similarities, in other welfare state jobs. It is with these themes in mind that I now turn to a consideration of other welfare state employees whom I interviewed in the course of this study.

4
The commitment of National Health Service CNDers

Introduction

In this chapter, I discuss the interviews which I conducted with National Health Service CNDers (doctors, nurses, therapists, etc.) and I show that their experiences of being part of the welfare state has affected them in similar ways to the interviewees in Chapter Three. It is argued that these welfare-state-employed CND members participate in a common form of life which engenders particular social and political orientations and a duty and proficiency to express them.

The doctors' commitment

Dr Jonathan Goole works in the obstetric and gynaecological unit of a large Scots City hospital and is married to a lecturer in child education. He joined Scots City CND approximately three years ago, shortly after he had joined the Medical Campaign Against Nuclear Weapons (MCANW). His work as a National Health Service doctor and his political activities do not leave him much time for disarmament protesting; to date, he has taken part in a 'die-in', heard Dr Helen Caldicott speak, and has attended a few of his group's meetings. Jonathan has not broken the law in the pursuit of disarmament protesting. However, he has recently been reading Gandhi's autobiography (*My Experiment With Truth*) and he admires his example and philosophy and feels that he 'would be quite happy' to be involved in Direct-Action protesting (that is, non-violent protesting) in the future. He described himself as a pacifist, but he was unsure whether he would be able to remain one if he were living in Poland or South Africa at the present time.

Dr Goole thinks that the majority of the population do not

support CND because they remember how close Britain came to being invaded in World War Two and because they believe nuclear weapons are a way of 'guaranteeing our freedom'. When I asked him whether he thought that members of CND were drawn from all walks of life he replied:

Uh huh. I've been impressed by the number of people who seem to me to have a much more solid working-class [background], perhaps in a university town, and also being a member of MCANW. I'm aware that there are a fair number of people from other social classes who are very interested in the issue. It's propaganda that says Tories aren't members, that CND members tend to be left-wing.

Jonathan believes that Britain could disarm unilaterally, although he is worried that the Labour Party (which he sees as the vehicle for achieving unilateral disarmament) would not be elected unless it adopted a more centrist position. Jonathan thinks it would be worth sacrificing some socialist principles in order to achieve disarmament. The son of a 'very anti-communist' Polish immigrant who thinks his son is 'mad' to support the Campaign, Dr Goole describes his own politics as 'slightly right to where I believe the majority of the Labour Party stand at the moment'. He has been a member of the Labour Party for the last decade and attends about five branch meetings a year. His location of himself on the right of the Party stems from his respect for the rule of law and for democracy: 'I'm a great believer in democracy, and I wouldn't do anything to bring the government down. At least I can express my views without worrying about somebody listening at the door.' Consequently, he found the miners' strike action without a (national) ballot 'a difficult issue'.

Perhaps predictably, Dr Goole disagrees with all of Mrs Thatchers Government's policies, especially the cutbacks in spending on health and education. The only exception to this is a reluctant agreement with the Conservative's championing of law and order (in the light of the miners' strike). Like many of the teacher members I discussed in Chapter Three, Jonathan references his politics to his work. For example, when I asked him whether he thought that matters of defence were best left to the government, he replied:

I don't see that the government necessarily has a monopoly view on what's right and I look at health, for example, where it seems crazy that we spend so much money on defence, the Falkland Islands, and yet here we are for the first time in our history, the Scottish Secretary of State actually reduced the budget to the NHS in Scotland and at a time when the population in the country are getting older, and with the medical advances, the NHS needs an extra one per cent just to stand still. And yet we actually had a cut! And so yes, I don't see the Government has necessarily made the right decisions.

For the past twelve years, Dr Goole has been a member of the Hosta Community (a Scottish campaigning Christian group with a retreat on an island off the west coast of Scotland) and he has deeply-held religious views which permeate his political conscious-ness: 'For me, one of the dilemmas is I can't see how capitalism fits in with deep Christian views.' He sees nuclear disarmament as an ethical question; '. . . for me it's a moral issue. Obviously, like all issues in life it has political implications.' The nature of Dr Goole's moral and political outlook was beautifully illustrated in his reply to my question on whether he belonged to any charity, organisation or group working in the Third World:

[Although not a member of any such group] I suppose like a lot of people I'm interested in what goes on in the world. I'm a great believer in, well, really, in these lines of J. B. Priestley in *An Inspector Calls* where he says, y'know, 'anything you do is going to affect everyone else, we're all intertwined, we're not all individuals', and I think obviously at the moment, very obviously, we are all worried about what's going on in the Third World in the sense of, y'know, how we make things more difficult for them and how the gulf is getting wider.

The lines from Priestley's play, to which Dr Goole refers, are from the Inspector's final speech, a warning to the Birling family:

INSPECTOR:
But just remember this. One Eva Smith has gone – but there are millions and millions and millions of Eva Smiths and John Smiths still left with us, with their lives, their hopes and fears, their suffering, and chance of happiness, all intertwined with our lives, with what we think and say and do. We don't live alone. We are members of one body. We are responsible for each other. And I tell you that the time will come when, if men will not learn that lesson, then they will be taught it in fire and blood and anguish.[20]

Priestley, the Vice-President of the original CND in its early years, wrote this play in one week during the winter of 1944/45 and the moral message of this play reflects the hopes of a large percentage of the post-war generation and perfectly captures the geist of CND. Interestingly, it was a moral 'call to arms' from Priestley in 1957 which acted as a major catalyst to the formation of the first CND and these themes – that we are all 'intertwined' and that we all have a moral duty to care for each other – could well stand as a motif for the

CNDers' form of life. And Dr Goole tries to practise his ideals; fighting against the closure of a hospital threatened by cutbacks, donating money to help alleviate suffering caused by the drought in East Africa, joining CND and working as a doctor. For Jonathan, all of these issues are of equal importance, all 'intertwined'.

However, Dr Goole was not born with the Inspector's warning ringing in his ears: 'As a boy, all my heroes were folk who escaped from prisoner of war camps, and I was interested in pilots and flying and my heroes as a teenager were men like Leonard Cheshire and stuff like that. For me, the peace thing is something that gradually developed as I got older.' Nor do his views reflect his parents' opinions; as I have already mentioned neither of his parents supports CND and his father thinks his son is crazy to belong to the Campaign. Similarly, his close friends do not agree with his disarmament views.

Nor was it the case that Jonathan possessed some innate urge to devote his life to the medical service of others. When he had completed his secondary education, Jonathan had no idea which subject he wanted to study at university and, after a completely unhelpful interview with his careers master, decided to read for a chemistry B.Sc. . . . simply because I was good at chemistry at school. That's all there was to it.' During his first vacation from the university he took a job in a commercial chemical laboratory in a nearby city and on his return to his home town in the autumn he informed his father that he was not interested in chemistry and was sure he wanted to change to a medical degree. I asked him what had prompted this change:

It wasn't the chemistry. I quite liked chemistry, and I could do it. But I'd always liked working with people. It was largely, there was one poor lad [in the commercial chemical laboratory] who wasn't getting on particularly well because he couldn't do his physics, he'd failed his physics exams a couple of times, and the boss took me aside and asked me if I'd like to tutor this chap for one hour a day. And I quite enjoyed that and it seemed to me that I was doing something worthwhile and I was doing it with a person and I think the contrast [with his chemistry degree and his likely future employment], and I think I realised I wanted to do something working with people. I think I'd vaguely thought about working with people when I was at school, personnel management, that sort of thing. I don't know why I chose medicine but I've never regretted it.

Dr Goole sees the formation of his social and political views as a long process of development, a process which included the embracing of Christianity. It may be thought that his 'vague' desire to work with people was present before he became a student and an aetiological analysis could be based on this desire. However, this line of reasoning predicates motives upon private innate characteristics rather than social relations. Without the existence of the university and the state-run medical apprenticeship, Jonathan could not have become Dr Goole – and it is as a doctor, as a welfare-state employee, that Jonathan helps others and expresses his political beliefs.

Jonathan joined the Hosta Community, the Labour Party, Medical Campaign Against Nuclear Weapons and Scots City CND after completing his medical training, as a doctor. And it is by reference to his welfare-state employment that he expressess his social and political beliefs (for example, refusing on principle to practise private medicine, concerning himself with hospital closures and joining the MCANW). It is as a part of the welfare state that Dr Goole tries to live out the moral lessons of Priestley and Gandhi and his membership of CND is one facet of this socially practised form of life.

Of course, and as I stressed before, Dr Goole must not be thought of as a stereotypical doctor CND member, nor must his experiences of the state be thought of as in any way the norm. Rather, such experiences and their effects need to be understood as bearing a 'family resemblance' to other welfare state activities which permit them to fall within a common category. Clearly, considerable diversity exists between different CND doctor members.

For instance, Dr Susan Stuart, a GP working and living in a small town on the outskirts of Scots City, joined an evangelical Christian group whilst at university and she still retains her faith (albeit in a somewhat tempered form owing to the lack of a congenial local church). Dr Stuart describes herself as a 'socialist, believing in more equality, but I'm not a communist' and admits to being 'very influenced by [her] husband who, being a social worker, votes Labour'. She joined Scots City CND three years ago and has taken part in a march and has done some door-to-door leafleting. Again, and in common with other women members, Susan has pressing calls on her time from her work and from her two young children.

Unlike Dr Goole, Susan is not a pacifist in that she believes 'in some sort of conventional weaponry'. Too young (at thirty-one) to have been a member of the original Campaign, she has never thought about her Campaign predecessors' fate. Susan agrees with the Campaign's non-party-alignment stand, for she fears that otherwise disarmament objectives might become associated with party policies which the majority find unacceptable. She thinks that the reason the majority of the British public do not support CND is because 'they stick their heads in the sand and think it's not going to happen. If they read a bit more about it and realised how close we are to it they might do a bit more about it.'

Although describing herself as a socialist, Dr Stuart is not a member of any political party and does not consider herself to be a particularly political person. When I asked her what she would call herself in political terms, she replied: 'I'm not very good at labelling myself. Well, y'know, where I live [there are] a lot of the upper, upper people and an awful lot of people, like farm labourers, with incredibly little. I'd like to see a bit more moving together. Again, I'm terribly simplistic about things, but there's a lot of injustice I see.' When I asked which of Mrs Thatcher's Government's policies, apart from defence, she agreed or disagreed with, she replied that there were none she agreed with but that the (then) imminent denationalisation of British Telecommunications was the only example of a specific policy which she objected to: 'I . . . I can't think of anything else at the moment'. It is perhaps fair to say that Susan's politics are more in the nature of a moral commitment to ease inequality rather than a studied political position. When I asked her if she thought that CND was a moral movement, she answered, 'Yes I do. Firstly a moral issue, it's got to be a political issue too. That people can contemplate destroying, it has to be a moral issue.'

Dr Stuart does not believe that Britain could disarm unilaterally. However, she feels that she has a duty to protest against nuclear weapons for the sake of her children. Susan told me that she thought that the reason she first became interested in the nuclear issue was 'probably thinking about having a family and a future, that sort of thing', combined with the publicity that the issue was receiving at the time (1981). When I asked why, if she thought that unilateral disarmament was not possible, she still protested, she answered, 'I don't think I could sort of live with myself without having tried to do something, particularly for my kids, and for their kids I suppose.'

Susan's parents and her brothers are all doctors and she studied medicine at university more as a matter of course than to fulfil any deep-seated ambition. As she said, 'I couldn't say it's a true vocation, it's just the direction I seemed to be pushed into.' At university, most of her time was taken up with studying for her degree and, apart from joining the evangelical group and meeting her husband-to-be, Susan does not think she 'experienced university life' and it does not appear to have been a politically formative period. Her views and attitudes, which she herself characterises as 'simplistic', would seem to derive more from her husband's influence and from a concern for her children's future.

Dr Stuart and Dr Goole, both religious, describe themselves as socialist and are both doctor CNDers. And both, in different ways, are moral in their outlook. Nevertheless, the meaning and form of their politics, religion and morality, and the spurs to the development of their views, are markedly different. Both try to live out their ideals (Susan sponsors a child through the Action Aid charity and contributes to Oxfam). Nonetheless, it is important to realise that their views on disarmament campaigning and their political perspectives bear a resemblance rather than identical duplications. Their respective ways of being doctors, and doctor CNDers, are akin to jigsaw pieces wherein each piece is unique and different from its neighbour and yet each piece shares features that allow it to be part of a single picture.

The remaining doctor CNDer in my sample, also from Scots City, is a psychiatrist with views and opinions which differ and converge with those of Dr Goole and Dr Stuart. Dr Kenneth Macman is acutely aware of the effects of the present Government's cutbacks in public expenditure. Due to retire, he finds himself having to submit a written report to the authorities justifying his work so that the hospital can apply for a replacement for him when he leaves. In the interview, Dr Macman's views and opinions clearly reflected his left-wing politics and his professional training.

Having previously joined the MCANW, Dr Macman joined Scots City CND in 1981. He agrees with the Campaign's non-party-alignment policy for he feels that the nuclear disarmament issue cuts, to some extent, across the boundaries of political allegiance and because CND needs as broad a base of support as possible. Kept busy with his work, Kenneth has only been on a few local marches and has only been able to attend a small number of his group's meetings which he found rather 'cliquey'. When I asked him if he thought that members of CND were drawn from all walks of life, he replied, 'Yes, but not equally representative. I know more people who are middle-class, social workers, socially-conscious types of people from the middle-ranking professional groups.'

Dr Macman is very personally involved with this work and intends to continue on a private basis when he retires from the hospital ('I don't want to give up work at all'). Describing himself as a 'socialist', he deplores what he sees as the present Government's attitude to people:

I strongly disagree with the present administration's attitude towards people. Towards their whole concept, their tendency to depersonalise people and to treat people as merely factors in the means of production, not to be concerned with people as persons but rather, as I say, factors to be considered in evolving policies. I think there's a lack of concern, a lack of caring for persons. And that to me, in my work, is fundamental! And I think that leads to all sorts of policies being adopted for theoretical reasons which don't have a brake put on them by caring for persons.

Kenneth 'would like to see twice the resources coming into the National Health Service. I think that most of the problems [in the NHS] are due to lack of funding and Government pressure.'

Kenneth's professional training has been internalised into a paradigm through which he interprets the world. Thus, for example, when I asked him why he thought it was that the majority do not support CND, he replied:

I think people tend to go on undisturbed as much as possible. I think there's a natural tendency in people not to look at conflict as much as possible and to, to have their own domestic security, unless they're forced to do so. Again, it's something I see professionally; people can cope with conflict unless it dominates them. They'll only come to see me if it takes them over . . . they hear the news and think, 'I don't want to hear about this'. It's a repressive mechanism. The more frightened they are, the more anxious they are, the more they tend to do that. That's the paradox. Again, it's for psychological reasons. The more anxious they are, the less likely they are to become involved, for psychological reasons. Becoming involved makes you more anxious; you become more aware of how awful the threat is.

(As I have already remarked in the context of discussing the interviews with teachers CNDers, the idea that the majority might *reasonably* disagree with the aims of CND does not seem to occur to Dr Macman.)

Similarly, when I asked him why he had chosen to do medicine at university (a necessary prerequisite for a career in psychiatry), he replied:

That's an interesting question. As far as I can look back I've always wanted to, and I've been curious to know where that want comes from and I think I discovered it. I think this had been a secret ambition of my father's. He used to take a funny interest in my medical work, and he used to pretend he knew more about it than he really did and so on. And I asked him one day what was his interest and stuff, and he said, 'Oh well, this had always been a secret ambition' but he'd never quite made it. And I have a feeling, before I was conscious of what was happening, and this was at least part of the origin of this.

In fact, Dr Macman's father was a civil servant, a job which represented, for him, upward social mobility from his manual working-class background. All of Dr Macman's family were of a left-wing political persuasion; his father was a member of the Fabian Society and Kenneth remembers as a boy listening to the family debating political issues. The family politics rubbed off on young Kenneth and as a child he helped distribute the League of Nations' pre-war peace questionnaire.

Going to university proved to be a very significant episode in his life: '. . . it focused my mind, finding people of a like mind, I look back to that period even yet as a tremendously important period, very creative, oh yes' (although he feels that it was somewhat dampened by the spectre of the Second World War). As a student, Kenneth joined the Communist and Socialist Societies and although never a member of any political party, he regards himself as a socialist. A life-long Labour voter, he would only be persuaded to vote for another political party if he thought that they would be more likely to achieve nuclear disarmament.

Clearly, Dr Macman's views and opinions have been shaped by both his family's political attitudes and by his career as a psychiatrist, a career made possible by a state (university) apprenticeship and the state professionalisation of medicine and mental health care. When I asked Dr Macman whether he thought that British unilateral disarmament was achievable, he answered, 'I doubt it. I'm not sure, I'm not too optimistic.' Nevertheless, he feels that he should protest, for violence in general, and nuclear war in particular, is repugnant to his political and professional outlook. When I asked him whether he thought that nuclear disarmament was the most important contemporary issue, he replied:

I would think it's the most urgent one. It's what I feel, on many levels, to be the most urgent one, not just because I've got a radical and emotional distaste for it, which I have, but, I mean, a professional objection. In fact, as a doctor I've been trained to try to foresee epidemics, lethal epidemics and stop them. This is what really one can see happening now and, as I say, I have political objections as well. There's all sorts of things. It's possible now to destroy the world.

A similar duality of perspectives, both political and professional, can be seen in his reply to my questioning him on what he thought were the main reasons for the existence of the arms race:

Well, there's various ways of answering that. I think it's an extension of basically a political power struggle. It's the logical extension of that. You can see it sort of extending from there, the massed armies of the frontier, to various ways of each side trying to increase its power. And I think it goes on because people don't step outside this and take an overview of what's going on, what's happening. They just go on, y'know, hmm, shouting their own slogans as it were, and I think basically each one hoping to win. Psychologically, I think this is a problem which arises when people exclude one side of an argument, a conflict, and seal their own side, and disassociate from the other half of the problem. So that instead of it being a problem on each side, y'know, you project one side into the other, into the enemy and feel you're entirely good and they're entirely bad, instead of feeling the good and the bad is in you and also in them, in which case you could negotiate. I'm a psychiatrist and this is the sort of thing I see with individuals all the time, and I suppose when you're dealing with groups and issues of tremendous concentrations of power that you tend to get an emotional regression; people behave in a less mature way than they do as individuals. And that is rationalised by all sorts of intellectual arguments to make it seem very adult and mature and so on, and you can talk yourself into believing anything and you talk yourself into believing that you're right and the other side is wrong.[21]

Dr Macman's answers to my questions very clearly reflect the two profound paradigmatic influences in his life – his politics and his profession. It would be misleading to imagine that his experiences of the state, as a student and as a psychiatrist, had caused him to join CND; rather, as with many of my interviewees, the effects of his contact with the state are imbricated within and co-exist alongside his own idiosyncratic and personal biography (which in Dr Macman's case includes the important political influence of his family). This interplay of individual experiences and state social relations produces the diversity and similarity which state-employed CNDers share. Dr Goole, Dr Stuart and Dr Macman are distinct men and women each with their own personal perspectives on the Campaign. Nevertheless, there exists an affinity between their professional concerns and their objection to nuclear weapons.

Indeed, it would be remarkable if at least some of the men and women who work in the National Health Service did not feel that nuclear weaponry was an affront to their professional ethics; the ultimate antithesis to their work. And in the revival of CND, the

MCANW has been an important element producing high-quality campaigning material which is often taken seriously by the media, for the social standing and non-political nature of their profession ensures that their views cannot be dismissed lightly.

The nurses' commitment

Not every National Health Service CNDer has been to university. For example, James Frier is an extremely active member of New Town CND, having held office in the group and the group's precursor, the New Town World Disarmament Campaign. James also co-founded a small, short-lived, local disarmament group called Peace Action which was intended to act as a radical fillip to New Town CND and he has taken part in many disarmament actions including blockades at American Air Force bases. James agrees with the Campaign's non-party-alignment policy, '. . . because I personally think that all the parties stink and the last thing I'd want is to be aligned to any of them'. However, he does see nuclear disarmament as a political issue and he dislikes having to work with Conservative and Christian members of New Town CND. Describing himself as a 'very impure' pacifist, James considers violence against people to be 'an absolute no-no' but he strongly favours Non-Violent Direct Action (NVDA).

James does not think that members of CND are drawn from all walks of life: 'No, I think New Town CND is very much those people who are either involved in other political campaigns in the town, those people who because of their Christianity have what they believe is a moral conscience, and those people involved in community politics.' He thinks that 'New Town CND operates way above the heads' of ordinary people and he believes that there is a high percentage of the population 'out there who are scared shitless' but do not join the Movement because they lack the confidence to take on the roles which the Campaign demands from new recruits. James feels that this failing is certainly true of New Town CND; he dislikes the bureaucracy of his group, (what he sees as) the dominance of old-timers on the group's executive, and the members' general conservatism and their unwillingness to engage in radical NVDA.

An ex-member of the Socialist Workers' Party, James would 'actually class [himself] as a socialist, but many people wouldn't'. He supports political separatism, 'self-organisation for oppressed groups', and votes Labour as 'an anti-vote' to the other parties. Although only twenty-four years old, James has taken part in a surprisingly large number of political campaigns and disarmament activities, including Amnesty International, a miners' strike support group and squatters' rights. During the interview he proudly showed me a scrap-book of press-clippings covering New Town CND from its inception. Many of the clippings mentioned James. He sees himself as more radical than the other members of New Town CND and he believes that politics should rightfully be based on the greatest possible democratic participation with the least amount of bureaucracy and élitism. James has a high profile in New Town CND and tries to mould the group according to his political convictions.

James first became interested in politics whilst living in a 'squat' in his parents' home town. At the age of fifteen he started to take part in self-help projects for minorities and his belief in non-formal democratic politics dates from these early activities. Two weeks prior to the interview, James had started working in the long-term ward of a psychiatric hospital. He has 'always been in the social work industry of some sort' and has worked with adolescents, old people on community projects. I asked him what attracted him to this sort of work and he replied, 'If I've got to work I want to be doing something that's fulfilling to other people and also has a good political input. I actually see social work as giving you the opportunity to work politically within any organisation you're working for.'

James has no educational or professional qualifications and his politics derive from his experience of voluntary social and community work which he undertook when he was younger. In the style of Sixties' left-wing activities, he believes in living out his politics in his everyday life and considers conventional politics to be corrupt. In addition, he feels himself to be a member of an oppressed minority and this social location gives an extra edge to his politics, promoting an identification with other minority group struggles. Unlike many of the interviewees I have discussed, James's political and social perspectives were already formed before he entered into formal state employment. Nevertheless, these views were engendered in the context of his experiences of voluntary social and community work. For James, there is no separation between his work and his politics and his membership of CND is an extension of his personal commitment, a commitment which includes attempting to reshape his local CND group into a form which squares with his conception of what politics and social life should be like. This conception, this ideal, developed in the course of his experience of social and community work, first as a volunteer, and now as a professional state employee.

Such commitment can spring from very different sources and may be expressed in a variety of forms. Tina Barth is a 32-year-old nurse and joined Scots City CND approximately three and a half years ago. So far, she has only been to one of her group's meetings which, although she did not wish to seem critical, appeared to her rather cliquey. In addition, she felt that she lacked confidence at the meeting for she thinks that she is insufficiently well-informed about the arms race and disarmament issues. In common with many women CNDers, Tina's disarmament activities are curtailed by her family commitments. However, she has been trying to remedy her supposed lack of knowledge by reading disarmament and related literature.

Her study involved reading books about Mahatma Gandhi and she believes that 'theoretically' NVDA is a good strategy but that in practice it would be impractical in all circumstances and this reservation prevents her from calling herself a pacifist. (Tina's reservation about NVDA and pacifism were both illustrated by the example of a hypothetical attack on her child, a circumstance in which she feels that she might well resort to defensive violence.) She believes that the Campaign's non-party-alignment policy is sound. Nevertheless, she thinks that '. . . just by its very nature more left-wing people tend to join, just because of Conservative policies'. Tina thinks that the arms race started as an attempt to secure peace by deterrence but that, with the escalation in the quantity of weapons, it has now become a 'mockery'.

Although, 'generally speaking', Tina would call herself a socialist, she does not favour political labels as 'I think you all believe in the same goal. It [labelling] often creates a lot of barriers I think.' Predictably, she is opposed to Mrs Thatcher's administration and thinks any alternative would be preferable: 'Anything but these Conservatives with these policies, and not just about disarmament, but obviously I'm very concerned with the running down of the Health Service, y'know they seem to be churning out, "Of course we care," but people have seen through all that and realise.'

Tina supports various charities, buys Campaign Coffee and works for the One-World organisation through her local church. She is a practising Christian and regularly goes to church, although she does not think that regular attendance is a sign of inner spirituality; rather: 'I think we all need, as in all walks of life, we all need to join together. We can't do things alone, and that you reach that goal much better by joining with other people of like mind.' Tina's parents do not support CND. Her father believes in the concept of nuclear deterrence which she finds surprising: 'I was absolutely amazed, and I said, "But dad, y'know as a Christian this can't be morally right." '

The daughter of a civil servant at the Board of Trade, Tina left school at fifteen without any educational qualifications and after five years working at various jobs joined the army, where she trained to be a nurse and gained an army nursing certificate. During her service in the army she began to take an interest in religion:

I suppose that I began to think about Christianity when I joined the army. I think I got involved with a Christian group when I travelled abroad. In fact, I was in Cyrpus in 1974 and this again made me think a lot about war and how ridiculous it was ultimately, and I saw the casualities of it in a military hospital, and we had both Greek and Turkish people with gunshot wounds. And, you know, when they're in a hospital bed, does it matter who they are? And you take care of them and this seems to me what it's all about.

Tina left the army after five years and, following a short stay with her parents in the South of England, she moved to Lancashire where she mixed with her student boyfriend's circle of friends, an environment which began to change her views and opinions. When she was in the army she:

was a different person if you know what I mean. I'd always liked the North of England and I moved up to Lancaster, this was before I met my husband, and I had a boyfriend who was at Lancaster University and I think that maybe meeting that group of people he was connected with, they were sort of into peace and harmony and that sort of thing. And a couple of really good friends we made sort of worked on organic farms and I think that probably, and one chap in particular, was very interested in CND, hmm, I think that probably sowed the seeds then, about five years ago, and I thought perhaps that's what I should be doing, joining this sort of Movement, but I hadn't I suppose thought it out properly why I was joining.

After living in Lancaster for about three years, Tina came to Scots City where she worked as a nurse with the physically disabled. This job opened her eyes to social class differences. As a preliminary to the interview, I had been discussing my research and telling her how interesting it was to interview the Campaign's members and she concurred saying. 'Many different people from different walks of life now, just from the people I've met in CND, completely different.' However, when I asked her later in the interview whether she thought that members of CND were drawn from all walks of life, she replied:

'Yes I think so. Hmm, I don't know, having said that. I don't think people know enough. One thing that bothers me, I used to work at the Clan Foundation at Moilfield [a working class area of Scots City]. It's a sort of community of houses for the disabled, and I'd never known areas like Moil-field or really run-down areas like this before and I got to know it really well and I got to realise that those sort of people are really not interested at all, that just their basic day-to-day life is just about all they can manage or all they're interested in. I'm not quite sure why that sort of thing is, and they tend to say, 'Oh, that sort of thing is just for the middle classes and we don't want to get involved in that sort of thing,' and I don't know whether that's true. Hmm, certainly when it started it did draw in more middle-class people and going back to the beginning, whether this was the reason it petered out, whether that was the reason; people thought it was too high-faluting and people thought they couldn't compete.

Such seeming inconsistencies of views were not uncommon in the interviews. Like many other people, CNDers do not always have clear-cut, coherent views and opinions. In point of fact, when I asked Tina why she thought it was that the majority of people did not support CND, she told me that she thought it was because they were too frightened to think about the issue, a reaction with which she sympathises. As in the case of most of the members I inter-viewed, Tina had not previously considered some of the questions and issues we talked about. Indeed, after the interview she kindly sent me a letter which began, 'Having just returned from my inter-view with you this morning, it has occurred to me that I didn't answer one of your questions very fully.' (The question was con-cerned with the possibility of achieving unilateral disarmament.) This is also true in relation to the events which prompt people to join the Movement; I have found that sometimes people simply cannot remember what event or feeling, etc. prompted them to join.

In Tina's case, a number of factors combined to persuade her to join Scots City CND. These included the birth of her baby, reading *Protest and Survive* and general media publicity on nuclear matters. However, these factors were predated by an earlier objection to nuclear power which arose from Tina discussing the ethics of nuclear energy with a friend who worked as a nurse at the Torness nuclear power station. In addition, Tina's Christian beliefs cannot be separated from her political standpoint and general attitude. She sees herself as having matured since leaving the army: 'In the past four to five years I started forming my ideas, my philosophy.'

Especially in the case of Tina, it would be foolish to attempt to identify a single causal event or factor which makes her a CNDer; rather, it is more profitable to see her biography as an entrance into social relations (as a nurse, mixing with students) which comprise a particular form of life. I think it pertinent to note that as a nurse in Cyprus and as a nurse in Moilfield, she perceived, respectively, the futility of war and the differences in class consciousnesses and ways of life – and that these perceptions were made whilst she was a state employee. It is perhaps not surprising that, when Tina found herself nursing the casualities of nation-state conflict in Cyprus, she began to question the nature of war and that this reinforced her newly-acquired Christianity. Nor is it surprising that she was 'amazed' at her father's support for the nuclear 'deterrent'; 'as a Christian that can't be morally right'. Unlike her father, Tina's state employment as an army nurse had shown her the effects of fighting and, unlike her father, her subsequent career was to promote a perception of herself and the world which involved protesting at the most monstrous manifestation of nation-state weaponry.

Conclusion

In the foregoing discussion of interviews which I conducted with CNDers who were employed in the National Health Service, I have tried to follow through the analytical approach which I used in the third chapter when discussing teacher CNDers. The intention is to show that the CNDers I interviewed are distinct individuals with idosyncratic biographies who enter into welfare-state social careers which are, in a variety of ways, conducive to them joining the Campaign. Such an analytical approach reveals a richer picture of the CNDers' form of life, wherein similarities which they share can be seen as the 'overlapping and criss-crossing' intermesh of categorisation to which Wittgenstein refers in his theory of 'family resemblance'. I now turn to the remaining respondents in my samples who were directly employed in welfare-state professions: social and community worker CNDers.

5

The commitment of social and community workers

As I remarked in Chapter Two, when discussing the interview with the retired teacher, Belinda, a commitment to the ethic of one's profession does not expire upon retirement. Mrs Patricia Wadely is a 62-year-old retired social worker and a member of New Town CND. She has never attended any of her group's meetings, but she has been on local and national marches, marches which seem to her less attractive than those she went on as a member of the original Campaign in the late Fifties and early Sixties. Patricia is unhappy with the atmosphere of today's marches and suspects that for some of the members, whom she refers to as the 'punks' and the 'noisy element', the CND logo is 'just another badge . . .' She thinks that yesterday's marchers were politer, quieter and better behaved. However, she believes that today's Movement has the merit of a more socially representative membership: 'nowadays there's a much broader band of the population. I think it was a very middle-class effort and this is a much more mixed bunch.'

Patricia thinks that, 'intellectually', nuclear disarmament is the most important contemporary issue even though, 'I don't do very much.' She believes that the majority of people do not support CND because they are 'afraid of communism' and because 'the majority of people do go along with the government, and not just the Conservative Government'. Disarmament is achievable, she believes, not just because of the efforts of the peace movement, but by virtue of a change in 'the climate of opinion' (a climate which the Movement helps to create). She is sceptical as to whether the Labour Party would fulfil its Manifesto policy on disarmament, for she suspects that this policy would be jettisoned if the Party came to power. Patricia agrees with the Campaign's non-party-alignment policy: 'I think it's a good thing that there are sort of things which are above politics and attract a broader spectrum of people.'

Mrs Wadeley first become interested in politics during the Second World War when she joined the Common Wealth Party[22] and became a member of 'Acland's Circus', contesting local by-elections in opposition to the war-time coalition. In 1948, following the demise of the Common Wealth Party, she joined the Labour Party and the Fabian Society to which she still belongs. Indeed, on the day of the interview she was preparing for a Fabian dinner party which she was giving at her home that evening.

It was in 'Acland's Circus' that she first met her husband-to-be who was standing as a Common Wealth candidate. After the war was over, she took a job as a domestic science teacher and after two years became a school dinner supervisor, a job which she left to marry the would-be Common Wealth politician. Whilst her family grew up, she undertook voluntary family planning counselling and then studied part-time for a Diploma in Social Work: 'I decided that's where I belonged.' After twelve years as a social worker, she retired. Nonetheless, she still works part-time for the Citizens' Advice Bureau, a local community association and a day-care centre for the physically disabled.

Patricia is opposed to Mrs Thatcher ('I can't stand the woman.') and she regarded the Government's policies of cutting back on public expenditure as a 'weakening' of the welfare state. A Labour voter, Patricia was an active member of the Party from 1948, when she joined, until approximately 1975 when she ceased to be politically active. However, a short time before the interview was conducted, Patricia had resumed her Labour Party activities, for she fears that her local branch is being taken over by members of the Militant Tendency. As a Fabian and ex-member of the Common Wealth Party, she finds the Militant Tendency's particular brand of politics distasteful. I asked her, 'What kind of socialism do you yourself favour?':

I don't know. I don't think that what I want to see is achievable because people would not let it be achieved. [What is it?] Well, it's incomes to start with. People are looking after themselves and trade-unions are strong and people are protected by their trade-unions until they're out of a job and then nobody wants to know and they don't belong to anybody. I mean, possibly as a result of working with the Citizens' Advice Bureau in particular, one again and again comes across people who can't afford to take a job; they'd be worse off than on supplementary benefit. It is subsistence. People can manage on it for a short time but not indefinitely, so that's got to go up, minimum wages have got to go up, and so some have got to come down. And people will not let their standard of living be eroded, and to produce socialism that has to happen. I mean, I have a very comfortable home here and a very comfortable life-style and so that's got to go. And I think I'm getting back to what one thought was achievable with Common Wealth. I don't think I've changed at all. I would still think I'm working for it, but whether one can realise it . . . [her voice tails off].

In the same way that she dislikes the Militant Tendency in the Labour Party, Patricia was unhappy with the presence of the Committee of 100 in the first Movement: 'There was a feeling it was going too far.' Patricia's political perspective prioritises the climate of opinion as the motor for change with which we could secure disarmament – rather than revolutionary socialism or Direct Action. And this climate of opinion must be produced by men and women responding to a recognition of their social duty rather than individual economic interest.

Mrs Wadeley did not adopt this social and political perspective solely as a result of her contact with the state in the form of social work training; rather, such employment training would seem to be a natural extension of her development from a Common Wealth supporter, domestic science teacher, family planning counsellor and Worker's Educational Association tutor; studying for a social work diploma 'didn't change my views. I realised that work would no longer be a chore and that it was where my real interests lie.' These interests first arose when she joined the Common Wealth Party ('I think it was very youthful, life before property, that sort of thing, the "Golden Age",') and remained with her, nurtured in her employment, for the rest of her life. At sixty-two, she finds herself still adhering to the Common Wealth ideals and rejoining the nuclear disarmament movement: 'Very often if I march from the old town to the new town it's because people will look at me and see I'm making my little bit of a stand.'

This notion of making 'a stand' against nuclear weapons would seem, from my interviews, to be of important personal value for CNDers. Naomi Jones 'would like to hope' that members of CND are drawn from all walks of life, 'but I think that people that actually join are drawn from middle-class groups of people who band together and talk about it in their private lives, at their dinner parties or whatever they do, or they go and see the movies about it'. I asked her, 'Why do you say it is the middle-class groups?':

Hmm, it's probably occasioned by the unison of the press they're likely to read, the newspapers they're likely to read and by more time they have to consider things outside of their daily lives. It [also] matters to some people who just don't have so much time outside their daily lives, they're not going to spend a lot of time worrying whether they can afford to go off on a peace camp this weekend, they're going to be worrying about washing nappies or something like that. Other people have more leisure time and more thinking time.

Naomi believes that the majority of people do not belong to CND for:

the same reason as me, a lot of time up 'till the point when I actually joined. Actually joining something is quite a commitment. Even if you do nothing after you've joined it, it says something to you about where you stand and I think a lot of people are wholeheartedly sympathetic with the aims of the peace movement and believe in a safer more peaceful world for them and their families – oh, and everybody else they hold close and dear – and they really believe in that, but *joining* something, it makes you feel as if you, well a lot of people don't join a party if they're left-wing, very few people actually put their name to the list.

Naomi was interested in the peace movement 'a long time before I actually joined. It took me a long time, I think it does with a lot of people, to get round to actually becoming a member. It's [her interest] probably going back a long way, ten or twelve years.' I asked her why she became interested at that time: 'It was the tail end of the Vietnam War, I'd become aware in my late teens at the end of the Sixties as to what was going on . . . I became aware of what was not coming on the screen [regarding America's involvement in the Vietnam War]'. Naomi actually joined Scots City CND:

about one and a half years ago. That's to do with the present situation. I've always felt like I do about it, but it's to do with the present situation, the present escalation of the Cold War y'know. [Was there any one event which triggered you into joining?] Not so much an event as a place; Greenham really triggered it for me. I haven't actually been, it's the feeling, it's the movement. For me, it was especially important as a woman that I actually signed my name up, not just to support it, not just to go along to buy something when they have sales and stuff like that, but actually putting my name to it as well.

Naomi has helped deliver Scots City CND's Newsletter, taken part in letter-writing drives and has been to two of her group's meetings which, she feels, should concentrate more on debating 'future modes of action'. For Naomi, Non-Violent Direct Action is the best way to protest against nuclear weapons and she describes herself as a pacifist. She 'is not totally decided' about the Campaign's non-party-alignment policy: 'I do feel it [alignment] might alienate some members who are members of other political parties from one that CND might affiliate with. It might alienate some people, I don't think that alienation is something we want to get in to.'

However, Naomi is interested in politics and sees herself as a 'privileged left-winger'. Although not a member of any political party, she has worked as a shop steward for the National Association of Local Government Officers (NALGO) when she was employed as a social worker. She sees the arms race as 'capitalist against socialist' and ranks nuclear disarmament 'alongside the sort of political party I'd like to see', as the most important contemporary issue. Although not a member of any charitable organisation, or any group working in the Third World, her 'job used to be social work. I used to be involved in the Scots City council for single homeless. I got considerably depressed by the Third World inside our world if you understand my meaning; the disadvantaged, the oppressed.'

Naomi's political stance is not derived from her parents: 'It's not something I got from my family. I worked it out as I went along.' Naomi went to Steelbrough University to study for a fine arts degree:

When I left home I didn't really have any idea about how I would vote except that my mother had always voted Tory. I thought that Winston Churchill was wonderful. I thought the Second World War was a great idea; we saved the world, really all that sort of stuff! – but with a few ideas that things were changing and that things were wrong in Vietnam, for example, with a few minor ideas like that. I used to argue with people at college on behalf of Tory ideas. But by the time I'd finished I really had lots of other ideas which weren't actually formed by being involved in a political party but which were really owing to knowing people who were left-minded.

Having left university with a degree, she spent two years as a self-employed artist and then went into a commercial artist's studio in the City of Cartcester:

I spent two years doing my own work and a year in a commercial situation, all the nonsense and the exploitation of it all, because it was in Cartcester in a very small non-unionised factory. The wages the girls were getting for standing about all day, every day, the general pay and the conditions were nonsense. I started getting involved in their problems while I was there. Y'know, they'd come and say things like, 'My dad and the [inaudible] say they can take my baby away from me. Can they take him alway from me?', things like that, and by the time I moved back to Scots City I was really much more interested in the people I'd worked with than the minimal bit of design work for Marks and Spencer I was doing. So then I wanted to work with people and I went into the social work department and said, 'How do I go about it?' At that stage you could go into residential care without formal qualifications.

Naomi was employed as a social worker for nearly five years, working with the elderly, the homeless and adolescents. During this time she took a diploma course in social work and met the man she was eventually to marry (also a social work student). Three months before the interview, she left her social work job to take a post as a director of a non-profit-making company which aims to assist aspiring artists and craftsmen. I asked Naomi if she 'was quite involved in her work?':

Totally involved! A bit beyond what I actually wanted to commit to. I wanted to be a bit less committed than I had been in social work but it's not possible, it's twenty-four hours a day. I don't know, I actually used to think it was me in social work, but I think it's me anyway, y'know.

As one would expect, Naomi does not agree with any of Mrs Thatchers administration's policies and strongly disagrees with the Government's cutbacks on social services expenditure and local council rate-capping. Naomi believes in:

the ideals of nationalisation. I support non-profit distribution, I support the ideals of redistribution of wealth, or I support the ideals of a National Health Service and I support the ideals of those who are healthier and stronger and better-off for whatever reason supporting those who are weaker and less healthy and less better-off so that not a general low standard of living is provided but a much higher standard is provided. I don't feel bad about the way I live because I just feel more people should live like it, reasonably well. But for those who don't, I wish that what I could do is help raise their standards to where they would like to be.

The daughter of a mining engineer, Naomi was not brought up with this point of view; her parents voted Conservative all their lives up until the 1983 General Election when their own worsening circumstances persuaded them to vote for the Alliance (in Naomi's words, 'a major change'), and we have seen how, as a young undergraduate, Naomi would champion Tory politics. However, meeting 'left-minded' people at university engendered a change in her political perspective and standpoint, a political point of view which found the exploitative conditions in the commercial artists' company repugnant. Helping her exploited workmates persuaded her that her interests really lay in the social work profession. Naomi is now fully

committed to her job. Indeed, in the course of the interview, which
was held in the evening at Naomi's home, we were interrupted three
times by work-related telephone calls. As Naomi says, it's a 'twenty-
four-hour' commitment.

Her membership of CND is an extension of this commitment. As
she told me, although Greenham Common was the trigger to her
actually joining the Campaign, her interest in the peace movement
dates from her late teens when she began to have doubts as to the
validity of the US involvement in Vietnam. Her biographical experiences involving her contact with, and employment in, the welfare
state have spawned a form of personal ethical commitment which, as
we have seen, is very important to her. I asked Naomi if she thought
that today's Campaign was a moral issue: 'Yes. If there's any deflec-
tion from that it's maybe because of the vast variety of people who
are involved in it, but for me it's *absolutely*, fundamentally a moral
issue.' This ethical orientation to nuclear disarmament is a reflection
and expression of Naomi's personal ethical commitment to her
work, a commitment also expressed in her political stance.

A similar biographical progression can be seen in the case of Mrs
Karen Landing, a 35-year-old single parent living in New Town.
Karen joined New Town CND in 1981 shortly after divorcing her
husband: 'I wanted to join for a long time but my husband worked
for Nearmorte Ltd [a large New Town company which manufactures
conventional weapons systems].' She has been on a few local
marches and has attended a few of her group's meetings which, she
feels, are 'very much steered by one or two people'. Karen has not
taken part in other campaigning activities and would not be prepared to break the law because of her children. As a single parent she
has little free time and in addition, as she says, 'I can't afford to get
arrested' for there would be nobody to look after the children.

Karen thinks that the Campaign's non-party-alignment policy is
'probably' a good idea because 'political parties can always let you
down'. She thinks that members of CND are drawn from all walks of
life and that the majority of people do not support the Campaign
because 'they don't think about it. If they saw *The War Game* and
really imagined it happening to them, maybe then [they would join].'
A principled Labour voter, Karen belongs to the Party and regularly
attends her branch's meetings. When I asked her what she would call
herself in political terms, she replied, 'At the moment I'm sort of
thinking around this sort of thing of Christianity and Marxism. I'm

sure that I'm the only divorced Catholic-Marxist you're likely to ask!' As a Catholic-Marxist, Mrs Landing does not agree with any of Mrs Thatchers Government's policies: 'Where shall we begin? You name a policy and I'll disagree with it.' She does not believe that nuclear disarmament is achievable: 'I felt very depressed after the last Election, from a CND point of view in particular, because here is Labour with their Manifesto, it's their policy and Callaghan turns round and backtracks. I don't feel very hopeful about it.'

The daughter of an infant school teacher and the Principal of a college, Karen left school at eighteen after taking 'A' Levels and went to work as an executive officer in the town's Labour Exchange. Although she enjoyed this job for the contact it afforded with people, she became dissatisfied: 'I found it frustrating in the Labour Exchange because you couldn't help the people, you just had to administer rules, pay them or not pay them, say to them, "Go and see the social security officer," and you'd know fully well what to do [to help them].'

As a consequence of this frustration, she decided to study for an Applied Social Sciences degree at a large Midlands college. I asked her whether being a student had changed her views:

Yes, thinking about it. It was quite left-wing. We did politics as a subject, we did different methods of elections and all that. Did economics, did sociology but I don't remember it having any effect on me at all. I don't remember sociology. Yes, I think it did, made me more politically, I wasn't very politically aware before I went.

After a year and a term as an undergraduate, Karen reunited with her husband, became pregnant, and had to leave college prematurely before completing her degree. Last year, having divorced her husband and with her two children now both at school, Karen started a Certificate of Qualified Social Work (CQSW) course at a nearby college. She enjoys this course ('It's very fascinating, it's all people') and when qualified she hopes to become a hospital social worker. In common with Naomi, Karen's biography reveals a progression of experiences which helped nurture the Catholic-Marxist social worker who joined CND. Because of the delicacy of some of the areas in Karen's life, and because she was obviously very tired (having only just returned from studying when I arrived), I felt it would be impolite to probe too much for details of her life. In particular, it is unclear from the interview how she is affected by her Catholicism (she became a convert at the age of twenty) and what influence her ex-husband has had on the formation of her views. Nevertheless, I have included Karen as a comparable example of how contact with the state can nurture social and political perspectives which can find expression in disarmament matters.

In the interviews with these three social workers it is clear that, in common with my other respondents, their social and political views which find expression in CND are best understood as an interplay of their idiosyncratic biographies and the influence of their entrance into the welfare state, mainly through their experiences of education and employment. This interplay generates and spawns a cultural category of considerable diversity embracing, for example, religious doctors, apolitical students and a Catholic-Marxist social worker. The remaining social and community workers in my two samples exhibited similar differences and commonalities.

Nigel, a 34-year-old, recently unemployed Scots City community worker told me:

The most important aspect of CND is the educational one; it's what people learn. What people can achieve materially is important, but looking beyond community politics, well, one has to realise that there are severe constraints on that. Just to jump back to Scots City CND, for example; there has been debate over a number of years as to what should be the role of Scots City CND, given the way in which the anti-nuclear movement in Scots City has got so many facets of groups that are geographically based, locality based, other groups that are based around areas of work or whatever. My own feelings is that an important role of Scots City CND is really to act as a resource, an educational and material resource, to the activities which are going on in those other facets. This is a model I've used as a community worker.

Nigel agrees 'with the position that it should not be party political. I don't think it's a non-political issue. I think it is an extremely political issue but there's no one political party I would trust to implement nuclear disarmament.'

He is uncertain whether nuclear-disarmament protesting should always be non-violent: 'The short answer is, I don't have a clear view on that.' Nigel has broken the law (a minor infringement) whilst on an anti-nuclear weapons demonstration and considers this to be 'perfectly acceptable in some cases and necessary in others. I don't think all laws are necessarily favourable to us.' He sees the nuclear arms race as a consequence of the superpowers defending their spheres of interest, geopolitical spheres which emerged in the aftermath of World War Two.

Nigel thinks that the majority of the British population do not belong to the peace movement because 'the nature of society is such that people are not encouraged, indeed they're positively discouraged, from becoming politically active'. Not a member of any political party, Nigel would vote Labour at a General Election 'without a great deal of enthusiasm' for he is sceptical as to what Labour could actually achieve if they came to office. He described himself as a 'socialist' and I asked him to elborate:

Hm, I'm not sure. I'm not a member of any political party or organisation, which is a contradiction if one thinks of oneself as a socialist. As to spelling it out, well, as I've said already, I don't see socialism as being brought about by purely parliamentary means I don't see the Labour Party bringing socialism about, or any other party by purely parliamentary means.

Nigel disagrees with all of Mrs Thatchers Government's policies, in particular their 'attitude to unemployment and the ways in which their policies affect women.'

The son of an English teacher (his mother has never been in paid employment), Nigel told me that he came from a background where 'it was assumed that one would go to university'. After six months spent working on a voluntary housing project in his home town, Nigel went to university to read for an economics degree but, after a year, switched to politics which he found more interesting. He does not see the time he spent at university as being the most important formative period in his life:

I see the period after I left university as being more formative. [Why was that?] It was because I had a job when I left university and in my spare time I became increasingly involved in sort of housing campaigning, and that became quite militant, and that really opened my eyes to a great deal, y'know, how politics and society in this country worked.

Shortly before the interview, Nigel had finished working for a three-year community housing project in a run-down working-class area of Scots City. As the community education officer on this project, he worked 'with tenants and housing associations, around housing issues supporting, education, advising, helping people to work out their campaigning strategies and so forth, a certain amount of education and advice work on a more individualistic basis, with a whole range of community groups.' Nigel has done this sort of work 'for the great majority of the time since I left university' and I asked him what attraction it held for him:

What interests me about the work is that what you are doing most of the time is working with people, helping them to develop a better understanding of how, for example, a local political system works and decisions about housing, how money is allocated, how decisions affect them, how they might become better equipped to become more involved in that sort of decision-making process. So what, very broadly speaking, interests me is the way in which it is about raising people's consciousnesses, raising people's questioning about how the world is, how they might perhaps be involved in changing it a bit.

Now unemployed, Nigel hopes 'to develop certain areas of skill around sort of writing or publishing or whatever, that has always been a sort of part of that work. Sort of information research work, I'm not quite sure, that's the sort of thing that interests me.' Not surprisingly, he brings his work-related experiences and perspectives to bear on CND and would like to see his local group 'act as a resource, an educational and material resource'. Unlike the majority of the population, whom Nigel sees as 'positively discouraged from becoming politically active', Nigel's social and employment experiences have positively nurtured a political concern for the well-being of others and have given Nigel a self-image whereby he sees himself as the raiser of other people's consciousness.

Like Nigel, Carol Cox, a 32-year-old Scots City community worker also feels that her work involves a duty to educate and inform. I asked her wehther she was involved in any organisation or charity working in the Third World or on community issues:

Well I'm a community worker, that's my occupation. So, yes, I'm involved in community issues. I think it's a really important part of my work to help raise these sort of issues at my work, and I do. Only last night I showed *The War Game* and *Protest and Survive* to a group of kids I'd taken to France on an international peace camp in July. So I'm quite involved like that. I've also shown *The War Game* at an unemployed workers' centre and a women's discussion group that I ran for a year. So, yes, I try to use my job like that.

Carol thinks that the majority of the British public do not support CND 'because I think the majority of people tend not to belong to things full stop. I mean, I think they can support it without joining. Not everyone has the time or commitment to join. Perhaps they don't join for that reason.' She thinks, speaking from her own experience, 'that the majority of people in CND are middle-class, educated people', which she feels is not peculiar to the Campaign; 'it's not just CND, it's endemic in lots of organisations. I suppose it's because of more confidence, more politically articulate.'

A life-long Labour voter, Carol has belonged to the Labour Party
for the past five years and is a 'very active' local ward member. She
disagrees with all of the Thatcher administration's policies: 'I just
don't like capitalism. It's about her basic philosophy. It's her
approach to politics I disagree with; it's about profits and capitalism
and not about people.' Carol is also on the local executive of her
union, NALGO, as is one of the officials of Scots City CND and they
'keep the issue alive. If anything to do with CND comes up it's
disseminated, and we send a delegate group to take part in demonstrations and so on.'

The daughter of Conservative-voting working-class parents,
Carol studied for a primary school teaching qualification at McCall-
ing House (a teacher training college in Scots City) and then took a
one-year course in youth and community education:

Teacher training college taught me the last thing I want to do is be a teacher!
The community work course gave me a lot of self-awareness and I suppose
that probably changed my life quite a lot. Just being at teacher training
college I realised how dry it was and how awful the people were and I
thought, 'I don't want to be part of this.' And that's when I thought, 'Well,
what else can I do?' So I did the community work course and I found the
lecturers there were a totally different breed of people; I was on first name
terms with them and it was a much more relaxed course. It was about
self-development, that was the difference I suppose. [What's 'self-development'?] Well, we did a lot of group-work stuff, and I suppose that a lot of the
placements I went on were places I'd never thought of or encouraged before,
so that was all sort of learning for me.

After successfully completing this course, Carol became a community education worker in a small town on the outskirts of Scots
City. In common with the majority of welfare state employees,
Carol's education was in the nature of an apprenticeship, an
apprenticeship qualifying her to legitimately work as an agent of the
state. Inevitably, the attitudes which she has assimilated in the course
of her state training and employment spill over into her orientation
towards nuclear disarmament; for example, feeling that it is her
responsibility to educate and inform people about CND – 'it's part of
the job'.

Of course, there are a myriad of ways in which the individual can
become involved in the state apprenticeship process. For example,
Ian Grant went to Southsea University to read for a degree in politics
and international studies, not so much out of interest but 'because I
was part of that education process and my parents expected it of me'.

Ian left university with a third-class degree and an urge to prove to himself that he could better this disappointing academic perform- ance. Shortly afterwards, he enrolled on a CQSW course (partly because, at that time, the entrance qualifications were not very demanding). His political and social views were shaped and changed during this time:

I suppose my views changed when I was a student, both on the undergra- duate and the CQSW courses. Hmm, I suppose now I'm still very vague on my idea of politics. In fact, talking about them just points out how vague I am. I remember when I first started university I was very interested in Red China and convinced myself I was a Maoist! I'm sure I didn't have a clue what being a Maoist meant at the time. Very rapidly I found at university that what I had thought of as political commitment disappeared. First of all I was finding out more about myself and clarifying my views about the world. It was only in the second and third year that I got into the hippy thing, all the sort of attitudes and beliefs that are seen as going along with that sort of culture. And when, as I say, I was a hospital porter [a temporary job] I decided I was interested in doing some kind of social work. When I actually started on the CQSW course I suppose my beliefs did begin to firm up. For the first time I began to see things in perhaps a more mature way. The first, what I would call adult type of like political decisions or awareness that I took was actually [when] doing the CQSW course when I realised that I couldn't be involved in social casework because that's crudely something that says the world's at fault because of the people in it, or a particular neighbourhood is at fault because of the people in it. I realised that the main problem is to do with the structure in society, and power and wherever it rests in society.

Upon completing the CQSW course, Ian moved from Southsea to Scots City, where he took a job as a community worker and com- pleted an M.Sc. degree in social administration. Not a member of any political party, Ian voted for the Ecology Party in the last Election, partly because he did not think the Labour candidate could unseat the Conservative MP in his ward. He describes himself as 'a vegetarian Luddite Digger' (he admires the Diggers for their commu- nal ideals):

I suppose basically in principle I'd vote for the Ecology Party. Hmm, I suppose I don't think the English Ecology Party is radical enough; it smacks a bit too much of the SDP approach – 'you don't have to be political, just join us' – and it's not hard-headed enough. I'd support an ecology party that was more hard-headed, but was also aware of some religious input, when I say religious I'm talking about some sort of Eastern religion, very informal.

Ian thinks that the British public do not support CND because, as a

nation, they see themselves 'as non-political and are not involved in
any social group. They seem to be more interested in CB radio or
stock-car racing than in changing the way society develops.' With
his interest in Eastern religion, the Digger and the hippy ideals, Ian
brings to bear on CND a rather, as he described it, 'eclectic' political
perspective. I asked him what he thought was the best form of
disarmament protesting:

It has to be peaceful. One thing that does worry me about the peace
movement at the moment is the, um, some of the more sort of aggressive
organisations that are showing an interest in it. I suppose being an ageing
hippy [Ian is twenty-nine], I tend to think the way that it spreads and the
way it should affect national policies is by the gentle art of persuasion and
impressing upon other people how many other reasonable people think that
the kinds of politics that CND supports are what we need the national
government to take on. It's [his campaigning prescriptions] rather vague.

Although he thinks that nuclear disarmament is a political issue, he
agreed with the Campaign's non-party-alignment policy, for he
believes that CND is a 'one-issue' Movement and that alignment
would mean taking on board all of the affiliated party's other
policies.

In addition to the idiosyncratic eclecticism of Ian's political
perspectives, he also, in common with other radical welfare state
employees, finds himself in a rather paradoxical socio-political
position. For Ian, his job is 'what the paper would call a vocation
rather than a means of getting money. It's important to me that I do
what I consider basically a competent job and I have something to
offer people in the area I work in.' I asked him if he was happy in his
job and whether there were any changes he would like to bring
about:

The structure in which I work is not sympathetic. Community work is . . .
[break in tape] . . . anti-state as it exists at present. Therefore, to be actually
employed by, in this case, the local state is a bit of a contradiction in terms.
That's not to say I see the job as being first over the barricades. That's not
the way the people I work with on the ground see things and you have to
start at the point where they're at. So, as I say, there's that kind of tension. It
would be OK if the state operated in the way I think it needs to. [Which is?]
More, a greater level of decentralisation, I think that's basically it. I
wouldn't describe myself as falling into the group of those who see
community work as being about advancing the cause of socialism, though it
tends to be seen as a left-wing activity, but that's because there are more
people who see themselves as socialists who believe in the decentralisation
ethos which is what community work is basically about.

This political 'contradiction in terms' is a well-known theme in social and community work literature.[23] Like many other welfare-state employees, Ian finds himself with a vocation to remedy what he sees as partly the state's own failings. And in common with his counterparts in other welfare-state professions, Ian is uniquely well-placed to perceive the failures and shortcomings of state policy. As we have seen in the discussions of some of the other interviews, coming face to face with the conditions in which people require the help of welfare professionals can act as a politicising experience.

Conclusion: welfare state CNDers

In the foregoing three chapters, in which I discussed the interviews with teacher, NHS and social and community worker CNDers, I have pursued an analytical line of inquiry which is underpinned by, in particular, Ludwig Wittgenstein's 'family resemblance' model of categorisation. My intention has been to show that this portion of the revived 'motley army of the good' is comprised of a great variety of individuals, each with their own idiosyncratic perspectives on the Campaign who share an intermesh of similarities as well as differences.

In my presentation of the interviews, I have focused upon the respondents' experiences of the state, primarily through education and employment, as an important factor in the biographical development of these CNDers' social and political ways of life. However, I have also stressed that, just as there is no one definitive characteristic which renders a person a CNDer, there is no one common experience of the state; as the interviews show, the effects of state education and employment upon the individual are varied and often need to be related to other features in their social histories. Nevertheless, in the majority of cases, their experience of the state are notably imbricated within their lives nurturing recognisably similar beliefs and attitudes.

Indeed, it would be extraordinary if it were otherwise. A doctor does not stop being a doctor when he or she joins the Campaign, rather, he or she brings to the Movement a doctor's socio-political experience. Typically, welfare state employees undergo a period of formal state-run training in order to qualify as legitimate teachers, doctors, etc. In contrast to the majority of students, their education involves a substantial amount of time being spent as trainees in their prospective places of work, for example, schools, hospitals or on social work 'placements'. In this sense, their education is more akin to an apprenticeship. In addition, as state apprentices, they also learn the ideology of their profession, the ethics and rationale of their work. For welfare-state professions, this ideology includes the notion that their employment is a vocation, a personal commitment to their profession's ideology and practices. In this way, welfare-state employees become *personally* commited to *socially* evolved and defined practices, and, as the interviews show, this commitment is often deeply-held and valued and spills over into other areas of their lives.

When welfare state employees join CND, when they create the Campaign, they also express the other social relations which they have learnt and live out in their daily lives. It can be seen from the interviews that such social relations and concomitant ways of thinking inform and act as reference points for understanding disarmament issues. Thus, for example, Dr Macman explains the failure of the majority of the British public to join CND in psychoanalytical terms, teacher CNDers advocate 'educating' the public about the dangers inherent in nuclear defence policies, etc. In addition, these social relations serve to distinguish welfare-state employees from other members of the community whom the interviewees often see as 'embourgeoisified' and intellectually benighted. (As Geoff Koelbach, the New Town teacher, expressed it, 'so many sheep'.)

Frank Parkin stated in his study of the original Campaign that:

Involvement in CND was a token not only of an individual's attitude to nuclear weapons but also of his [sic] position on a wide array of other radical and humanitarian issues. Identification with CND could be taken to be a capsule statement of a distinctive moral and political outlook, and support for its activities a means of affirming this outlook through symbolic acts.[24]

I believe that Parkin's observation is pertinent to the revived membership but that it stands in need of further clarification and a grounding in social life. When individuals create CND they are also creating a particular form of life, or culture, and this culture is moulded from wider social relations, in particular, welfare-state social relations. Thus CND also expressed the ideology and politics of the state and this partly accounts for the fact that membership of CND acts as a 'capsule statement' of particular socio-political attitudes and stances.

Furthermore, it can be seen from the interviews that the CND culture also embraces other ideologies and political beliefs, in particular, Christianity and socialism. That this variety of beliefs can happily exist within the CND culture is a tribute to the 'fuzziness' of the CND category. Rather than a category with sharply defined and excluding boundaries, CND shares similarities with other forms of life so that, for instance, the ethics of NVDA can strike a receptive chord for Christians.

In the next chapter, I discuss those campaigners whom I interviewed who did not hold a welfare state position and were not necessarily fortunate enough to have experienced higher education. It will be seen that their reasons for belonging to CND are engendered by other socio-political factors and that, concomitantly, their form of commitment varies in character from that of their welfare-state peers. Whilst the welfare-state CNDers are an important and pronounced facet of the Campaign, CND must be seen as a *composite* of only *partially* complementary perspectives and positions co-existing in both harmony and tension.

6

Other commitments: members of CND not employed in the welfare state sector

Introduction

In this chapter I discuss those respondents who were *not* employed in the welfare-state sector. It will be seen that, in contradistinction to their welfare-state CNDer counterparts, these members exhibit attitudes and opinions which have often been engendered by experiences shaped by forces such as social class or religious conviction that may retain a vitality which does not always live happily with the CND cause and culture. Consequently, these members' commitment to the Movement often assumes a form which is, in varying ways, of a different character from that of the welfare-state members.

Other commitments

Simon Thomas, who is thirty-two, joined New Town CND in early 1984. He does not think that the membership of his group is drawn equally from all walks of life:

No. I think a lot of them are middle-class, semi-professional. The ones I've met are fairly, shall we say, teachers, doctors, that sort of thing. It seems to be a middle-class clique. That's what's happened here. This is one of the reasons I suppose I did join, but with everything else that's going on I haven't got a chance to get in there and stick the boot in. The Church seems to have a lot to do with it, which is probably one of the reasons it's still not political.

Simon believes strongly that it should be a political Campaign and disagrees with the non-party-alignment policy:

You've got Tories Against the Bomb etc., etc. Yet if they really wanted the country to be brought to a stage, by what they would consider a bad government, whereby to rebuild it into a nuclear stockpile would cost too much, they would really have to vote Labour. Really they ought to swing their votes behind the Labour Party, whether they agree with their economic policies and so forth, in order to achieve getting rid of these nuclear weapons.

Simon's political activities and hours of work do not leave him much time for CND campaigning:

I meant to go to a meeting but it clashed with a Labour one and, in my view, the Labour Party gets major concessions because the Labour Party, should they get in, are going to get more or less what CND are asking for. So it's better to try and get something done rather than go round the country having Easter holidays, holding hands round nuclear bases, if you know what I mean.

He believes that the policies of Mrs Thatcher's Government have, 'unfortunately, pushed us into the position where you have to break the law to get your voice heard' and he feels that, 'ideally', peace protesting should be non-violent, 'but I'm afraid her [Mrs Thatcher's] new secret weapon in blue tend to often aggravate to a point where people can no longer be passive shall we say. I mean, someone like myself, I can be extremely violent if provoked. Y'know, basic working-class background.'

For Simon, the arms race is a consequence of self-interest on the part of arms manufacturers ('making a few readies I would imagine') and he thinks that even if nuclear disarmament was achieved there would still be a conventional arms race because Britain's conventional forces have been allowed to deteriorate in order to pay for nuclear weaponry. The majority of the British public do not support CND, Simon thinks, because:

They don't like to be seen as pacifists, I think that's one of the major reasons. You start talking about peace to men, so-called men, all swigging beer at the bar and that, and they think you're a poof. Y'know, 'What about those lassies at Greenham Common?' and all that stuff, it's unbelievable. And of course they don't read any newspapers as such; they read The Sun – that's a comic. Well, they don't read it: a quick glance at the headlines, Page 3 for a quick drool, then to the back page for the sport and then back to the middle in case there's a few more tits hanging around. But that's the mentality of the majority round here for a start. Unbelievable. Their own little concepts are confined to keeping up with next door. Next door have double glazing, they've suddenly got to find the money, or the credit, to have double glazing. They're so tied up with their stupid little world they can't see what's happening around them and of course the literature they get through the door, as I say, The Sun and The Express and that sort of stuff, my God!

An active member of the local Labour Party, Simon is hoping to stand as a councillor and he describes himself as a 'hard-left socialist'. Not a member of any charitable or voluntary organisaton, Simon makes the occasional donation to Oxfam and tries to live out his socialist principles, for example, shopping only at the Co-Op and making his own wine in order to avoid inadavertently donating money to the Conservative Party. With regard to Mrs Thatcher, he disagrees with 'virtually everything she says and does'. Although Simon thinks that the case for nuclear disarmament is 'morally correct', he sees it, of necessity, as properly a political campaign.

Simon was brought up by 'pro-Tory working-class' foster parents in New Town. He left school without any educational qualifications and worked for some time in a variety of dead-end jobs spending his leisure time as a 'biker', riding down to the ritual clashes between mods and rockers at English seaside towns in the Sixties. Having become dissatisfied, he enlisted in the Royal Air Force and became a skilled ground-crew propulsion engineer. In 1972:

... they threw me out. They don't like socialist thinkers there, especially when they're getting lots of their little fascist rules questioned. I guess I've always been a rebel. [Did you go in as a socialist?] I went in as a Labour supporter, er, a sort of righter of wrongs shall we say, that sort of childish principle. Some of the things the military make you do are so moronic. You're supposed to obey without question, and of course when you do question the order then it's a disruptive influence and you don't fit in with the team.

Simon came out of the RAF a socialist and his perspectives on CND reflect the primacy he ascribes to his political commitment. For him, unemployment is the most pressing contemporary issue, 'unemployment first and then the nuclear issue'. Although proud of his working-class origins, he sees himself, as the above quotes make clear, surrounded by unthinking, materialistic and sexist individuals in contrast to whom he is enlightened; a self-perception which accords with the view of many of the more middle-class members of the Campaign.

Like Simon, Harold Aitchison, a member of Scots City CND, is also thirty-two years old and is also an ex-RAF man. Joining the RAF had been a boyhood ambition and at first the life of a ground-crew officer appeared to live up to his expectations, 'wearing a uniform, strutting about, people saluting you, that sort of thing'. However, after a while, Harold found himself teaching new recruits and his views began to change:

When I had to teach new people when they came in as recruits, I began to question what I was actually teaching them. And at the end I really could not do that, I just *could not teach* what I did not believe in and did not agree with at all and I had to leave. If I had not sat down and thought about it [he pauses], when I was teaching I had to plan out the lessons and things and I thought, 'I don't believe in this, so I'm damn well not going to teach it'.

The final straw came on the day of the Queen's Silver Jubilee celebrations at Harold's RAF camp:

Would you believe it, Her Majesty the Queen, she had to pick the station I belonged to and, er, there was a large influx of other officers and things. And I remember having a discussion with a man I hadn't seen in years. I'd trained with him, and he's a great believer in 'drop the Bomb first before they drop it on us' and I just could not understand this attitude. Not just limited to him, it was all around me. And if it hadn't been for that I suppose I could have soldiered on for a while. But when I heard the attitudes and I saw the attitudes that I was actually helping to develop, y'know, it was time to get out.

Upon leaving the service, Harold:

. . . swanned about for a year, I had my gratuity which I spent. Travelled a lot, went to America and Russia. Went to Moscow. I flew straight from America to Russia. I'd never been to America and the opportunity came and I had the money to go. I'd been teaching that the Russians were 'baddies' and the Americans were 'goodies' if you like, in this sort of simplistic attitude, and I thought I'll do this. And when I was in America I saw this [flight] advertised, straight from New York to Moscow. I just wanted to compare the 'goodies' and the 'baddies', if you like, at first hand. I found plenty of 'baddies' in America but I didn't find many 'baddies' in Russia [he laughs].

On returning to Scots City, Harold took a temporary job as a teacher in a secondary school, which he left to try to become a free-lance journalist. On his return, he also joined Scots City CND.

Harold believes that members of Scots City CND are drawn from all walks of life and he thinks that the majority of the British population do not support the Campaign because:

I think a lot of it is sheer apathy, bone idleness, and *not wanting* to get involved, this reservedness of not wanting to get involved, of being interested – 'Yes, it's doing a good job but; yes I agree but I *don't want* to be *involved*.' There is in Britain this terrible reservedness and I think this comes out in everything . . . it's foreign to them.

Since joining his local group, Harold has helped with leafleting, attended local and national demonstrations and has been to a few of his group's meetings, which he dislikes intensely for he feels that far too much time is taken up with deciding who should do what campaigning task. He thinks that the arms race is a consequence of 'distrust, complete and absolute distrust and fear of the unknown', and he favours mass non-violent Gandhian-inspired demonstrations as the best form of protesting.

Harold's father is a member of the Liberal Party, whilst his mother is non-political ('she picks a name with a pin'). Never a member of any political party or trade-union, Harold would vote Labour in the event of a General Election and he describes himself as a 'democratic socialist, I am a socialist. I do believe in democratic ideals so I would say I'm a socialist.' He does not agree with any of Mrs Thatchers administration's policies, for he feels that 'her whole policy is a *complete disregard* for *people*'. Harold supports the Campaign's non-party-alignment policy,

... because if you get linked in with the Labour Party or the Conservative Party, SDP or anything, it will be tagged on with a political tag it shouldn't have. It should be open to all members of any political persuasion. I know Conservatives that are members of CND, I know Liberals that are members of CND. That's fine, it should be open to all of these and if it becomes tagged on all it will do is attract adverse publicity. It shouldn't have a political philosophy because it's not there to decide policy. It's only there for one specific issue.

Although not a member of any charitable or voluntary organisation, Harold buys Campaign Coffee, goes to Anti-Apartheid and Chilean Aid concerts and he argues that the arms race impoverishes the Third World. For Harold, nuclear disarmament is the most important contemporary issue and he would be quite prepared to be arrested in the pursuit of Non-Violent Direct Action protesting. I asked him whether he thought that nuclear disarmament was a moral issue:

Yes, I would say it's a moral issue. Disararmament to me is tied in with the entire morals and ethics of violence. All I really see nuclear weapons as is an extension of man's violence. The thing about man is that he must dominate, I don't know why it is. The only way we can achieve disarmament is if we learn to control our own violence, our attitudes to other people. So it is a moral issue, a very moral issue.

Clearly, for both Harold and Simon, their experiences of the state, in the form of the RAF, was highly important in their lives and in the formation of their views. Nevertheless, the effects of their contact with the state are disparate: for Simon, it has resulted in a hardening of his nascent socialist politics; for Harold, it provoked a reassessment of his beliefs and attitudes. In both cases, their experiences of the RAF acted as a catalyst in their biographical development. Simon sees himself as working-class, although not benighted and material-istic, and his political commitment takes priority over his alle-giance to CND; nuclear disarmament is something to be fought for by and through the Labour Party. For Harold, on the other hand, nuclear disarmament ranks as the most important contemporary issue to be achieved by a mass non-political single-issue movement. Becoming an instructor in the RAF inadvertently rendered Harold personally responsible for the policies of the state – a personal moral responsibility which became repugnant to him. Both men's personal commitment has been engendered by their experiences of the state but, whereas Simon's commitment is overtly political, Harold's commitment, which is closer in character to the commitment expressed by many of the welfare-state CNDers, is overtly moral.

Of course, there are a multitude of ways in which an individual's work or profession can act as a catalyst to personal change. For example, 24-year-old Shirley Murray joined Scots City CND in the summer of 1983 and since then she has been to a few of the group's General Meetings which she dislikes, for she finds that 'nothing really gets done'. Sceptical about politicians in general, Shirley favours the Campaign's non-party-alignment policy despite the fact that 'I sway towards Labour', and she is unclear as to why we have an arms race: 'I'm not really very sure. I think it's just distrust; they [the Superpowers] won't sit down and trust one another.' She thinks that the majority of the British public do not belong to CND because:

There's still a lot of people in this country who like this glory, y'know Great Britain, get the flags out, we're one of the top countries. And I think there still is, especially in Britain, they like, they seem to thrive on, the War, y'know, the fact that we won. The British Empire and all that. Some of them still think that. And they're brought up to think that Russia is the enemy.

In her opinion, members of CND are probably drawn from all walks of life:

I think so. I'm not very sure. I think probably they are. But most of them tend to be, oh I don't know now because I've met miners who support it, so I would say they are drawn from all walks of life. A lot of people have the opinion that the peace movement is just the plaything of the middle classes, but most of them I know aren't.

In the event of a General Election, Shirley would vote for Labour and she would like to join the Party but is unable to do so because her membership would be conditional upon her bringing her union back-payments up to date which, at present, she cannot afford. Describing herself as 'left-wing' ('If I was a member of the Labour Party I think I'd be in the centre'), Shirley disagrees with 'everything she [Mrs Thatcher] does', in particular, the Government's economic and immigration policies and the running down of the Health Service. For Shirley, nuclear disarmament is 'a big political issue', but not the most pressing contemporary issue: 'No, the state of this country, unemployment like, does come into my mind more. That's why I have to get involved in the Labour Party.'

The daughter of a now unemployed construction engineer, Shirley left school with five 'O' Levels and went to work as an electronics component assembler for Fearland Ltd., one of this country's largest electronics companies, with a heavy involvement in military production and research: 'When I left school I worked in Fearland. But I eventually got to sort of thinking, I mean everything that Fearland built was all military and that's when it all started, y'know. I left there and decided to change my job altogether.' Shirley's questioning of her work was prompted by a company training visit when she was taken from her assembly desk to see the finished product of her labour power:

It didn't really hit me at all until one day there was a few people from every department taken to McHeath Airport. And I happened to be one of them and I got sat in the Warrior jet and I saw it all and thought, y'know, this actually gets involved in, I didn't really – I mean I was still too interested about what I was doing, just went along and done it – and that really started to, y'know, I thought about it, this is a *fighter* plane, this *kills* people, and I thought, it started to prey on my mind for quite a while.

Upon leaving Fearland, Shirley '. . . started working for a company that did medical electronics, ultrasound scanners and that, so I felt that was OK. But now this company I'm with, now they're starting to trade with South Africa, for the military and that, so I am actually leaving it at the end of the month.'

For welfare-state CNDers, the ideology and practices of their professions does not entail a separation of labour and morality. Indeed, their professional ideology seems to encourage them to feel personally responsible for their work. For most workers in capitalist industries this is not the case; a high division of labour, the cash nexus and the production of commodities serve to alienate the labour force from the moral qualities and ethical implications of

their work. Thus, Shirley could escape the full import of her elec-
tronic assembling and only a chance encounter with the finished
product, a fighter plane, caused her to question the validity of her
employment. This questioning led her to the conclusion that such
employment was morally unacceptable and she gave in her notice.
She appears to have retained this attitude, for now, faced with
another ethical dilemma, she is on the point of again resigning her
job as a question of principle – a courageous personal stand in these
times of unjustified high unemployment.

From my sample of Scots City respondents, I also had another
Fearland employee; 38-year-old Adrian Nash joined Scots City
CND in 1981. He has never been to any of his group's meetings, and
his only campaigning activities to date are having taken part in two
local marches. Brought up by working-class foster parents (his father
was a postman), Adrian is, in formal activist terms, a nominal
member of the Movement. He believes that the arms race is a
symptom of 'greedy mankind' and he supports the Campaign's
non-party-alignment policy and non-violent protesting. Adrian has
not broken the law in the pursuit of disarmament protesting and
found it hard to imagine himself doing so. He believes that the
majority of the British public do not support CND because of
'tradition, traditional views. The establishment. We come from a
background of a patriotic nation', and he ranks nuclear disarmament 'on a par' with ecological concerns as the most pressing
contemporary issue. A Labour voter, Adrian was a member of the
Party from 1980 to 1981, leaving out of disillusionment with what
he saw as the other members' narrow-mindness. Politically, Adrian
described himself as 'very near to Neil Kinnock, so I suppose it's
slightly left of centre', and he strongly disagrees with Mrs Thatchers
administration's economic policies, which he feels are the 'capitalism
of a bygone age'. In preference, he would like to see public expenditure used to reduce (in a Keynesian fashion) the level of unemployment.

In the interview, Adrian tended to give clipped, one-word answers
and seemed reluctant to express his views. Consequently, it is difficult, from the interview material, to reconstruct his biography and its
relation to his disarmament and political perspectives. Nonetheless,
when speaking of his employment history, Adrian gave an interesting insight into the ethical dilemmas faced by a Campaign supporter
forced, by capitalistic circumstance, to manufacture military

equipment.

Adrian left school without any qualifications and became employed as a sheet-metal worker, a job which he left in order to undertake a government retraining scheme with the intention of becoming an electronics assembler. He then joined a small company which manufactured medical equipment but, six years later: 'It's a bit ironic, they got into financial difficulties and I had to leave that.' Adrian then went to work for Fearland Ltd where he helps to assemble the flight-deck instrumentation for the Revered combat plane. This unsought-for change in his employment is not to Adrian's liking: 'The conditions [in the two companies] are about the same. But you felt as if you were contributing something towards society, a wee bit proud, y'know. Now I don't feel I'm contributing anything towards society, using up world resources for nothing.'

Adrian has a few workmates who are also opposed to nuclear weapons and share his distaste for their work:

There's two or three people I can talk to, who are sympathetic towards it and realise it's . . . in fact, there's a bloke who works beside me who was in Hiroshima for about three years after the war and it was still flat, no tar on the roads. He said it looked like, reminded him of one of these films you see of the Klondike where the mud's up to there.

Adrian thinks that most of the workforce at Fearland are aware of the dangers of nuclear war. Even so, they are not sympathetic to the peace movement: 'I know that there's people I work beside at the moment and when Greenham Common was on and the girls were trying to rip the fence down and that, what they saw was a load of hippies and yobbos. They did na' see the actual thing, the actual thing they were trying to do, trying to explain and get over.' I asked Adrian what he thought could be done to gain the support of such people: 'It's hard to say really. How do you change people? People are influenced by The Sun newspaper. The depth of their political thinking comes from there.'

In the foregoing interview with Adrian it is unclear as to why he, unlike the majority of his workmates, feels ethically perturbed by his present employment. It seems reasonable to speculate that the change from manufacturing medical equipment to producing fighter aircraft may have heightened his moral perception. This difficulty notwithstanding, I feel that Adrian's remark on his work allows an insight into his position as a CND supporter, a position he has 'taken up in the world'.[25] It is only by placing the commitment to CND within the social world of the members of the Campaign that one can understand its fuller meaning. A commitment to CND is not discrete, it lives alongside, and is an expression of, the individual member's other social stances and positions.

Matilda Acorn joined Scots City CND a year ago after watching *The Day After*[26] on television. Matilda's only contribution to the Campaign is her subscription and she has never attended any of her group's meetings. She believes that the membership is drawn from all walks of life and that the majority of the population do not support the Campaign because: 'I don't think they know much about it.'

Matilda is first and foremost a Labour Party activist and she believes that the most effective way in which CND could achieve its aims is by getting:

. . . more involved in political issues. That's why I said I didn't think I'd be a great help to you because I'm not actually an active member of CND. As far as I'm concerned, after seeing that film I was really quite horrified and I felt I had to make some form of commitment but it was purely financial. I do get the Newsletter every month which I pass round at work, so my involvement is purely financial. Mainly because I don't have time to get more involved. I'm very active in my local Labour Party, in my local branch and in the constituency, and I'm also very active in my trade-union, and I do hold a position in my union and that takes up most of my free time. So I really don't have a lot of time left for CND. But I feel that the organisation isn't political enough and, hmm, I've often been rather irritated about CND especially during the last General Election campaign. Everybody in the local Labour Party was working very hard to try to get a Labour government elected, who certainly have peace more in mind than a Conservative government do, and yet CND were busy organising mass demonstrations down South. I was really annoyed. [You know the official CND policy is not to be aligned to any party?] Oh, I appreciate that. But I do feel that during the General Election campaign, hmm, to me, they were playing into the hands of the people who are against the peace movement. [Do you think they should be aligned?] Personally, I think they should. But I can understand why there are people involved in CND that don't want to get involved in political issues, but I would say that it's probably lack of information that makes them feel that way.

Matilda's parents are both 'out and out Tories' and, until recently, owned and ran a small hotel. Matilda left school with three 'O' Levels and went to work as a receptionist for a large nationalised hotel in Scots City, an experience which radically altered her political outlook:

At work I used to complain about the conditions, and I used to say 'they' should do something about it. It's quite amazing, you hear people say 'they' should do something. And one day someone turned round to me and said, 'who are they? Why don't *you* become they?' and that's why I decided to get involved in my own union. And I think it's the same with CND. There's no point in sitting around waiting for someone else to do something. If you feel strongly enough you should do something about it yourself.

When Matilda first became active in her union she still held faith with her parents' political outlook. However, a little while later her union sent her on a training course:

I was very active in my union and they sent me on a summer school . . . and at night I used to go down to the pub with the Kent miners [who were also attending the school] and there were quite a few members of the Labour Party. We started having political discussions with miners and they said they couldn't understand how someone who was so active in the union could vote Tory, and I said as far as I was concerned – this is maybe something a little like CND – what I did in my union had absolutely nothing to do with politics. And it was just absolute ignorance on my part that I'd never *connected* the two together, but it was the way I'd been brought up. It was just everything I'd heard from my family and my parents, that being a Conservative it was up to yourself how you progressed through life. It was everything I'd been brought up to believe and I'd never thought there was any other way until I went to the summer school and actually started to *think* about it.

'For a few months' after the summer school:

. . . little brown paper parcels kept arriving through the door from Kent and other places in the country. It was people on my own course and miners sending me books. I was getting sent things like *The Ragged Trousered Philanthropists*. I was sent things like this and I started doing a lot of reading and then I decided that I was right and my parents were wrong and I was going to join the Labour Party.

Matilda now feels that she 'would never go back, no matter what happened. I would *never, ever* leave the Labour Party' and she describes herself as 'a left-winger, I'm a great supporter of Tony Benn.' As one would expect, she does not agree with any of Mrs Thatcher's administration's policies and she believes that the present high level of unemployment is a deliberate and classic capitalist policy designed to oppress and exploit the working class.

In contrast to the more middle-class respondents, Matilda's main concern is with the local effects of the cutbacks (for example, street-cleaning, local housing conditions) rather than with wider welfare-state issues such as education and the NHS. In addition, and again in distinction to the interviewees in the preceding chapters, Matilda is not prepared to subordinate her political aims for the sake of the nuclear disarmament cause. I asked her why she thought some members of CND did not want to be involved in politics:

I think there's still the old-fashioned bogey, about the Labour Party anyway, about reds-under-the-beds and all this sort of nonsense that frightens a lot of people. Whereas they genuinely believe that working for a peace campaign is maybe not giving them quite as much commitment as it would if they joined a political party, whichever one.

Matilda's own form of commitment makes for an interesting comparison with those welfare-state members who, like her, were politicised by their experience of work. Unlike, for example, teacher and doctor members, Matilda became committed to a political party rather than to her world of work and its ideology. Indeed, Matilda is committed to changing her world of work rather than merely protecting it.

In contrast, 76-year-old Michelle Nairn, a member of New Town CND, has been to university and, although never a teacher, doctor or social worker etc., she has been in an akin form of employment and her commitment to the Campaign more closely resembles that expressed by welfare-stand CNDers. (The welfare-state category is blurred at the edges and it is not always possible to locate unambiguously occupations within it. I have chosen to discuss Michelle, who has worked in local authority housing management, in this chapter for comparative purposes.)

The daughter of a civil servant and a mother who undertook voluntary work until starting a family, Michelle went to university in 1929 to read for a degree in mathematics. Like many undergraduates, Michelle chose her degree subject on the basis of it being her best subject at school, and she now wishes that she could have done a course in social work: 'I think I would have done something a bit more, but in those days they didn't have degrees in social work. It was too early.' Upon leaving university with her (titular) degree, Michelle spent a year as a voluntary worker in an Approved School and then went into housing management, which remained her field of employment until her retirement: 'I was a socialist, and I thought it was terribly important to administer things humanely and housing was a good example.' In addition, Michelle had become an admirer of Octavia Hill's housing policies and, although now retired, she still receives literature from the Institute of Housing.

Whilst at university, Michelle had also been involved in the Labour Society, had joined the League of Nations and was interested in contemporary political campaigns of the time (for example, home rule for India). She 'has always been a Labour voter, and I shall go on being a Labour voter. Mrs Thatcher has made me even more determined. There was an argument at one time that there wasn't much between them, but you can't say that now.' Describing herself as a socialist, Michelle thinks that 'things should be run for the good of the community and not for profit' and she disagrees with all of Mrs Thatchers administration's policies: 'It's all, um, all profit motive isn't it. And these cuts too, it's increasing unemployment by cutting services, spending money on all the wrong things.' Not a member of any charitable or voluntary group, Michelle supports their aims but: 'It's a matter of time. I'm very much in favour of the world development movements, and I subscribe to these things, but I think you have to decide what you give most of your time to and I give mine to CND.' Similarly, Michelle '. . . goes to ward meetings [of her local Labour Party], and I canvass when the Election comes along. Again, it's a matter of what is most important, the Labour Party or CND. I mean they're both important, and it's very, very difficult. This is one of the difficulties I think.'

Michelle dates her interest in the peace movement as starting with her student involvement in the League of Nations and, although she had been 'in sympathy' with the original Campaign, she did not become a member because, as the Housing Manager for a local corporation, she did not wish to be seen as 'politically' involved. In the late Seventies she attended a meeting of the World Disarmament Campaign in London and she subsequently joined this Campaign's New Town branch (which evolved into New Town CND). An active member of her local CND group, she regularly attends meetings, goes on demonstrations and 'mans' the group's bookstall. Michelle thinks that peace protesting 'should always be non-violent, yes, definitely' and believes that, in the right circumstances, it may be necessary to break the law in the pursuit of nuclear disarmament.

Michelle thinks that the arms race is a consequence of '. . . fear, largely. I know it's augmented by people making profit, but I think that wouldn't in itself make an arms race if the public weren't convinced it was the way to keep the peace. Unfortunately, it's the public that support it.' Relatedly, she believes that the majority of the British public do not support the peace movement because they fear that disarmament would render Britain vulnerable to attack. Michelle thinks that members of New Town CND are drawn from all walks of life: 'Yes, I think so. it's a difficult thing to answer, but I think, as far as age group and background and so on, I think we're pretty varied.' Although Michelle 'approves of a lot of the things that Greenham Common women do', she is worried that:

... some of them are over-emphasising. I don't like placards up against men. I think it's a pity that some of the Greenham campaign has become that type of feminism. After all, a lot of women are jolly militaristic, and a lot of men who, after all, were conscientious objectors because it was men who were called up, they've been foremost in the peace movement. There's a lot to be said on the feminist movement on other things, I'm not decrying that for a moment, but I think it's a pity to bring that too much into CND because I think for one thing it's divisive.

And, despite being a member of the Labour Party, she agrees with the Campaign's non-party-alignment policy 'because you want the support of people in other parties'. Michelle sees today's Campaign as '. . . moral primarily, but you've got to get it through politics haven't you. But I often think that the best arguments come back to the moral one. The nuclear bomb is immoral full stop, and it's immoral to talk about pressing the button and killing millions of Russians.'

Michelle's father had been a Liberal Party supporter, her mother was a socialist, and Michelle remembers as a child listening to her parents discussing political matters.

After leaving university, and spending a year as a voluntary worker, Michelle took up a post in housing management which allowed her to put into practice her political and ideological convictions, convictions which she retains to this day. Although hers is an ambiguous welfare vocation, Michelle's local state employment, her experience at university and the symmetry between her work and her political convictions closely resemble those of, for example, teacher members of the Campaign. In addition, her perspective on, and commitment to, CND is in sympathy with the welfare-state CNDers' position. Like them, she is prepared to give priority to disarmament campaigning and is opposed to what she sees as divisive or partisan strategies. In this sense, her campaigning position is close to that of the welfare-state CNDers and notably different from the overtly political (left) stance of Simon or Matilda who both believe that CND should be incorporated within the Labour Party. It could be argued that this is a consequence of class differences in that Michelle is 'middle-class' whilst Simon and Matilda have working-class biographies. However, it is, I suggest, more analytically precise and heuristically useful to view the former pair's biography and class location as being akin to the welfare-state CNDers. Clearly, Michelle's views and opinions have little in common with, for example, the traditional 'petty bourgeoisie' (a social group notably absent from the Campaign's membership). Like the welfare-state CNDers, Michelle does not favour partisan politics; humane policies are, in common with the NHS, education and the social services, for the common good. In this socio-political paradigm, the nuclear disarmament cause can take priority, for it is not in conflict with other aims. Instead, it is the most pressing issue in a set of interrelated threats to the common good.

A commitment to a Campaign which transcends partisan politics or ideologies may, of course, derive from a variety of sources. For example, Walter Mitchell is a young lawyer and a member of Scots City CND who kindly agreed to take time off from his busy legal practice to be interviewed at his place of work. Walter first became interested in nuclear disarmament in the late Seventies: 'largely through the development of my religious beliefs, through becoming a Christian and becoming concerned with broader issues in general. And also through being at university.' He had recently joined Scots City CND and Christian CND and had attended the preliminary meeting of the (then) fledgling Lawyers Against Nuclear Armaments group. For Walter, the best form of protesting is through 'consciousness raising' of the general public and he believes that any disarmament protesting must be non-violent as a question of principle.

Walter holds the opinion that the majority of the British public do not support CND because:

. . . perhaps it's perceived as anti-establishment, anti-government. That may be a fault of the way CND presents itself; it may be a fault of how CND is presented by others, particularly the Conservative Party, but I think it probably is seen as anti-establishment in some ways, and for the vast majority of people their lives are within this fabric of establishment and if you start attacking any one corner of the establishment you're threatening to attack the whole thing, you're left with no certainty or structure . . .

He believes that:

. . . there's a certain picture of the average CND member in the press, the sort of, y'know, vegetarian, quasi-anarchic, woolly-hatted brigade, which in my

experience is true of only a very small minority. I mean, there was eighty odd
folk at the meeting I went to for the proposed Lawyers Against Nuclear
Armaments thing and these were lawyers in private practice and one or two
senior members of the Bar. The Medical Campaign Against Nuclear
Weapons is large and strong and these are not all quack doctors or weird
types at all but ordinary people. Probably on balance there's a slight
preponderance of left-wing political views, but I think it probably is true to
say that people concerned with the peace issue are drawn from all walks of
life.

Having vacillated between voting for the Liberal and Labour
Parties in the past, Walter would now definitely opt for the latter
and, although never a member of any political party, he classes
himself as 'a socialist of some description. I was going to say a
"progressive socialist" but, um, I'm not sure if that's the right term.
Let's say I'm mildly right socialist if that's accurate enough.' As a
'mildly right socialist', he:

. . . disagrees with one of the fundamental principles of Conservative
philosophy which is; if you leave people to get on with their own thing, give
them as much freedom as possible, it will all work out OK in the end. I agree
with them that there's selfishness in human nature but I strongly disagree
with their conclusion that you shouldn't fight it, because the results are
disastrous for the majority who end up at the receiving end. So on that basic
level I disagree with them.

Walter's father worked 'in life assurance' and his mother has been
a secretary with a number of private companies. Both parents are
agnostics. Walter went to university to read for a degree in law, an
experience which:

. . . didn't particularly change my views. It would be truer to say it gave me
an opportunity to do some prolonged reflecting and thinking which I don't
think I would have had if I'd gone straight into my job. So, in that sense
particularly, it changed my views. But also there were opportunities for
discussion on issues in a way that doesn't quite happen in a full-time job . . .

During his time as an undergraduate, Walter became interested in
politics and disarmament issues. His interest in religion, however,
predates his student years. It is his religious faith which allows him,
unlike in his opinion the majority of the population, to live outside
'the fabric of the establishment.'

Walter's religious conviction is the pre-eminent feature of his
personal socio-political paradigm and it provides him with a
transcendental authority which can act as a court of appeal in
matters of personal and political ethics. For Walter, the existence of

the arms race can be explained '. . . in religious terms. The basic reason has got to be human sinfulness and self-centredness and a combination of fear of others and fear of the differences in others and innate hostility and aggression. I think these basic and psychological facts are reproduced in international relations as well.' In his personal life, 'the primary issues are Christian and spiritual issues, but that's not to say that CND and nuclear disarmament is not part of that because it is, very much so. So it's an important issue for me *because* it's a part of that.' He sees the nuclear disarmament cause as '. . . a moral issue, and a spiritual one as well. And a political issue. It has many dimensions. At root, I think it's a moral and spiritual issue, and political issues are concerned more with the details and practicalities. But it certainly goes deeper than a political issue.' Consequently, he supports the Campaign's non-party-alignment policy:

If CND was to be aligned to any of the official parties, presumably it would be the Labour Party. Now I don't object to the Labour Party, in fact I vote Labour myself, but I feel that the issue of nuclear disarmament is a broader one than a party political issue and, um, that in a sense would be to play into the hands of those who would like to reduce it to a party political issue.

I asked Walter how he would feel about breaking the law in the pursuit of nuclear disarmament, a provocative question to put to a practising lawyer:

I really don't know. I think in principle there has got to be a higher law than the mere law of the state, and – whether you're talking about moral or divine law – there's something about that and the law of the state is not absolute. I think for a Christian that's clear. The law cannot be the last word, and if the law is in fundamental conflict with what one believes to be correct then, in certain circumstances, I feel I would have to break it. I wouldn't on principle say I'd never break it, I would have to be careful.

In common with Walter, 74-year-old Heather Young and her husband, both members of New Town CND, also place their commitment to CND within their paradigmatic religious witness. Although very articulate, Heather was somewhat prone to wandering away from the subject under discussion and is physically infirm. Consequently, this interview was truncated. Heather and her husband hail originally from the East End of London where Heather worked in the print trade and her husband was employed as a salesman for a bakery company. Like Walter, Heather and her husband see their commitment to CND as an extension of, and concomitant with, their strong religious faith. I asked Heather,

'When did you first become interested in the peace movement?':

Well, you see, it goes back to when I felt Jesus or God or whoever you call Him was talking to me. I was watching my daughter getting married and I felt I'd got to do something more about my Christian life. That's my opinion about it. From then onward, er, I made inquiries about going to, er, a Christian community for my holidays. I felt that something seemed to tell me that that was the right thing to do, which we did and, er, we went to Calvary Abbey [a Christian holiday centre], went there several years running, and I was greatly impressed with them. They're quite Evangelical, although it's an Anglican base, as we're Anglican, but it was very Evangelical. This daughter, she had a lot of trouble with her husband . . . so I was going to the Abbey one night and I thought to myself well, perhaps these people – this is leading up to, I'm going a long way round, but this is my way of explaining why I threw myself into all these peace movements – and I wrote on a piece of paper 'Please pray for these people' and they asked me who they were and I said, 'my daughter and her husband' and they said, 'Would you like us to intercede for them? Can you tell us anything about them?' and I said, 'God knows all about it.' You see, I think my peace movements with the spiritual thing. Anyway, as I was having this laying on of hands as they call it, I felt, 'I'm not going to worry anymore,' and I don't now, y'know, even if it worries me, I just put it in God's hands. From then onwards I seemed to hear of different things. World Development was one of the first ones; somebody told me about that, and I became quite concerned. I read the papers quite a lot and listen to the radio and I was hearing about these people starving and all that, and I got involved with the World Development lot. My husband got this job as a verger and caretaker and we used to have a lot of meetings. People used to come there from different meetings, Amnesty International and all that sort of thing, and I used to go into them because he was working quite late at night, and I got involved with them and I felt that if only we could become a more spiritual country we wouldn't have to worry. I support a lot of them. I support the miners and all that sort of thing and I feel, you see, I link mine to the spiritual thing.

Heather and her husband regularly attend their group's meetings and they think the members of their group are 'good and sincere' and they admire the other members' activism. Heather's husband thinks that the majority of the British public do not support the peace movement because 'they're frightened of the red bogey'. Heather has a somewhat different, and familiar, point of view: 'That's my husband's opinion. But I think a lot of people are apathetic, especially when they're not doing too badly for themselves. People are fools. Carlyle said this. People are mostly fools, people are idiots. The more I look at mankind, the more stupid I think they are [she laughs].' Both Heather and her husband think a 'good cross-section' of the public are represented in their local group and they cite the membership of both an avowed communist and an ex-Justice of the Peace in support of this opinion. Heather does not:

like politics pushed too much, John [the author]. I think it would be quite a good idea to make it Christian. My daughter belongs to what they call Christian CND. They did speak about it in this area but they didn't get enough support for it really because quite a lot of good people wouldn't call themselves Christians. But I think Christian CND would be better than political CND myself.

Not members of any political party, Heather and her husband describe themselves as 'Christian Socialists', vote Labour and 'don't like the capitalist system', which they regard as immoral, materialistic and un-Christian. As Christian Socialists, they 'don't think much' of Mrs Thatcher's administration:

They're so much against our point of view that we feel rather sorry that the people were *stupid* enough to put them in, and it will be years before we can get them out. It's a selfish, unfeeling, unthinking lot of people. That John Gummer who she's recently given five thousand pounds extra to, we've had tea with him! He's only an ordinary man, they don't need all that money. There was a man named Peter Tatchell. He was going to be put forward for Bermondsey, and he said if he was elected he'd have been willing to accept £8,000 instead of, I think they get about £15,000. He wasn't even accepted. You see, this country worships money, especially Mrs Thatcher, especially the Conservatives, and you can't worship God and Mammon, Mammon being money, and people do worship money. I don't think much of the Conservatives.

In addition to supporting CND, Heather and her husband also belong to, or support, an atonishingly large number of other campaigns and causes, including Amnesty International, the Anti-Apartheid movement, the Greenham Common women, and the (then) striking miners, to name but a few. They visit the sick in hospital, correspond with a jailed South African priest and are disgusted by the working conditions of Indian tea plantation workers and the existence of the EEC surplus food mountains. A devoted couple, they see themselves as different from the materialistic, money-worshipping majority: 'When we had this social worker come along the other day she said, "You're rather unusual everybody else moans about their lot and how much they want and how they haven't got enough." We said we were quite comfortable and happy about it. Apparently, we must be something out of the ordinary to think that way.'

In their personal lives, in their approach to social and political

issues, Heather and her husband try to express their conception of
Christian witness, a witness incorporating a strong component of
moral duty. Heather has a firm faith in this transcendental moral
force: 'I'll tell you this. Take my advice, John. If you do the right
thing in this world you never get let down. There's a higher power
than ours. You can call it a moral law of the universe. If you do the
right thing, things work out and I've found this all through my life.'
Their membership of CND is an expression of this witness, a
commitment which is one facet of their religious way of life. Heather
and her husband's religious beliefs serve to engender a personal
stance similar to that of welfare-state CNDers: both the transcendental Christian moral law and the universalistic ideology of the
welfare state separate their adherents from the everyday acquisitive
and self-seeking ethics of British capitalist society. This is, I feel, a
more useful formulation of the distinction which Parkin draws
between 'instrumental' working-class politics and the supposedly
'expressive' politics of middle-class radicals.

Sarah Jackson, who is forty-four, is also a working-class member
of New Town CND. The daughter of a baker ('thirty-six years on
nights'), Sarah has been unemployed for the past four years, during
which time she has undertaken voluntary work for a local unemployed person's group and a, now defunct, local organisation which
helped to provide facilities for the town's West Indian youth. Sarah
is, obviously, a political activist and her kitchen, where the interview
was conducted, was festooned with evidence of her activism. At the
time of the interview, Sarah was especially preoccupied with the
miners' strike. Sarah's parents were Labour voters but her own
political awakening took place two years after she started work as an
office junior:

I was called 'a red' when I was eighteen. I was working in a department, there
was a guy who was a trained architect, he got the job over the 'phone. And
they [the management] said, 'Well, come up and see us and we'll talk about
your holidays, etc., etc.' and when he turned up they said, 'Sorry, you haven't
got enough qualifications.' He was West Indian, he was black. And he came
back, told us what happened, and I went *loopy*. And I only knew one black
family, so I didn't have, I wasn't surrounded by black people, I didn't know
any black people apart from this family. I didn't know what West Indians
were. I thought West Indians came from West India, I really did. I was that
naïve. And I just thought it was *immoral*, and somebody said to me, 'You're
a red,' and I said, 'Pardon?' and they said, 'You're a red,' and I thought,
'What do you mean?' I was literally looking at my skin, I was that naïve at

eighteen. And he said, 'You're a bloody communist,' and I didn't even know what a communist was! That's how naïve I was about politics. My father would never discuss religion or politics at home, never. [How did you get interested in politics?] It was after that, and I thought, well, if that's what a red is, and then I met up with an old boyfriend of mine – and I mean I didn't know his father was a member of the CP [Communist Party of Great Britain]. We used to have discussions, and Alan and me *always* used to argue against the others in the kitchen and I used to agree with everything he said, and I thought, 'I'll never join,' and then I met my first husband, and I hadn't known him very long, and I literally thought, 'Right, this seems to be the party for me,' it's the party that seems to have the most things I agree with in it, like non-racialist . . . so you can say I'm a socialist or a communist, you can put names on me, but basically I'm concerned about humanity but I like to have time off to enjoy myself.

Marching under the flat of the Young Communist Party, Sarah took part in the 1962 Aldermaston March (on which she was arrested and subsequently fined): 'I literally jumped in feet first. I'm like that.' For personal reasons, Sarah went into the 'political wilderness' until the late Seventies when she became reactivated and joined New Town CND which she thinks is:

. . . very different from when I first joined. I would say I was one of the very, very few that were not of the sort of the duffle-coat brigade, and I'm not sort of putting anyone down. But they were basically professional people. There were only one or two people, although their parents may have been working-class they were very thinking backgrounds, they had been involved in things. It's widened out now. I think it's broadened out into incorporating people from a lot of areas. Most of the people that I knew in the [original] New Town CND were teachers, but that was because my husband [and hence the people she was likely to meet] was a teacher. My husband came from that sort of background where he was always surrounded by books and thinking. I came from a completely different kind of background. So I suppose in some ways I was the odd one out because most of them, as I say, were professional people. There's one or two people in the town who, ever since I've known them, have been lecturers at college. But that might be peculiar to New Town, it's broadened out far more in New Town than when I joined in '61.

Sarah thinks that the majority of the public do not support the Campaign because:

I think the British are peculiar to themselves. They've never ever, unlike Europe, lived under a fascist régime. Therefore they haven't been occupied for hundreds of years and therefore, we also tend to be insular, being an island, we tend to be. Certainly in Europe, I think we're the most unpolitical, non-political. Basically, we're ignorant about politics. But then basically, once again, it comes back to education. Our young people are very different

from the young people in Europe. We flounder for a lot longer. We get
thrown out of school at sixteen and it's twenty-one, twenty-two, twenty-
three before we've shaken off that silly little, er, I mean, our attitude towards
sex is very, very childish. We tend to regard it as smutty. It's an unsophisti-
cation we tend to have here.

Sarah would be quite prepared to break the law in the pursuit of
nuclear disarmament and she supports the Campaign's non-party-
alignment policy because:

'I think it might be politic not to because it does embrace people from all
parties. Yeah, I think it's good, because if people know you belong to a
particular party, up go the barriers straight away. Whereas if you talk to
them it could be that you're both agreeing on the issue, party politics may be
different. Educate them into seeing it's part of a system that is producing
these things for their own ends, maybe you'll get the education through.

She sees the arms race:

. . . as part of, well, my own theory is that there is no manufacturer of nuclear
arms that wants a nuclear war. They keep the fear going so that they can
make a fast buck and also I think it's part of the policy of the American
government to economically break the Soviet Union. I think that's the main
reason we've got an arms race. In face, I think that's the only reason we've
got an arms race.

No longer a member of the Communist Party, Sarah now belongs
to the Labour Party and votes Labour 'because I see it as an anti-capi-
talist vote'. Not surprisingly, she strongly disagrees with all of Mrs
Thatchers administration's policies which she regards as perpetuat-
ing inequalities of power. I asked her what she would call herself in
political terms:

I don't know because I've been accused of so many different things. I'm an
atheist in so far as I don't believe in God. I believe in Christ as an historical
figure and if what he preached is true then I believe in that 100 per cent. So
I've been called a Christian. As I say, I don't believe in God, I'm an atheist. I
have certain moral things, whether it comes from conditioning, I'm not sure.
I was a member of the CP. My first husband still is. I never actually left . . .
after my first divorce I sort of went into a political wilderness. When I came
back to New Town I thought I'd never join another political party. I joined
the Labour Party because I thought it was the way to get the, the kind of
world I'd like to see. I suppose the best way, by working through a large
movement. Hmm, I suppose basically, yeah, I believe in the ethics of Christ
but I'm not a Christian. I believe that you can call it pure Christianity, pure
communism, pure anarchy, as, if you like, a sort of utopian world. I think it's
immoral that people are going hungry while us in the Western world are
going on diets. And yes, it has to do with politics. It's the politics that make

that situation arise in the first place and that is born out of greed and man not giving a *damn* for his fellow human being. That to me is pornography, that to me is immoral. We all do it to a degree, I mean I throw food away so I'm immoral, but I *try* not to do it.

Clearly, Sarah's moral form of politics bears an affinity to the Christian witness of Heather and Walter (the Christian lawyer) and shares a 'family resemblance' to the welfare-state CNDers' socio-political stance. Sarah believes that the original CNDers saw the Campaign:

. . . in that narrow context of being a moral issue. There were obviously people within it who saw it as part of an immoral economic system and that's how I see it; it is part of an immoral economic system and I didn't see it then, I saw it as a separate thing: 'Get rid of the Bombs and everything in the garden will be lovely.' I didn't realise why these Bombs were there, y'know, political naïvety.

Twenty-five years on, Sarah sees herself as more politically sophisti-cated and now imputes immorality to the 'economic system'. Never-theless, her political opposition to nuclear armaments retains the ethical thrust which resonates throughout the composite forms of life which go to make up the Campaign's culture.

In the foregoing interviews I have been concerned to show how various other forms of life (political and religious) and various social experiences affect the members' perception of, and participation in, the culture of CND. Despite the diversity of influences and experi-ence, the generative contexts, all of the above members are recog-nisably similar. Once again, it is similarities and differences which form the cultural category of CND. In particular, there exists a notable similarity between the personal stances of these members and the stance of the welfare-state CNDers. Crudely expressed, this is a moral posture in which those who do not agree with one are seen as apathetic and benighted.

In his study of the early Campaigners, Frank Parkin noted that a number of his adult middle-class respondents had 'creative', profes-sions. Unfortunately, Parkin's data is not sufficient to permit one to discover precisely what form of creative employment these respondents engaged in (see Appendix C). However, the literature on the original CND would seem to suggest that the musicians and artists who supported the first Campaign were, in the main, politi-cally orientated. As the following interview shows, support for CND may well owe more to social influences than to the creative muse.

Malcolm Ross is a professional musician and a member of Scots City CND. His disarmament activities include benefit concerts for the Movement and he has also played in productions staged by a left-wing theatre company. Malcolm thinks that disarmament protesting must always be non-violent and not:

. . . over-dramatic, die-ins, that sort of thing. I'm always afraid of alienating the average person who hasn't given it much thought. Marches, debate, reasoned publicity, that's the sort of thing I'm interested in and also, because I'm a musician, I look very hard at songs and theatre. I used to be a member of the Red Act Theatre company, that's the world I'm in. I think very much of music and arts in general as a method for changing people's attitudes. Protesting by blockading would work in the short term but you've got to change people's attitudes to bring their awareness up.

A pacifist, opposed to all weaponry, Malcolm thinks that the existence of the arms race can be attributed to the working of a 'self-perpetuating system'. He believes that the Campaign's non-party-alignment policy is correct because 'you just keep away from all the nonsense of party politics. It's a one-issue thing and no party would look at it as a one-issue thing; they'd look at it as part of their package of policies.' The majority of the public do not belong to the Campaign, he thinks, because of apathy. There's a possibility that they might feel alienated from that sort of thing, they might feel worried about it. Don't want to commit themselves.' Malcolm does not believe that members of CND are drawn from all walks of life:

No, I don't. I think they seem to come from a certain *kind* of person, not just to do with income class. It usually seems to be the kind of person who are fairly heavily motivated anyway, that are joiners. Hmm, you often find that they often work hard at something else. I don't know, the kind of people that don't seem to be involved is the lower middle class, to use that very broadly, people who have decided to buy a house and have a family. So, not from all walks of life, no. But from, I suppose, from the middle-class, working-class people who have been to university and mixed with other ideas are more likely to be in it.

Malcolm comes from a religious family, his mother is a housewife and his father is a director of a medium-sized Scots City company. Both parents are 'Tories'. Malcolm went to:

. . . an all male [private] school in Scots City with military traditional style and attitude. I was never at one with it. I hadn't really mixed with people except like that. It was quite a shock when I went to university and found all sorts of different people and found the questioning of attitudes. That wasn't desperately encouraged at my school . . . [break in tape] . . . It came as quite a shock. There were International Socialists. At first I thought it was a bit of a laugh, but, yeah, it definitely did, not so much the content of my courses, but the social life.

Malcolm studied English and Psychology, with the intention of becoming a journalist. Unfortunately, he failed to gain a sufficiently good class of degree for this profession and upon leaving university he worked for a short time in an audio-visual library and then became a professional musician. In addition, he forsook his parents' Conservative politics and he now considers himself to be 'a small '1' liberal, a trendy leftie, I don't know. I've never given it much thought. I mean, I vote socialist or ecology if there's a chance.' An inactive member of Equity, he is:

... worried, particularly worried about their [this Government's] whole attitude to the, well, welfare state's a broad word, but the whole government caring agencies. I fear that, although they say this is just the operation of the free market, they would prefer, I think at bottom I'm afraid that they want to create a prole class, a worker-bee class of people that are given sufficient to keep them alive but are kept away from the centres of education and decision-making. Rather than any one policy, that's what would worry me.

Malcolm has never belonged to any political party and, as his foregoing remarks show, he does not consider himself to be a particular political animal. Nonetheless, he performs at various benefit concerts ('not always CND, but that sort of thing'), and he has persuaded the initially reluctant members of his present band to do likewise ('at first it was just Greenpeace but now we do all sorts'). His interest in the nuclear disarmament issue dates from 'discussion at university rather than reading a particular document or seeing or hearing a particular speech and becoming converted or anything like that' and he joined his local group 'because I had been living with a group of people who got the Newsletter and I moved away and went to live on my own and I wanted to keep in touch'.

For Malcolm: 'the main thing in my life is my job'. However, in the formation of his views it has been his experiences of university which promoted his political awakening and his political interest and awareness has been furthered by his engagement with the left-wing theatre company and the social culture of musicians: 'Other issues do get brought up. Er, feminism, world development, you know, you hear more about it, hmm, the whole concept of the way the police behave is brought into question.' It would seem that it is these influences, this particular form of life, and not merely the creative

muse, which has rendered him susceptible to forming a commitment
to campaign.

As Malcolm observed, members of CND tend to be 'a certain kind
of person . . . it usually seems to be people who are fairly heavily
motivated anyway . . . you often find they often work hard at something else.' In the preceding interviews, it can be seen that the
respondents often have a commitment to other forms of life, political
or religious, the moral import of which closely resembles the ethical
stance which welfare-state CNDers have internalised from their
state-apprenticeships and vocations. However, as I have discussed, a
commitment to another form of life may lie somewhat uneasily with
members of CND. Of the remaining five respondents in this
chapter,[27] three fall comfortably into this heuristic pattern: thus,
73-year-old Elizabeth Duncan, a Catholic working-class member of
New Town CND joined the Campaign after 'we had a meeting about
Christian CND at my local church and that's what made me go to my
first meeting'; Keith Eagles, a hard working Labour Party and community activist personally knew the founders of New Town CND.
Although he feels that the disarmament issue is '*very* important', he
is more concerned with the issue of old-age pensions and the 'poor
getting poorer' and cannot spare the time from his political and
community activism to attend his groups' meetings; Philip Kent has a
long history of political trade-union activism and, as a 'revolutionary
socialist', has '. . . always been critical of CND on its restricted
policies. I know the argument about restricted single issues but it's
demonstrable in my eyes that single issues will not survive on single
issues; either they die or they're driven into discussion of other
political issues. Life is a good deal more integrated than CND
realises.' Nevertheless, this stalwart revolutionary socialist told me,
'I must say that my own reaction to Hiroshima – I'm arguing against
myself to my own surprise – my reaction to it was totally moral. It
was the immorality of it that totally staggered me.'

However, the remaining two respondents from my samples do not
conform to the heuristic approach which I have developed in this
study: neither respondent participates in any other complementary
form of life and they have not been influenced by state education or
state ideology. In this sense, they can be seen as counter examples to
the analytical arguments I have put forward.

Ronald Green joined Scots City CND in 1983: 'Things began to
look a bit dodgy with Reagan and all. They had a stall outside The

Academy in Fuller Street, signatures, y'know, so I signed it and gave my address and then I got an introductory thing. So that's what it was really.'

Since he joined the Campaign, Ronald has not taken part in any disarmament activities but he thinks that the best form of protesting, 'the thing I would most like to see, is such a dramatic increase in membership that it would just be impossible, that they had to, sort of sheer weight of numbers.' In favour of NVDA, Ronald thinks that he is too old for protesting and, besides: 'I don't feel strongly enough about it.' He believes that the Campaign's non-party-alignment policy . . . is almost essential. If you were restricted to one party, you'd get a drastic fall in the membership. I don't know, I've no idea of a breakdown of the figures, but I would imagine that most of them would be Labour or left-wing of Labour, but there must be a considerable proportion of SDP, Tories, all sorts.

In the light of his memories of the Second World War, Ronald feels ambivalent about pacifism but he would like to see all nuclear weapons abolished: 'I know it's possibly an idealist dream, but that would be my wish.' He sees the arms race as a consequence of a 'struggle of power' and he thinks that the majority of the British public do not belong to the Campaign out of:

. . . fear, they're afraid of the situation as it is, but they're more afraid of facing up to the realities of an about-turn in the situation and the uncertainty attached to it. And I think, the people I come into contact with anyway, that's the impression I'm left with anyway. It's, er, 'The *status quo* is bad but God knows what would happen if this was all reversed.'

Apart from three years' membership of the Scottish Nationalist Party between 1975 and 1978, Ronald has not belonged to any political party. In the event of a General Election, he would vote Labour and, politically, he locates himself on the left wing of the Party. Ronald 'disagrees with so much' that Mrs Thatcher's administration has accomplished and '. . . in the present time what I disagree most about is, whatever economic arguments she can bring forward for unemployment, there was no need to do it on the scale that she's done it. That's the thing I hate most about what she's doing, what she's done.'

The son of a building worker, Ronald was employed for most of his working life as an accounting clerk in the civil service. Ronald would have liked to attend university but he was forced to leave school at the age of fourteen in order to help support his family: 'I don't know what I would have wanted to study, but just the thought of it, the thought of books. I was always glad to get books in my hand. As a schoolkid I used to read a lot, even mathematics which I detested.' A young victim of the Thirties' Depression, Ronald has no formal educational qualifications, but he has attended some evening classes out of interest. Reticent in the interview, Ronald lacked the privileged confidence which underpins the middle-class articulateness of many of his Campaign counterparts. A decided atheist, and never a member of any other campaign or group, Ronald's membership of CND is not linked to any other form of life, nor is it augmented by a complementary moral posture or by an ideological stance inculcated by his experiences of education or work. Unlike the majority of the membership, and contrary to Malcolm's observation, Ronald is, in his own words, 'not a joiner at all'.

The final interviewee and counter case was, at ninety-four, the oldest respondent in my two samples. Despite his age, Dr Claus Stein is an articulate man, at ease in interviews – an ease probably born of experience, for Dr Stein is a distinguished classical composer and author of several books on music. Dr Stein thinks that as nuclear disarmament 'is a question of existence or non-existence, it certainly is the most important' contemporary issue, and he believes that 'mutual fear' underpins the arms race. In his judgement, members of CND are 'probably' drawn from all walks of life, however: 'I mean people who are able to think are in a minority and they've always been in a minority.' Never a member of any political party or trade-union, Dr Stein has 'always been a Liberal, all my life' and, in the event of a General Election, would vote for the Liberal Party. He supports the Campaign's non-alignment policy: 'It's perhaps better to be outside the party and not to be influenced by decisions taken by the party. It is outside politics in so far as the idea of the nuclear armament is simply unacceptable in every respect. One cannot inflict this, one cannot accept it.'

Dr Stein thinks that there may be some link between male attitudes and nuclear weapons: 'I think this is the truth: in some respects men are more stupid than women and this may be the cause of it.' With regard to the possibility of achieving nuclear disarmament, Dr Stein thinks that 'reason should prevail if it were sufficiently well-known to everyone [but] I'm old enough to have become sceptical with regard to my fellow human beings.'

Dr Stein has personal and reasonable grounds for this scepticism.

The son of a doctor of medicine, he studied music at a continental university and, when he graduated in 1912, turned professional. His career was interrupted by the First World War, after which he returned to composing and performing and, in 1929, he took an appointment as a director of a music college. Shortly before the Second World War he was compelled to emigrate to Britain where he has lived ever since. An erudite and cultured man, Dr Stein:

... belonged to CND ideally before it existed. Practically, since one of the worst days in my memory, August 1914, when the First World War started through a coincidence of idiocies. Since then I have become mistrustful with everything that happens in this world because worse couldn't happen. In 1914 the chief forces were the coincidence of chance events connected with personal stupidities, this is what leads of catastrophes.

Dr Stein 'would never trust any government with things like that [nuclear weapons]' and he holds the opinion that faced 'with a distrustful and heavily armed enemy it is a lesser risk to be unarmed. That is a simple fact for me.'

Very clearly, Dr Stein's membership of CND is not an expression of the social influences which impel his younger counterparts. In his own words: 'If I think back to the catastrophes of my life – 1914, 1918, the end of the First World War with its incredible catastrophes for central Europe, 1933, 1938 – I have lived through four catastrophes. Uprooted every time. And in a practical sense having to start again, every time. It's a little much, for one man.' Sadly, at the end of his life, Dr Stein is witness to yet another conflict between nation states, the outcome of which may well eclipse even these catastrophes.

Conclusion

In the preceding chapters, wherein I discussed the interviews with welfare-state CNDers, it was clear that these interviewees' views and opinions on nuclear disarmament matters (and social and political issues in general) were an expression of their wider social position. Typically, these interviewees had formed their political opinions whilst undertaking a state apprenticeship at an institute of higher education or in the course of their employment. These interviewees personally identified with their vocations and were politically and ethically committed to the welfare state. In this sense, the welfare-state CNDers' participation in the Campaign culture is an expression of their social position.

By virtue of their educational histories and their relation to the state, the welfare-state CNDers share in a common form of life. In contrast, the respondents in this chapter, with their various jobs and educational experiences, are more diverse; these respondents have social class locations whose effects are not nullified by a common form of life. In this chapter I have pursued the same analytical approach which I employed when discussing the welfare-state members of the Campaign – relating the respondents' politicisation, socio-political views and membership of CND to their social biographies. In contrast to the majority of welfare-state CNDers, the respondents in this chapter do not necessarily enjoy the educational and vocational underpinnings which have nurtured their welfare-state CND peers' socio-political stance. Instead, the spur to a commitment to CND has been generated by, and is an expression of, their affiliation to other religious and political forms of life. This is particularly true of those respondents from working-class backgrounds who have not had the privilege of higher education.

As I have stressed in previous chapters, there is no one common defining CND essence; the members share complementary similarities and differences. This is true of both the relation between members and the relation between CND and the affinitive religious and political cultures which combine to form the Campaign. In terms of a sociological heuristic, the affinity existing between the members is best understood as one of a similar stance towards the social world. In the same way that welfare-state CNDers feel responsible for their work, the respondents in this chapter, in various ways, see themselves as ethically accountable and concerned social agents. Just as the welfare-state CNDers work for, and identify with, the public good, so too the respondents in this chapter identify with some transcendental moral aim. This affinitive concern finds expression in a similar personal stance and a similar socio-political commitment which involves a personal responsibility for the social world.

The generative context of an individual commitment gives it a particular character and form. In common with their welfare-state counterparts, most of the respondents in this chapter support the Campaign's non-party-alignment policy. The exception to this support comes from those interviewees whose primary commitment is to the Labour Party rather than to a transcendental authority, such as a moral law or religious ethic. Pertinently, regardless of any criteria of social class, all the respondents in this chapter see non-supporters of the Campaign as benighted and/or materialistic. It is in relation to those perceived of as furthest outside the cultural category that the members' expression of a commonality of commitment and shared identification is clearest. Unlike themselves, the members see non-supporters as crassly materialistic and morally remiss, lacking a 'proper' personal stance.

It is this shared personal stance, this common commitment, which, in harness with an unspoken fear of nuclear weapons, acts as a cultural glue binding individuals in a common cause. Faced with an indiscriminate nuclear threat, and championing a unilateral policy, CND can accommodate otherwise divisive political and religious ideologies, for the commonality of commitment is predicated upon a transcendental aim which subordinates partisan strategies born of only, in the last resort, partially compatible perspectives.

However, as the interviews in this chapter clearly show, the affinity of commitments contained within the cultural category is a subtle matter not easily paraphrased or captured in the language of formal, Procrustean sociological analysis. For the purposes of understanding social life, description, rather than obfuscating explanation, can yield the richer picture. In the next chapter, I discuss the interviews I conduct with those respondents who hold elected offices in either Scots City or New Town CNDs.

7

The elected officials' commitment

Introduction

Unlike most other analysts of the peace movement, I have not focused solely upon the Campaign's 'activists'. All the interviewees in the previous chapters are 'lay members' of the Movement, as are the majority of the Campaign's supporters. These interviewees did not regularly attend meetings of their group, nor did they engage in very much formal campaigning (such as leafleting, publicity drives, etc.). Most of the administration and organising for both New Town and Scots City CNDs is undertaken by a small minority of the groups' members.

I am unhappy with any *a priori* equating of formal activism with greater personal radicalism. A prerequisite for being an activist is a fair amount of free time and, as can be seen from the interviews in the previous chapters, this is unavailable to many, especially women and welfare-state CNDers, who have occupational and familial commitments which militate against the degree of activism in which they would *wish* to be involved. Holding a post, such as Secretary or Chairperson, in a CND group is not an opportunity which is open to everyone; mundane reasons such as being too shy, or simply living too far away from where the group's meetings are held, play their part. Nevertheless, as the foregoing chapters show, lay members often campaign informally at their place of work and amongst their family and friends.

An analytical focus upon activists seems to suggest that these individuals will possess a greater, or stronger, degree of radicalism than the lay members. This, albeit implicit, argument is only credible if one believes that there is a common, uniform essence of CND radicalism; if this were not true, of what could one say the activists were a stronger case? This essence of 'CNDism' clearly does not exist in lay members who share only partially complimentary similarities and differences, and this is also the case for activists. What is interesting about the office-holders is that they must organise and administer a campaign, the composite factions of which exist in a state of both harmony and tension. This involves pursuing a policy of building a non-partisan Movement designed to attract the greatest possible public support.

For the sake of confidentiality, I have not specified the group to which these interviewees belong, nor the office which they held. The respondents in this chapter were sent a draft of their particular interview, together with a letter inviting them to comment upon what I had written. Seven of the interviewees replied to this letter and were happy with the draft and suggested only minor changes or clarifications which I have incorporated into the text.

The elected officials' commitment

Sally Almond's support for the anti-nuclear cause dates from the official formation of CND in February 1958; her membership of the national Campaign has never lapsed and at the age of sixty-six, she is one of her group's most active and energetic members. Sally's perspective on nuclear disarmament reflects her long involvement with the Movement, an involvement which has convinced her that if CND is to be successful it must remain primarily a one-issue campaign.

The daughter of a shipyard engineer, Sally left school in the mid-Thirties to take a job as an executive grade clerical officer in the Civil Service. Shortly after the end of the Second World War she married and, under the Civil Service regulations pertaining at the time, had to resign her job and she has never been in paid employment since. Naturally, Sally was relieved when the war ended and she was pleased with the outcome of the election: 'We thought, with this Labour government, 1945 and all that, [we'd] never have to worry again.' However, this feeling of security was to prove fairly short-lived:

I didn't think about politics until Suez [1956]. We were in London, and I'll never forget waking up that morning and hearing the radio people say that the British Air Force had bombed Cairo. That was what set me off. And the first thing I did then was that I rushed away and I thought, 'I must *do* something.' Here was all these kids that we thought were safe and this blinking government's dropping bombs and we picked the kids up – I remember putting the baby in a carry-cot – and we got into the car . . . we said, 'We just *can't* sit here, something's bound to be happening in London,' and we went into London. We parked the car near the Embankment and the whole place was seething with people. It was a most amazing experience, and this was the big Trafalgar Square demonstration against Suez [October 1956]. That was what, I suddenly realised, 'God!, we *could* have another war, these *stupid* people, and I blame myself for not thinking more about it.' So anyway, that triggered me off and I went and joined the United Nations Association.

Shortly afterwards, in 1957, Sally and her husband moved to their present home:

We were just getting settled here, and I opened the paper one night, I think it was January 1958, and there was this advertisement for the Hockton Hall meeting [the inaugural public meeting of her original CND group] and so I went along to that and you signed the usual piece of paper and before long I was on the Committee, and that's been that ever since.[28]

Although Sally had not been politically active until the Suez debacle, she came from a family which had lost relatives in the Great War and in the interview she speaks of the 'sadness' of her mother's generation in the inter-war years. Consequently, she became a pacifist, opposing conscription ('I was in the Civil Service, it was my friends, my generation, that were being conscripted'), and these personal experiences made the cessation of fighting in 1945 all the more precious and heightened her disgust at Eden's gun-boat diplomacy during the Suez affair. As for many of her generation, 1956 was to prove a watershed year, a time of political awakening.[29]

From 1958 until 1963, Sally actively campaigned in the original CND and in the early Sixties joined the 'Liaison Committee for Women's Peace Groups'.[30] From the earliest days of the original Campaign, Sally has been concerned that the Movement should not be party political but should concentrate solely upon the one issue of nuclear disarmament. She believes that the original national Campaign went into decline because many members of the movement were under the impression that the 1963 Labour Party Manifesto would commit Wilson's administration to a renegotiation of the Nassau Agreement and the scrapping of Britain's Polaris Force. Consequently, many of the early CNDers diverted their energies into working for a Labour electoral victory.

Of course, when they came to office, Labour went ahead with the Polaris programme, albeit somewhat reduced in scale, and the promises of the 1963 manifesto were largely forgotten. Sally believes that this disappointing performance disillusioned many, especially younger, CNDers who subsequently left the Movement to work for other causes such as the Anti-Apartheid and the Anti-Vietnam-War campaigns: 'This disaster after 1964 completely disillusioned a whole generation of young CNDers and they would have nothing to do with them [the Labour Party].' This sense of disillusionment and betrayal was deeply felt by Sally herself and in the interview she spoke at some length about national and local politicians she had known who, after the 1964 General Election, had foresaken their commitment to CND in favour of what she sees as political opportunism. Sally has come to the conclusion that 'in politics your career is more important than your conscience'. Sally's mistrust of conventional politics and politicians has remained with her and she tries to use her influence to prevent the present day CND from falling prey to the errors of its predecessor.

Sally thinks that members of CND are drawn from all walks of life ('Oh yes, even more so now') and that unlike in the early Movement, CND now has the added strength of support from specialist subgroups such as the Medical Campaign Against Nuclear Weapons and the anti-nuclear-power lobby. She believes that the majority of the public do not support the Movement because of 'lack of information' and that the government tries to suppress public debate on disarmament matters unless provoked by CND. Sally agreed with Bruce Kent's view that to possess and to threaten to use nuclear weapons is illegal, 'so it's a human right and a public duty to object to an illegal act', and she has always supported Non-Violent Direct Action (NVDA) protesting. As one would expect, she thinks that the Campaign's non-party-alignment policy is 'absolutely essential, from the very beginning and now', for disarmament is 'primarily a moral issue. It's also a very practical issue; people of differing views can work together in CND.'

Also predictably, Sally does not support the policies of Mrs Thatcher's administration, which she considers to be 'possibly the worst government we've ever had'. Not a member of any political party, she would vote for the Labour Party if they would firmly pledge themselves to implementing their present (1983) Conference policy on nuclear disarmament and she describes herself in political terms as:

. . . agnostic. I suppose I'm just obsessed with defence. I could never vote for the Tory Party. I suppose I am a socialist in the basic sense that I believe in social justice and that there should be things like equal rights, basic sub-sistence wages for everyone, dramatic things like that. But I've not time for the political wheeling and dealing of the political system as it is now and I applaud people like Tony Benn who've tried to clean it up. To my mind he seems to be bringing some sort of principle back into the thing.

Sally thinks that, 'unfortunately, politics has got a bad name. People don't go in with shining armour any more as they did in our gener-ation when they thought to go in to politics was the best possible public service you could do . . .' In contrast to the sordid political world of 'wheeling and dealing', Sally sees CND as morally untain-ted, 'there's nothing for people in CND except hard work', and certainly Sally works impressively hard for the Campaign's cause. Nevertheless, despite her grave reservations, she thinks that if the disarmament issue had not existed she would have gone into the Labour party 'because, despite the failures of the past, it is the Party for social justice'.

Sally's parents 'always voted Labour, but I wouldn't call them political people. The atmosphere in our house was always anti-war.' As I have already remarked, Sally and her family mourned the 'lost generation' and as a young woman she saw her friends conscripted into the army. Naturally, the post-war peace and the promise of the Attlee Government would have been especially precious to her and the crass handling of the Suez crisis came as a deep shock to her expectations. Once again, the lessons of war had not been learnt. Once again, the state was failing to live up to its ideological image.

In contrast to Sally, Clive Thompson's perspective on CND is born of a distinctly working-class biography. In 1979, Clive co-founded the local branch of the peace campaign which was to evolve, in 1980, into his local CND and he has held two elected posts in his group. He believes that the majority of the British public do not belong to the Movement. '. . . because the majority of people don't see clearly the danger. And when they do see it they don't feel they can do anything about it and they're so immersed in the problems of daily living, and the media encourages this way of thinking, and they just shut it out.' When I asked him about the members of CND, he replied, 'There are people from all walks of life, but it's activists, dominated by people like myself.'

For Clive, the arms race is a direct consequence of the drive for profit by the companies involved in arms manufacture. He sees nuclear disarmament as an essential prerequisite to any other political or social ambition and he believes that the aims of CND are 'the most important political issue of the century'. Clive completely agrees with the Campaign's non-alignment policy because:

We are not a political party, we are a pressure group, but one of the most powerful pressure groups that's ever existed. If we get large enough, if people understand that such a group can really influence government, and providing that it works hard enough, it can change government policy and can, in my way of thinking, which might be a bit exaggerated, save the world. And therefore, if you're going to involve the majority of the people, you've got to recognise from the start that people have different politics, different standpoints, different religions. And you *can't* allow these differences of opinion to dominate. And we do have this problem in ----, and people *don't realise it*. They just don't realise how they're tending to bring their ideas and prejudices into it. I have prejudices, which I struggle to overcome. I do believe that you've got to submerge your prejudices.

Clive believes that 'we have all got to work together and try to understand the other person's point of view' and that the problem of people bringing particular prejudices and 'sectional ideas' into the Campaign can be seen on both a local and national level. Instead, the members of CND should remember 'that this is the central aim, nuclear disarmament, and we should keep this aim in front'.

However, Clive is certainly not apolitical. Indeed, he believes that his lengthy experience of working in the British Communist Party helps him to overcome his own prejudices. Born in London in 1917, his father (whom he described as 'a skilled artisan') died when Clive was only ten years old, leaving him to be brought up by his mother who worked for most of her life as a waitress. Clive became politically involved in the Thirties:

The reason why I joined the CP [in 1937] eventually – because I toyed with pacifism and I toyed with the Labour Party, and I joined the Left Book Club, but I found in the Communist Party the most sincere, the most understanding people, I felt had an *answer*. They weren't waffling, they had a clear-cut answer. [Why did you get interested in politics at that time?] I don't know, it's a question you can ask anybody, I think it's part of your make-up, that's all, a rebel I suppose. I think it's partly because what I saw happening to my own mother and the way we were treated, and the landlord, and we went through all that saga of the rentman calling. And I used to get very angry. I can remember, although I was only a youngster at the time, really getting angry with him at the door when he was calling for the rent and I could see my mother struggling to keep the place together and there was this man calling for his arrears and I thought that was wrong. And I suppose I had that in me, and I still have. I just *can't stand* oppression of any kind whatsoever, wherever it might be, and I'm old enough in the tooth to recognise that all things aren't rosy everywhere, anywhere. Human nature has its strengths and weaknesses in the Soviet Union and in the United States of America.

Now retired, Clive has worked all his life as a skilled engineer and has served as a shop-steward in his union, both when working in London and in – – – –. Still a member of the CP, Clive would wish to vote for a Communist Candidate in the event of a General Election, but if no such candidate were standing he would vote Labour, 'as I always have done'. As one would imagine, he strongly disapproves of Mrs Thatcher's Government:

Well, her whole policy is aimed at turning the clock backwards in my opinion to one where sheer personal advantage is the sole arbiter of success, which brings in its train all the evil things which society has always been subjected to. That's the whole point about it; if you leave human gain, personal gain, profit, whatever term you want to call it, to be the sole arbiter then it's the law of the jungle. And the ultimate result of the jungle is nuclear weapons of course, but everything else goes with it, the attacks on the trade-unions, the run-down of all the facilities of the so-called welfare state. You name it, it's being hived off for the private enterprise. And the people with the least moral concepts, whose main aim is self-advantage, are the ones who come out top-dogs everytime. It's the law of the jungle, and that's what Mrs Thatcher wants us to get back to. Whatever she might think she's doing, that's what it boils down to.

Clive believes that on occasions in the past his views have been misrepresented by the press and he was perhaps understandably cautious when I interviewed him, for he is aware that his membership of the Communist Party may provoke prejudice. I found Clive articulate, sincere and tolerant of other people's points of view. As a very active member of CND, he tried to live out his belief that nuclear disarmament is the supreme contemporary issue and that members of the Campaign must not, albeit unconsciously, allow their personal political or religious attitudes to dominate the Movement. I asked him whether he thought that CND was a moral Movement:

It's difficult. Yes, it's a moral Campaign if you like, but like every other word in the dictionary it gets a connotation and gets stuck-up so people can decry and say, 'Oh, you're a moralist,' or whatever. Ultimately, whatever people want to say about it, all the great achievements of humanity in the history of mankind, in the sciences, the arts, and in trying to build a caring and loving society, are being defended in this Campaign. If that's moral, then yes, it's a moral Campaign, but it has to be practical and deal with the realities of the situation in which we live.

Unlike Sally, Clive's biography and politicisation is decidedly working-class in character and is not referenced to experiences of state education or employment. Both Clive and Sally express strong support for the Campaign's non-alignment policy and see nuclear disarmament as 'above' party-political considerations. The threat of nuclear genocide seems to call for a subordination of personal politics – the issue seems too momentous, too all encompassing, to allow such potentially divisive factors to come to the fore. Of course, this is not just a characteristic of the elected officials, nor of just today's campaigners; this belief was much in evidence in the original Movement. This attitude permits very diverse individuals and attitudes to merge in a common culture.

In the interviews with welfare-state CNDers, I noted that a commitment to their professional ideology spilled over into other areas of their lives and it was seen that such commitment was often deeply felt and positively evaluated. This commitment constitutes an ethical stance and can be engendered by a variety of sources. For instance, as a boy, Derek Sox won a scholarship to a private school where he joined the Anti-Apartheid campaign (AA): 'I felt especially at the school I was at, there was a thing, er, some people's attitudes really disgusted me and I felt it was important to show the way you felt about something like that.' Derek's participation in AA was, he told me, an act of schoolboy rebellion against what he saw as the privileged attitudes at the school and only amounted to a nominal membership. His political activism was to begin some years later:

I sort of felt all the time I was at school, and after I started university, that I'd never really *done* anything, and I felt guilty about that but I felt I hadn't really found anything in which I could really direct my energies usefully, mainly 'cause I'd never come across anybody. Some of my friends were in the Communist Party for instance, but I didn't want to join any political party because I didn't really trust any political party at that time and I felt at that time very reluctant to join anything because I was scared stiff of getting too involved because I knew there was *so much* out there which needed changing that if I joined anything I would *have* to commit myself to it and I wasn't ready to commit myself to anything. I was afraid of getting into something I'd have to commit so much time to, I'd have to lose everything else. It wasn't 'till a friend said, 'Come along to this Oxfam group,' which I joined. And that was when I started getting involved and of course it did happen: I thought that things have got to be done, you've *got* to change people's minds before it's too late and, hmm, for quite a number of years I was very active in the Young Oxfam group in --- and that was where I met my girlfriend in fact.

In 1982, Derek and his girlfriend[31] became joint office-holders in their local group, 'because I thought that we should be able to handle it, and y'know we wanted to *do something* and we felt we could probably do it reasonably well'. Derek believes that members of CND are 'predominantly middle-class, professional or semi-professional', which he thinks may be a result:

. . . of the image we present because of that; the working class in general, who we haven't been so successful in drawing into CND, are not in such a good position to be able to go out and join groups and go to meetings and maybe broaden their education at an earlier stage as we are, they're more concerned with going out and earning their daily living.

Derek thinks that that majority of the British public do not belong to CND because:

. . . the majority of people that you ask on the street would say, 'Yes, I think it's absolutely wrong that you allow people to starve in the Third World,' and would say, 'Yes, I think nuclear weapons are a terrible thing,' but when it actually comes down to actually doing something about it they are scared stiff about *committing themselves*, because once they do they would feel that their cosy little life-style isn't the same any more; they can't go on ignoring it any more. So people are very willing I think to believe the sort of propaganda that's put out to justify nuclear weapons. The government have a far greater opportunity to get their message across than the peace movement. I think if people *really* understood the reasons behind it, they would be members of the peace movement.

In his own biographical progression from rebellious schoolboy, Oxfam worker and now CND activist, Derek has lost this debilitating fear of becoming 'committed'.

A Labour Party member, Derek supports the Campaign's non-party-alignment policy because 'CND is a single-issue Campaign, and CND's policy should be to win as many political parties to its policy as well as many non-political people.' He sees the task of CND as being one of convincing the public of the need to get rid of nuclear weapons and thinks that 'if we've done our jobs properly', people can be credited with sufficient political common sense to vote for the party which seems most likely to carry out CND's aims. In common with some of the other CNDers who I interviewed, Derek found it hard to draw a clear-cut distinction between ethics and politics. However, he told me that he thought nuclear disarmament '. . . is first and foremost a moral issue. For us involved in the Movement it's a moral issue, but for the people who are building the Bomb, for the government of the day, it's a political issue. So it's a political issue whether we like it or not. But wanting to get rid of them is a moral issue.' Derek's personal involvement in the Campaign stems from his slowly evolving commitment to activism, and it is not difficult to perceive how this ethical stance finds resonance with the moral standpoint which is fostered, by state apprenticeships and employment, in the lives of welfare CNDers. This intermeshing of similar perspectives allows a commonality of culture to exist for CNDers, a culture of individuals committed to non-partisan ethical protest. This moral commitment, and the subsequent wish to 'make a stand', may derive from a variety of social sources and idiosyncratic experiences; notably, and as recognised by Parkin, it is very similar to the notion of religious 'witness'.

Alec Right, a 43-year-old CND office-holder, joined his local group four years ago and has been a member of Pax Christi (the Catholic Church peace campaign) for the past twelve months:

I'd always been thinking about the issue, I think through a Christian concept through the morality or immorality of the arms race and the arms race in general, and they got Bruce Kent down to speak and I signed a piece of paper saying I'd been to the meeting and every month they pushed the Newsletter through the door, and he [Bruce Kent] was at the national demo of 1980 and I thought, 'Right, I must get off my backside and do something', and I went to the local meeting and signed on as a member and that was it.

Alec thinks that the Campaign's non-party policy is essential: 'I think it has to be. Who can trust politicians? One can support a political party because you think that will be the party that will bring about a more just society, but when it comes to so-called defence I don't think I'd trust anyone.' He sees himself as in the process of becoming a pacifist and believes that disarmament must and should always be non-violent as a question of principle. The existence of the arms race is, for Alec, a product of profit-hungry capitalists in the West and the fear of invasion in Eastern Bloc countries.

When I asked Alec whether he thought that members of CND were drawn from all walks of life, he replied:

I was thinking about this the other day, and I can only speak from my own experiences. We've got no members from the council estate [the particular estate close to his home]. There isn't *one member* from that estate. I get the impression it's all middle-class people. I think that in the main that they're people who've thought about it, who've taken the time to think about the issue and joined. But there is a very strong Christian element in ---- CND and that's become very pronounced in the past twelve months.

He believes that:

... the majority of the British people are apathetic, always have been. Its been shown. It takes something quite dramatic to stir them into action. The last time was in the Second World War when the good old British spirit came to the fore. And I think it's a sad reflection of our society that it takes something like that to, despite all the education that people have had over the years. They don't *want* to think for themselves and they object and attack people who do try and make them think about it.

Alec left school with seven 'O' Levels and one 'A' Level and entered the Civil Service. He was not involved in the first Campaign, or in politics, until quite recently ('too busy enjoying myself to get involved in political things'). However, he is a practising Roman Catholic and, prior to his joining CND, had been one of the founding members of the local Ecumenical church and was very involved in Church-sponsored charitable projects in the Third World. For Alec, disarmament and Third World issues are 'all interrelated, no matter how you look at it. It's all robbing the poor. The money that's spent on armaments is so obscene. It's depriving people all over the world as well as in this country.'

Alec now channels his energies into CND campaigning, which he sees as the most pressing contemporary issue. His political awakening came about, in a truly Marxist fashion, during the course of an industrial dispute: 'It was when I was Chairman of our union branch and we were involved in strike action. And that was when I became politically aware. That was when I became really politically aware. Then I joined the Labour Party. Then I joined CND.' Alec regards his experiences during this strike as educative. I asked him what had prompted him to become active in his union: 'I don't know. Maybe I've always had this sense of justice, y'know, that if you want anything done you've got to get up and do it. Obviously, if things are unfair *we* should be doing something about it and 'we' starts with yourself. It's just finding the courage to get up and do it.' For Alec, this 'courage' was forged in the course of the strike and it is a resource he can now draw upon for CND campaigning. He says he would class himself as a socialist: 'I believe in a more equal and equitable society, each according to his needs', and predictably, he dislikes Mrs Thatchers administration's policies and Mrs Thatcher personally; 'she's just got no consideration for other people's problems'.

In common with the other CND office-holders whom I

interviewed, Alec told me that 'most of my close friends are now from CND'. He decided to take on the office, which he has held since joining, because 'I'd had a lot of experience as a trade-union activist, Chairman and Secretary of our branch, and I felt I could use the experience I'd had over many years for helping ---- CND. I just felt it was something I could contribute to it.' Alec found that his new duties quickly came to occupy all of his free time. Before joining the Campaign, Alec had not known anyone in the Movement but, in the four years in which he has been a member, he has become acquainted with most of the town's activists for, as he told me, 'We've got a lot of members, but ---- is a funny place; it doesn't matter what you're involved in it's still the few who do all the work.'

Alec's parents were both Roman Catholics. He was brought up in the faith and his Church campaigning and involvement in the Ecumenical movement predate his membership of CND. His religious faith, his sense of justice and his political awareness (deriving from his union activism) are all intermeshed in his participation in the culture of CND. They are resources which he employs and which intertwine with the social relations that other members exercise in the creation of the Campaign. Alec's biography has engendered a personal ethical commitment and the confidence to express it. CND embraces this commitment, which bears similarity to the personal stance of other members who view the Movement as a non-party crusade for survival. Clearly, however, it is distinct in character and origin from the world view of Clive (whom I discussed earlier in this chapter). Interestingly, when I asked Alec what sort of work he would choose to do, he replied, 'I think I'd like to be a teacher, to influence the younger generation.' I have been struck by the career choices of respondents such as Alec and Sally; notably, the choice is often a welfare-state post.

Gloria Smith also belongs to the Ecumenical movement, chairs her church's Social Responsibility Group and sponsors a child in the Far East. Gloria supports the Campaign's non-party-alignment policy for she feels that CND 'should embrace everybody', regardless of their political views, and she believes that the profile of her group is 'quite representative, with a large Christian membership'. For her, the arms race is a consequence of, 'fear, pure fear on both sides'. She thinks that the majority of the public do not support the peace movement because:

. . . they don't like to think too deeply about it, it becomes uncomfortable. It's a bit like a drug. You sort of go into CND not knowing very much about nuclear weapons and then you start finding more and more out and then you can't stop. I think most people don't want to be disturbed. They've got enough problems of their own, they don't want any more.

Gloria joined CND four years ago: 'They had a thing down the town, a video, and I thought I really must join and it dragged on from there.' She took up her present office six months ago: 'They just asked me to do it and, as there was no one else who wanted to do it, I said, "All right." ' I was present at the meeting which elected Gloria and it was clear that she is a popular member of the group, a popularity stemming, at least in part, from her vivacious personality and her record of activism. Previously employed as the manager for a firm of insurance brokers, Gloria is now a full-time housewife and she told me that, if she could choose, 'I suppose I would probably like to do social work.' Not a member of any political party or trade union, she describes herself as 'generally socialist' and would vote for the Labour Party at a General Election 'as long as they stuck to their present defence policies'. She does not agree with any of Mrs Thatcher's administration's policies and she told me that she doesn't 'like to see the way the welfare state is going, education, health services, the social aspects of life today, it's going so bad. I find that really worry.'

As the Chairperson of her church's Social Responsibility Group, Gloria brings matters of social concern to the attention of the congregation and it was my impression that it was her religious conviction, rather than a political or work-induced perspective, which forms the basis of her campaigning stance. It was unclear, from the interview, what exactly had prompted Gloria to take an *interest* in Christianity. Fortunately, in her comments on the draft of her interview, she clarified this for me:

It's not an 'interest' in religion, that sounds like a hobby or something. My Christianity has always been important to me, as a young child I enjoyed Sunday School and stopped going only when, at the age of ten, I discovered horses! As the riding lessons were on Sunday mornings, religion took a back seat for a few years. It was when I was sixteen that I realised how much I missed my Church. There was no sudden event or happening in my life, tragic or otherwise, which some people think one has to experience before finding religion. I'm not being over-sensitive here, but it's hard to explain how strong my Christian convictions are and how, even as a child, it was so natural to follow Christ's teachings. Indeed, it is my Christian conviction which is the cornerstone of my peace activism.

She believes that disarmament is achievable:

. . . otherwise I wouldn't be doing it. It's going to be a long, long struggle but it's just like any other issue that a minority have taken on, like the slave trade or anything else. It's going to take a long time, let's hope we've got long enough. If only people are not to be blinded by the media which is terrible. It's got to come politically, I suppose; I wouldn't like CND to be used for political purposes but I'm not opposed to using politics for CND purposes.

This rejection of, or ambivalence towards, party politics helps atheistic Communists and non-political Christians to work together to prevent the potentially divisive ideologies and perspectives which exist in the Campaign coming to the fore. In this endeavour, the socio-political ethic of the dominant culture in the CND form of life, the contribution of welfare-state members, is clearly of value. CND itself is, in this sense, ecumenical, embracing any individual who believes in the aim of disarmament regardless of their other political or religious predilections, and, as in Ecumenicalism, it is inappropriate to champion a partisan form of witness which may jeopardise the ability of others to share the faith.

Marianne Weston, a 57-year-old CND office-holder, joined the Campaign approximately three-and-a-half years ago. She finds herself 'in a bit of a dilemma' with regard to the Campaign's non-party-alignment policy: 'I believe we're never going to get anywhere unless a political party is strongly supporting us. But at the same time, I do think there are people in different parties who can unite on our aims. So I feel we should welcome everyone.' Describing herself as 'ninety per cent a pacifist', she 'would strongly oppose involvement in anything that wasn't going to be non-violent'. Marianne believes that members of her local CND group are reasonably representative of the population at large:

We have a fair range; we have men and women, we have varied classes. I think it's reasonably well-spread. We have people from churches. I think perhaps it's weaknesses – oh, I don't know if it is a weakness – it is very largely Labour Party, although we have a few Liberals and SDPs. But I think a better spread than I would have expected. I would have expected it to be sort of rather middle-class, middle income and so on.

Drawing upon her experiences of talking to people who are not supporters of the Campaign, Marianne thinks that:

. . . there is an attitude of 'it's so awful it doesn't bear thinking about, so I won't think about it'. There's others who think we must be able to retaliate and there's the awful feeling of revenge that people have; if they're going to hit us, we're jolly well going to hit them . . . but I think it's mainly fear that if we haven't got it [the Bomb] we become a sitting target.

Marianne joined the Labour Party fifteen years ago. She 'attends the ward meetings, canvasses before the Elections and that's about the extent of it' and she regards herself as 'moderately left, but I'm not Militant Tendency'. For Marianne, 'there was no major political thing that made me join [the Labour Party], it was just a gradual feeling that I must stand up and be counted'. At this time, her brother-in-law was standing as a parliamentary candidate in the 1970 General Election and she had just moved from a Conservative Cornish constituency to a more left-wing environment in the North. Marianne deplores Mrs Thatchers administration's 'general attitude of, 'You pull yourself up by your boostraps,'' an attitude which she thinks 'seems to work out in just about every policy, on privatisation and education and health and social services and moving as much as possible away from public ownership and public control'.

Upon leaving her secondary school, Marianne went to university to read for a science degree. Unfortunately, a recurrent illness prevented her from finishing her degree course and she had to leave university prematurely. Shen then went to work in the office of a firm of solicitors, studied for law 'articles' and practised as a solicitor until the mid-Seventies when, once again, her recurrent illness forced her into early retirement. Since her enforced retirement, Marianne has been the Secretary of the (now defunct) local World Development Movement, has been involved in her church's Third World charity projects, undertaken voluntary work for the Citizens' Advice Bureau and is currently the Secretary of a residential housing organisation for the aged. The daughter of a Methodist minister, Marianne is herself a practising Christian: 'I've always had an interest in Third World issues. My parents were missionaries, and I've sort of grown up with that idea. I've worked for a missionary society myself in this country at one time.'

In the last three years, Marianne has held two offices in CND: 'I was pushed into it. I was sort of pressing for getting more people involved so someone suggested, sort of pressed the job onto me.' A stalwart member of her group, Marianne would appear to devote most of her time to CND and her voluntary social work. She lives with another voluntary worker and during the course of the interview, which lasted about one hour, we were interrupted several times by telephone calls concerning her voluntary duties. Clearly, in her biography, Marianne's religious faith, presumably learnt from her missionary parents, has been a great and continuing influence. But not all of her friends in her church share her views on disarmament, dissent which she finds somewhat disturbing:

There are certain close friends who are active in the peace movement. There are others who I just assume, they may not be active but I just sort of assume [their support for the nuclear disarmament cause]. But there are others, and this is where I feel my greatest anxiety in a way about what I *should* be doing, people within my church who definitely are not. They may not be my closest friends in the church, but they are friends, people for whom I feel a great respect in many ways. And I find it very difficult with them to try to press my views, for it seems to me to be sort of impugning their faith; they see their religious faith leading them in one way and it's very difficult to impugn those beliefs. And yet I feel very strongly that Christianity should lead one into this [that is, support for CND].

I asked her whether she saw today's Campaign as a moral issue: 'It is for me. I think that nuclear arms are immoral, and that even to threaten to use them is immoral. It is a moral issue. For me, irrespective of whether or not it makes ourselves a target, I just say it's *wrong*. And I would stress that as one of my arguments against armaments.'

Marianne, in common with the lay members whom I interviewed, takes a socio-political stance which is only partially complementary with that of other supporters. Her ethical commitment is nurtured and finds expressions in her religious life and in her voluntary work, and it is interesting to note the inner conflict which Marianne experiences when she finds the ethics of some members in her church do not completely square with the morality of the CND culture. Given the choice, Marianne would wish to be employed as a social worker.

Celia Watkins, the remaining CND office-holder in my sample, has not worked since 1963 when she gave up her job on the shop-floor of an electronics company to become a full-time housewife. Now that her children have grown up, she occasionally helps her husband with his small business. If she could choose, Celia would plump for 'something in the "caring" . . . I think I'd find something in the social services, something in welfare, interesting'. Unlike Marianne, Celia comes from a working-class background (her father was a building worker and her mother worked in cotton mills and served in building site canteens), and she describes herself as a 'left-wing socialist'. An active member of her local Labour Party, instrumental in getting her town declared a nuclear-free zone, Celia blames 'money, power, the big monopolies' for the arms race: 'They're not interested in disarmament because they're making too much profit. It's down to capitalism really. That's a personal opinion really, and a lot of people would be horrified, but that's what I really believe.'

She thinks that the majority of the British public do not support the Campaign, 'out of ignorance for a start. Many people think that governments know better and that Russia is such an awful thing.' For Celia, 'governments are a puppet of capitalism' and if matters of defence were left solely to the government, '. . . they'd go on rising and rising out of the public purse and the Health Service and education and the Third World are suffering greatly through it. We've got the technology to bring these people water yet we spend it on bloody destructive things. I don't know – I'm an idealist – but it just screws me up.' Celia thinks that members of CND are drawn from all walks of life and she does not support the view that nuclear weapons are merely an extension of male aggression. Although she recognises that social institutions of war are traditionally male-dominated, she is: 'not a feminist. I've got mixed feelings. I can't really say so when you've got people like Thatcher, not really. I don't go with that line [of thinking].'

As a young woman, Celia did not belong to the original Campaign: 'I was very unaware really. I was one of those people that annoy me now. I was too busy having a good time I suppose.' She joined CND:

. . . about seventy-nineish, I suppose. What it was, I was one of those people who hated the thought of nuclear weapons but believed in nuclear deterrence, burying my head in the sand really. I think it was when they started on about Cruise, I thought, 'Jesus, this has gone too far.' I joined the United Peace Response [the precursor of her local CND] and I became involved from there. Then more and more active.

At the same time, she joined the Labour Party, and she now sees herself as a left-wing activist, using the language of contemporary radical left politics. Celia was elected to her present office in CND following the resignation of her predecessor some eighteen months ago. Since joining the Campaign she has become increasingly interested in radical politics and she believes that, as a result of her political activism, her telephone is 'tapped' and that, following a visit to Greenham Common, she is being spied upon by the Ministry of Defence. Celia's mother died when Celia was eighteen:

So I don't really know what she was politically. She was quite rebellious in lots of things. I've got a feeling she may well have been a socialist because she was *always* on about the Health Service, how wonderful it was and that sort of thing, so I would think she would have been a socialist, especially coming from Cottonbrough at that time. My father I think used to vote Liberal. He now votes Labour. I've sort of educated him.

Twenty-five years after her mother's death, Celia is witness to the current attack on the public sector. She agrees with none of Mrs Thatcher's policies and especially, and emphatically, disagrees with 'privatisation, cuts in health services and education. I don't agree with any of her bloody policies!' As I have already remarked, Celia is very active in her local Labour Party, sees herself as a political animal, and employs a left-wing perspective and lexicon when discussing nuclear disarmament issues. Even so, when I asked her opinion of the Campaign's non-party-alignment policy, she replied:

Yes, I think it is good in a way because CND is a non-political organisation. You've even got Tories in it, Liberals, Communists, Labour Party. Yeah, I think they've got to keep that line. It can be off-putting for other people who might be interested because either it's a socialist organisation or whatever. Yeah, I think it needs to be non-political.

Although she donates money to, and supports the aims of, Amnesty International and Greenpeace, Celia has never been involved in any charity or undertaken any voluntary social work, for she feels that it is better for her to concentrate her energies on what she sees as the more pressing issue of nuclear disarmament. In addition, her political commitments take up a lot of her time: 'My family didn't see me for months on end before the [General] Election!' The only other post which she holds is that of School Governor. Celia left school without any qualifications and she clearly believes that, with improved facilities and better teachers, she would have been capable of passing exams but '. . . our education was very poor . . . Y'know, secondary modern school, that sort of thing. Now I look back on it, it was disgusting. We didn't even have a chance to take them [exams] unless you were in the top class.' As a School Governor, Celia feels helpless in the face of the recently imposed cutbacks in education expenditure:

As I say, in the Sixties it did become, I noticed at that time because my Amanda was born in '66, and Paul was a couple of years older, and they went to school and you *just couldn't compare* their schools; theirs was a private education compared to ours. I mean it was incredible, the amount of resources. My kids just missed the cuts y'know. Amanda caught the tail end of them, so she was fortunate. But the kids that are coming up now; I'm a School Governor and I feel like throwing the towel in, because there's nothing you can do as a School Governor except write letters. We really ought to get organised on that one.

Celia thinks that her local CND group is 'fairly successful. I think it could be more successful.' I asked her, 'What would you do to make it more successful?: 'Well, we rack our brains all the time. Education, that's what it is, educating the public.' In common with her more middle-class counterparts, Celia sees those who do not support CND as 'ignorant', benighted and duped by the media:

You get a few each time you have a stall or something like that, you get a few. An awful lot of people can't bear to even think about it so they bury their heads in the sand. They'd rather not even discuss it. What annoys me, what I can't believe, women with kids passing our stall and looking the other way. But it is horrific. All they want to do is to get on with their lives. They don't want to worry about war and destruction. It must be nice to be like that. I can't be like it I suppose.

Before joining CND in 1979, Celia knew very few members of the local peace movement and had not been involved in any form of political activism. The media publicity surrounding the siting of Cruise missiles and a meeting of the United Peace Response provoked a political awakening and five years later she is a heavily committed political activist and CND office-holder. In common with the majority of CNDers whom I interviewed, Celia's primary objective to the present Government is directed against the running-down of welfare-state provisions and, in her capacity as a School Governor, she tries to resist the erosion of state educational services – a political right of which she feels herself deprived. Celia's political views, which are intertwined with her perception on disarmament issues, have a decidedly and particular ethical character, as does her personal commitment. It seems likely that Celia was influenced by her mother's political views, although without unwarranted speculation it is not possible, from the interview, to decide that this was the origin of Celia's present stance. Regardless of origin, Celia's commitment, her belief that non-supporters of the Campaign are benighted and her advocacy of the non-alignment policy have a place within the culture of CND – a culture which has, without doubt, nurtured her political development.

Conclusion: the office-holders' task

In the foregoing chapters, I showed that CND is a composite of only *partially* complementary ideologies and perspectives. In this composite, the welfare-state CNDers' contribution is notably pronounced. However, even the welfare-state Campaigners are characterised by similarities and differences and this incomplete commonality is accentuated when supporters of CND who are not employed in the welfare-state sector are also taken into consideration. Although I have highlighted certain features of the Campaign's culture (for example, the belief that non-supporters are in some sense benighted, and the ethical nature of the Campaigners' commitment), these elements should not be thought of as a necessary set of defining qualities which comprise an essence of CND; rather, they are like prominent threads in the tapestry of the Movement's culture.

The office-holders whom I discussed in this chapter are also characterised by similarities and differences. They joined the Campaign in various way, became office-holders by disparate routes and have diverse socio-political stances. As I argued in the Introduction, they do not express a uniform radicalism and they are not *necessarily* more committed to the nuclear disarmament cause than their lay member counterparts. Like many of the interviewees in Chapter Six, their commitment to campaign has been engendered by their participation in other forms of life such as the Church or party politics. These generative biographical experiences and commitments are not always fully compatible with each other.

Nonetheless, despite this diversity, all the respondents in this chapter are pledged to building a non-partisan Movement. Faced with a truly indiscriminate threat and a multi-faceted membership, they strive to nullify potentially divisive strategies and political differences in order to build a Campaign that is open to the greatest possible public support. This is done despite, in most cases, their own strong allegiances to sectarian party politics or religious beliefs. Thus Labour Party, Catholic and Communist office-holders consciously champion the transcendental ethic of nuclear disarmament in their attempt to unify the Movement. However, this ecumenical strategy proves especially appealing to only a particular *minority* of the population, a minority whose vocational morality also features a transcendental ideology – welfare-state employees. Paradoxically, championing an ecumenical ethic actually serves to attract a socially *unrepresentative* basis of support for CND.

8

State class radicalism

Introduction

In the first chapter I gave a detailed critique of two of the major studies of CND (Parkin 1967; Taylor and Pritchard, 1980). I argued that, whilst these studies constituted valuable resources and contained promising insights, the authors failed to develop an adequate sociology of the Campaign and were prevented from doing so by their theoretical approaches and concomitant analytical tactics. It was also noted that both these studies focused solely upon activists. Both works tended, in various ways, to devalue the CNDers' own reasons for their campaigning and membership of CND and both studies, although recognising the moral character of the first Campaign, failed to further our understanding of this important characteristic of the Movement. Moreover, neither study developed a satisfactory heuristic to relate the members' social class location to their protesting and neither study recognised that it was the fact that the crucial group of members were welfare-*state* employees, rather than merely the 'middle class', or 'middle-class radicals', which held the key to understanding CND.

The limits of this study

From the outset, I decided that this research should be focused solely upon the revived CND, rather than attempting to encompass other organisations which fall under the umbrella term 'peace movement'. The principal reason for this focus was a wish to compare and contrast my research with that of Parkin, and Taylor and Pritchard, and a wish to supplement my modest sample with a secondary analysis of Nias' and Byrne's data on the current Campaign's membership. Moreover, the theoretical perspective which I favoured

demanded detailed ethnographic analyses of the interview material
and I did not consider that I could reasonably increase my sample
size to include a significant number of interviews with members
drawn from other peace groups. In addition, CND is the largest
component in the revived peace movement and the only major
component with a history.

As a consequence of this focus, the heuristic developed in this
research is not applicable axiomatically to other peace groups such
as European Nuclear Disarmament, or to specialist sub-groups, for
example, Scientists Against Nuclear Arms (SANA). Nonetheless,
there would seem to be no reason in principle why these organisations should not be studied in the same manner employed in this
study. Of these neglected component forms of life, perhaps the most
sociologically interesting is the women's peace movement and the
Greenham Common settlement.[32] The intentionally non-bureaucra-
tic and non-hierarchical character of Greenham Common, which
confronts social analysts searching for recognisable leading activists
and an 'essence' of the Greenham phenomenon, would seem to be
more analytically approachable if considered as a composite form of
life and if the women protestors' social praxes were related to their
generative social contexts. Clearly, for practical reasons, such
research would be more easily accomplished by a female researcher.

Of necessity, in this study there is an in-depth focus upon individual Campaigners. The analysis requires this focus for it demands
detailed consideration of campaigning and context which, as I have
shown, can be a subtle relationship without essentialist uniformity.
Nonetheless, the available data contained in Appendix C, which
highlights the preponderance of welfare-state and student members
in the peace movement, gives every reason to believe that the arguments in this study could be extended to cover the social bases of
support for the peace movement in general.

Other accounts of the revival of CND

In terms of the strongest original research component (and subsequent resource value for successive researchers) Peter Nias's 1983
study[33] of 'the recent rise of the Nuclear Disarmament Movement in
Britain' is the pre-eminent academic work on the present peace
movement known to this author. Revealingly entitled *The Poverty of
Peace Protest*, the study draws upon the author's large-scale survey

data (see Appendix C) in support of his claim that 'the nuclear disarmament movement in general, and its component organisations in particular, cannot legitimately be called a mass movement because the membership base is too narrow . . .' (1983, p. 3).

Nias argues that in the Seventies a number of events and influences emerged which provided an atmosphere conducive to the growth of 'protest movements in general and nuclear disarmament movement in particular'. These events and influences include the Russian intervention in Afghanistan, the publication of *Protect and Survive* and the debates on the introduction of 'new' weaponry (the Neutron Bomb and Cruise and Pershing missiles). In addition, following the arguments of Tony Benn, Nias cites the demise of consensus politics in the Seventies as responsible for provoking a re-examination of political ends as well as means. In his survey data, the social class of the members is categorised in accordance with Registrar General definitions and consequently Nias did not notice the high profile of welfare-state employees in his samples of CNDers. He argues that 'The movement's chances, by itself, of changing society sufficiently for such nuclear disarmament in Britain to take place are limited both because it is not a mass movement but a loose coalition of social groups and organisations, and also because there has been concentration upon protest rather than upon dialogue or social change' (1983, p. 4).

All available data on the Campaign's membership supports Nias' claim that CND is not a 'mass movement' in the sense of attracting support from a wide social base. However, it is debatable whether the Campaign's being a 'loose coalition of social groups and organisations' disqualifies it from being seen as a 'proper' mass movement. Nias experiences theoretical difficulty when confronted by the problem of categorising peace movements and remarks (1985, p. 1) that 'the modern peace movement is quite different from many of its predecessors, and in many ways defies conceptual labelling'. It would be fair to say that Nias' work is more in the nature of a commentary on his survey results than a fully developed analysis. Nevertheless, as a source of data on the Campaign's membership it is most valuable and, as he points out (1985, p. 1), whilst 'many social movements have been studied only after they have gone into decline, or succeeded in their aims . . . this study was carried out during a period of intensive campaigning'.

One difficulty in Nias' work, in common with many other

accounts of the revival of CND, is that whilst he describes the events and influences that could have proved conducive to the growth of protest movements, this wider context is not drawn upon to explain in detail the content of CND politics; a form of protest which is notably similar to its predecessor in the late Fifties and early Sixties. Furthermore, he does not draw upon this wider social context to account for why it is that only some people (and not the whole population) chose to respond to these events by joining CND. Consequently, these events etc. remain only a catalogue of historical incidents.

Another example of this problem can be found in the Introduction to *Debate on Disarmament*, wherein Clarke and Mowlam state that 'there are some very obvious and immediate reasons why disarmament should have become such a live issue since 1979' (1982, p. 1) and then present a very comprehensive list of national and international events which formed the back-drop to the growth of the peace movement. But again, what is not analysed is why the Campaign proves attractive to only a minority of the population drawn largely from a particular social stratum – without whom the Movement would not exist. Nor is it clear why the present peace movement has assumed its present form, which is so akin in character to the original Campaign. Similarly, Pamela Bartlett, in her 1983 study of *The Nuclear Disarmament Movement* in Scotland, traces the history of the Campaign and its revival, cataloguing the growth of the Scottish Campaign and related events in the Seventies. However, Bartlett attempts to explain the revival of the Movement by reference to Down's five-stage 'issue-attention cycle' and she does not incorporate into her account the Campaign's socially unrepresentative basis of support.

This focus upon allegedly precipitating events is naturally also to be found in activists' own accounts of the revival of CND. Understandably, peace movement activists often regard the need to protest as being palpably obvious and are more interested in further encouraging support than engaging in sociological analysis. In fact, the dramatic revival of the Campaign, between late 1979 and early 1980, appears to have surprised the Movement's national leaders and was certainly not planned for in terms of organisational capacity. As Monsignor Bruce Kent stated in his General Secretary's Report to the 1980 Annual Conference of CND, '... the vast increase of interest in disarmament issues in this country in recent months has left most peace movements trying desperately to keep up with the endless (and welcome) demands of all sorts. There has not been much time for reflection on what has been going on.' Accounts of the peace movement's revival, written by activists, are usually catalogues of the disturbing nuclear issues which surfaced in the Seventies, reports of particular protest actions and calls for support.[34]

Analyses of the revived Movement focusing more specifically on politics have been provided by Day, and Robbins, Keane, and Taylor. Day and Robbins's study is based on contemporaneous original research (see Appendix C). Given this, I find it particularly encouraging that there are several convergences between their findings and mine. Entitled *Activists For Peace: The Social Bases Of A Local Peace Movement*, Day and Robbins' study of the Aberystwyth peace movement is an attempt to 'examine some features of the peace movement as it appears at a local level to see how far it can be said to exemplify the "new politics".'[35]

Day and Robbins criticise Parkin's study of the original Movement for an over-reliance on secondary sources and for 'a consistent unwillingness to take CNDers' motivations on their own terms' (1987, p. 219). This unwillingness to accept CNDers' avowed motivations is, the authors believe, a reflection of a 'fundamental restriction arising from the imposition of a particular conception of political action which he [Parkin] shares with many others' (1987, p. 219), in other words, a methodological and analytical myopia engendered by Parkin's allegiance to what Day and Robbins term the 'old politics'.

Acknowledging the important influence of writers such as Poulantzas and Gramsci, Day and Robbins appear to regard the 'new politics' as a welcome 'loosening up [of] the connections between determining conditions and political outcomes: the "relative autonomy" of the political argues the need to pay attention in detail to the way the political is constituted' (1987, p. 221). This conception of political analysis is in contrast to the 'old politics', of which Parkin is said to be an adherent, in which, it is implied, a deterministic tendency exists and in which 'formalised bureaucratic institutions, systematised doctrine, and strategic policy formulation' are held to be the proper means for achieving political change. In contrast, according to Day and Robbins, '. . . both theoretically and practically, the new politics is alert to the importance of limited, transitory,

shifting struggles of highly disparate kinds, and the need for continuing efforts to achieve some sort of controlling direction over the
diversity of practices, ideas and grouping (1987, p. 222).

Following on from this distinction between 'old' and 'new' politics, Day and Robbins provide an interesting ethnography of the
Aberystwyth peace movement, noting the wide range of different
ideologies ('Welshness, socialism, libertarianism and Christianity'),
the educative role which membership of the peace movement serves
to sponsor, and the tensions caused by the members' ideological
diversity. They conclude their study by suggesting '. . . that in its
attempts to bring together a variety of ideological themes and
negotiate appropriate organisational structures, the peace
movement is rehearsing many of the problems that will be faced by
any broader alliance of the left. The success or failure of such efforts
is likely to determine the fate of the new politics' (1987, p. 236).

Day and Robbins's acknowledgement of the educative and formative effects of peace movement campaigning – of the way (not
sufficiently recognised by Parkin) that peace campaigners may not be
the 'same people' as they were before starting to campaign – is
analytically important. However, in a sense, I feel that they fall into
the same trap as Parkin and other 'old politics' analysts in that
disarmament and the members' own reasons for campaigning, and
the distinctive content of their politics becomes somewhat subsumed
beneath their attempt to present CND as an exemplar of the 'new'
politics.

Day and Robbins's substantive findings closely and encouragingly
replicate mine. In their 'Profile of the Activists', the authors:

. . . find a notable absence from the scene of the working class. In occupational terms, CND activists belong squarely to the intellectual/artistic/edu-
cational middle class: getting on for half (forty three per cent) of our
respondents are teachers, lecturers, researchers or involved with the arts.
The remainder include nurses, secretaries, librarians, civil servants,
ministers and students. In common with other recent studies (Mattausch,
1987 and Nias, 1986) we find that those in waged work are *overwhelmingly
employees of state agencies* concerned with health, education or welfare.
Their education profile is remarkable: only three have not been involved in
further or higher education . . . (1987, p. 224), emphasis added. See also
Appendix C)

Day and Robbins believe that this socially specific base of support
is a reflection of 'the crisis of social democracy' in Britain; a crisis

which has seen state resources shift from welfare to 'repressive' and militaristic funding. This shift, they argue, has been accompanied by a concomitant change in state ideology and thus, 'In the face of this material and ideological threat it is hardly surprising that the peace movement provides an avenue of mobilisation that is particularly attractive to members of the 'caring' professions.' (1987, p. 232.)

Richard Taylor's recent writings (1983 and 1984) on the revived CND are consistent with his analysis of the original Movement and true to his pervasive belief that, if CND is to be effective, it must adopt and pursue his particular conception of New Left socialism:

The persistent and fundamental problem of the movement since its inception has been its inability to translate its undoubted popular appeal into real tangible achievements. Although the movement has had a very considerable impact on public opinion, and thus, arguably, indirectly upon formal political structures and policies, it is quite clear that its central objectives have not been achieved . . . The problem then is essentially political: how to articulate with effect the peace movement's dynamism and strength. The inability to find a solution to this problem was one of the central reasons for the movement's decline and disintegration from the mid-1960s and threatens again to undermine the strength, dynamism and self-confidence of the movement in the 1980s, both in Britain and elsewhere. (1983, p. 121)

Taylor recognises (1983, pp. 138–9) that British political life has moved on from the 1960s. In particular, there has been a 'partial disintegration of the seemingly stable and secure Western economic system' and, in Britain, the 'era of crisis' has meant that 'the material base of the 1950s and 1960s, within which the integration of the working class has been rooted, has been significantly eroded', leading to 'political demoralisation and disorientation'. With regard to the middle class, Taylor, drawing upon the work of David Coates (1984), argues that:

. . . there has been a considerable expansion in the number of radical tertiary educated professional and intellectual employees *whose public sector occupations and general background of critical thinking, have resulted in an ideological stance opposed to the market individualism of competitive captialism.* Such a disaffected, radical middle class has of course existed throughout the twentieth century. It has been from within this consistuency that most of the impetus for direct action movements in the past has stemmed. The crucial development in the 1970s, however, has been the *expansion* of this social group, as a result primarily, of the expansion of higher education and public sector employment . . . (1983, p. 139, emphasis added)

Taylor (1983, p. 139), again drawing upon Coates and writers cited by Coates, identifies three major groupings involved in the growth of the contemporary radical middle class:

... trade union activists in the white collar unions (white collar union membership has grown from one million nine hundred thousand to two million six hundred and ninety thousand in 1964, and four million two hundred and six thousand in 1974); new artisans ('a set of often college educated young people denied access to bureaucratic occupations because of the recession, who have turned instead . . . to petty commodity production – in wood, textiles, paint and so on – ') the welfare bureaucrats (those working in schools, welfare agencies, etc, who as Cotgrove and Duff have observed, have rejected, at least to an extent, the ideology and values of industrial capitalism and opted instead for careers 'outside the market place').

This growth of this radical middle class is, according to Taylor, a source of political hope, and the '*structural* strengthening of the basis of the radical middle class left' augurs well for the development of a 'humanistic socialist' political strategy; the very strategy which the original New Left working in the original CND failed to articulate.

Leaving aside the validity of Taylor's political position and the problems associated with his characterisation of CND and the peace movement as an organisation which must politically articulate its disarmament demands (analytical standpoints which I have considered in some detail in the first chapter of this study), Taylor's remarks on what I have termed the 'state class' are both interesting and stimulating. However, I feel that Taylor has not adequately related the distinctive political and moral orientation of this expanding group to its social class location and, as in his earlier work, his main point of reference remains the development of 'humanistic socialism' rather than an initial understanding of the forces in capitalist society which have spawned the newly enlarged constituency upon which he pins his hopes for political change and the realisation of British nuclear disarmament. Crucially, Taylor does not give adequate analytical weight to the significance of a high profile of welfare-state employees (or those likely to have been influenced by their experiences of the welfare state, especially of higher education), and consequently his analysis relies on concepts such as 'critical thinking' and 'disaffection' to account for their susceptibility to radical politics and the characteristic form which it takes. In this study, I have argued that by focusing upon the CNDers' relationship to the state we can make their membership of the

Campaign, and the expression of their protest, sociologically intelligible. The viability of this approach is borne out by the analysis of the interviews in this study and suggests rather different political lessons from the ones which Taylor urges us to learn from the demise of the first Campaign (this point is elaborated upon in the final chapter).

In an interesting paper cited by Taylor in his account of the revival of CND and entitled 'Environmentalism, middle class radicalism and politics', Cotgrove and Duff (1980, p. 343) note '. . . the almost complete omission of any discussion of the particular faction which has been identified in this analysis: those operating in those subsystems of industrial societies concerned with the pursuit of non-economic values, and functioning outside the market, and in this sense, non-capitalist elements persisting within capitalist societies'. Comparing samples of 'environmentalists', 'industrialists' and the 'public', the authors (1980, p. 340) find '. . . particularly striking . . . the high proportion of environmentalists in our sample occupying roles in the non-productive service sector: doctors, social workers, teachers and creative arts'.

Cotgrove and Duff's study is heavily informed by Parkin's conceptualisation of 'middle class radicalism':

> To the extent that schools, hospitals and welfare agencies operate outside the market-place, and those who work in them are dedicated to maximising non-economic values, they constitute a non-industrial enclave within industrial societies and are the carriers of alternative non-economic values. And they may well provide a more congenial environment for those for whom the values and ideology of industrial capitalism do not win unqualified enthusiasm and unquestioning support. In short, those who reject the ideology and values of industrial capitalism are likely to choose careers outside the market-place. (1980, p. 344)

This adherence to Parkin's work means that Cotgrove and Duff are not alert to the possibility that there may be a connection between welfare-state and environmentalist forms of life. In addition, it is unclear what is meant by the phrase 'subsystems of industrial societies', or how 'non-capitalist elements' could exist in capitalist society. Such phrasing suggests an analytical understanding predicated purely upon the level of values and ideology without a consideration of the specific social influences experienced by environmentalists. Moreover, as can be seen in many of the biographical histories of the interviews in this study, it is not simply the case that welfare professionals choose this area of employment because they reject the values of industrial capitalism. This study suggests that state apprenticeships and/or vocational practices, that is to say *the welfare state itself*, encourages the identification with, the assimilation of, the distinctive ethic which finds expression in disarmament campaigning.[36]

Writing from the perspective of a political analyst (and END member), John Keane offers a novel view of the relation between the peace movement and the British state. Keane argues that the contemporary movement '. . . in respect of its anti-statism undoubtedly constitutes an important and new phase of the struggle for renewing and enriching old British traditions: parliamentary democracy, independent public criticism, and suspicion of overextended state power'. Keane proposes that the peace movement not only implicitly challenges the power of the state but, in addition, its own decentralised and diverse internal organisation stands in strong contrast to the bureaucratic apparatus of the state itself. This leads Keane (1984, p. 6) to suggest: 'If these anti-state and pluralistic features of the new British peace movement are considered together, it is not implausible to suggest that the decisive significance and political potential of the movement lies in its militant defence of a democratic civil society against the state.'

In Keane's article, members of the peace movement are characterised as agents of civil society resisting the imposition of newly extended 'state power' issued in under the guise of strengthening the British deterrent. Keane, after castigating the peace movement for its 'tendency to moralism', its chauvinistic aspects and negative aims, proposes an END-inspired strategy involving wider European political goals and the adoption of the recommendations contained within the report of the Alternative Defence Commission, *Defence without The Bomb*.

Keane's article is undoubtedly thought-provoking and original. However, it rests upon the questionable belief that members of the British peace movement are best seen as defenders of 'civil society'. All the available evidence on the social bases of support for CND, and the peace movement in general, seems to contradict Keane's central position; in the membership of the peace movement, welfare-state employees have the highest profile. This is especially true of the European Nuclear Disarmament movement; END, as Peter Nias' research shows, is very largely compromised of teachers, lecturers and students. Rather than an opposition of civil society to the state, the peace movement can be more accurately described as one *section* of the state (the welfare section) protesting against the practices of its 'warfare' counterparts. That British post-war society should have evolved in this fashion, spawning its own fiercest critics is, I believe, the most significant implication of my study.

Welfare-state radicalism

The Campaign for Nuclear Disarmament is a composite, and the constituent ideologies and praxes share both similarities and differences. That they exist in a state overlapping harmony and tension is a most important characteristic of CND. Nevertheless, one of the strands that goes to make up CND is of particular importance: the social basis of support for the Campaign is largely drawn from a socially formed constituency which has a special relationship to the welfare state.

The genesis of the 'welfare state class' ('state class' for short) with its distinctive politics points to a post-war duality in the structure of the British state, a significant and possibly insufficiently recognised social dynamic. (If, as seems likely, this 'state class' has provided the membership basis for the 'new' social movements, then their political impact has already been marked.)

The British state is both welfare Dr Jekyll and nuclear Mr Hyde: the concomitant problems of legitimacy to which this potentially gives rise might have been containable in the past, but in a period of increased weapons deployment and attacks upon the welfare state this problem becomes more acute.

Recognition of the dangers of a nuclear 'deterrence' policy and its political ramifications seems to have eluded many social analysts. Like the actual historical event itself, the crucial decision to build a national nuclear deterrent does not figure as a major factor in standard political and social histories of post-war Britain. Not until public concern mounted over fall-out from weapons-testing, Duncan Sandys made Britain's reliance on nuclear weapons explicit in his 1957 White Paper on Defence ('Outline of Future Policy'), and the British government exploded their first hydrogen bomb in May of the same year, did the Mr Hyde of the state make a truly public appearance. This duality in state functions, and the growth of a social class of welfare employees who were to prove the sharpest critics of the state's defence policy, merits further attention.

9

Beveridge and the Bomb

On 14 August 1945 Sir William Beveridge, the architect of the British welfare state, wrote to *The Times* arguing that:

The decision to use the atomic bombs against Japan has no doubt hastened the end of the present war and has thereby saved countless lives in China, Burma and elsewhere to set against those it has destroyed. The ultimate justification will depend not on this, but on its service in showing to humanity the danger to which we are all exposed if we allow the war to recur. The decision has brought us to the necessity of abolishing war. This cannot be done by reducing the occasions for dispute between nations, by measures for increasing economic prosperity and economic cooperation. Such measures are desirable in themselves, but irrelevant to the main issue.

Nor can abolition of war be obtained by negative means, by merely renouncing or prohibiting war. It depends upon finding a positive alternative to war as a means of settling disputes between nations. This alternative method must be world-wide: no nation can be content any longer to seek peace in its particular region and disregard the rest of the world. The only alternative method which can be world-wide is compulsory arbitration by an impartial tribunal applied to all disputes between all nations and backed by overwhelming international force. Only in this way can peace be reconciled with liberty and national self-government.

Tragically, Sir William's hopes and recommendations were not to be realised: as in the past, the lessons of war were not learnt. Once again, politicians of all countries set about the task of restoring an international order based upon the building-block of the nation state. In this process, nuclear weapons came to assume a crucial role in international politics: the Bomb became a weapon of sovereign nation states.

In Britain, the electorate had gone to the polls a month before the destruction of Hiroshima and Nagasaki. The subsequent, famous Labour Party electoral victory heralded a new, warmly-welcomed political era. Although the reasons for, and the scope of, these changes are the subject of academic dispute, the progressive nature of Labour's welfare reforms is generally accepted. This commendably progressive ethos was, however, addressed primarily to Britain's *domestic* front and Labour's 1945 Election Manifesto (*Let Us Face The Future*), drafted whilst the war against Japan was still being pursued, reflected this bias, concentrating largely upon the Party's domestic aspirations with only a short section devoted to foreign and defence matters.

Even if they had wished to, the Labour Party could not have presented a defence programme to the nation which incorporated a policy for nuclear weapons. Unlike Churchill and a tiny, select number of scientists and civil servants, the leaders of the Labour Party were entirely ignorant of Britain's initiation of, and collaboration in, the American-led Manhattan Project which had produced the first atomic bombs. As Professor Gowing, the official United Kingdom Atomic Energy Authority historian, notes (1974, Vol. 1, p. XI): 'at the end of the war a Labour Government came to power, not a single member of which knew anything about the very secret war-time atomic affairs'. Upon coming to power, the Attlee administration faced a new and unexpected challenge, for which they had no guiding policy or prepared strategy.[37]

On the domestic front, Labour was in a somewhat better position. As Kenneth O. Morgan relates, in his (1984) excellent history of the Attlee Governments, although the new Labour administration lacked specific, detailed plans for the practical implementation of their political programme, the Party could draw upon traditional socialist ethics of equality, their war-time governmental experience and the principles of the 1942 Beveridge Report. In combination with the widespread desire to create a better social order from the ruins of war, these resources proved sufficient for Labours' expansion and consolidation of the welfare state and for their economic goals of Government planning and nationalisation. In the six years of Labour rule, the ethic of social welfare was successfully articulated and practically implemented: the new welfare state was built upon foundations which subsequent Conservative Governments were obliged to accept for the next quarter-century. In the post-war decades, the domestic political agenda revolved around competing Party claims to manage the reformed capitalistic economy; an agenda set by the Attlee governments which would hold good until the late seventies and the advent of 'Thatcherite' politics. A concomitant of the expansion and consolidation of the welfare state was the generation of a new and fortunate social class comprised of individuals working for, and imbued with the ethos of, their welfare-state professions.

This specific social location has clear implications for these individuals' social class position and political outlook. In truth, employees of the welfare state cannot reasonably be classified as 'working-class': in terms of status, lifestyle and general market situation, teachers, doctors, social workers etc. do not meet the criteria of what is normally recognised as working-class. Similarly, they do not own or control the means of production, nor do they engage in self-alienating labour; a strict Marxist understanding of class is unable to encompass their distinctive social grouping. Attempts to locate welfare-state employees between upper and lower classes, a literal middle class, are equally unproductive: the distinctiveness of the welfare-state employees' social position becomes lost in a category which must include those groups, for example, craftsmen, mercenaries and the self-employed, who do not fall happily into whatever criteria are proposed for defining the upper and lower classes.

These attempts to capture the class position of welfare-state employees deflect attention away from that which makes for the distinctive social position; namely, their relation to the state. Educated, apprenticed and paid by the state, and responsible for the implementation of welfare policies, these individuals *are* the welfare state. They do not, however, conform to the Weberian picture of rational bureaucrats, nor to the Liberal concept of impartial administrators. Rather, I suggest, they are better seen as active citizens of the state, an institution which, therefore, requires our careful examination.[38] Crucially, this examination must include a recognition of the fact that, in the words of Michael Mann (1987, p. 59): 'The modern (Western) state is not single but dual, its domestic life separable from its geopolitical.' Welfare is only one function, and one component, of the British state; Britain's state is partly defined and influenced by its place in the international system of nation states. This external dimension, with its concomitant spheres of foreign and defence policies, was also forged decisively at the same historical juncture which gave birth to the modern welfare state.

Attlee's new administration faced dilemmas abroad which were at least equal to the domestic challenges. Whereas, in the field of domestic politics, Labour could meet the challenges by drawing upon the resources which I have outlined above, in the international arena they were relatively weaker. There were two main reasons for this weakness: firstly, Labour lacked considered, socialist, guiding foreign policy principles (a problem which has dogged the Western Left); secondly, the war-torn world of 1945 presented *new and unforeseen* challenges which demanded urgent attention. In particular, the war had shattered the previous boundaries and patterns of the international nation-state system. The wish for a stable peace and the, at least initial, hope for a united international response needed to be implemented in the insecure and uneasy aftermath. And, as a corollary, questions of defence – defence of nation states – came to the fore. In the post-war world, the shape of defence policy was largely to be governed by the new atomic weaponry.

In Britain, in September 1945, a secret research programme, approved by the equally secret and exclusive General Committee 75 (Gen 75), was established at Harwell, near Oxford, to produce plutonium from a water-cooled reactor.[39] In early January 1947, the even smaller and more exclusive Gen 163 (which had superseded Gen 75 and which existed only for this purpose) took the momentous decision to initiate a British atomic weapons programme. Both these decisions were taken in complete secrecy with no discussion or Parliamentary debate whatsoever. Except for a disingenuous and cursory announcement to Parliament by A. V. Alexander, the Minister of War, in May 1948 (an announcement which attracted no interest and which was covered by a Government 'D-Notice'), Parliament, including most members of Attlee's own Cabinet, remained in total ignorance of these new developments. The decision to build a British Bomb was taken by an élite handful of Government ministers, scientists and civil servants and the immense cost of the nuclear programme was 'hidden away in the accounts'. Professor Gowing (1964, p. 56) reasons that:

The prime reason for this treatment of atomic energy, so exceptional by any of the usual constitutional tenets, was awe and fear. There may have been other reasons. For example, Mr Attlee and Mr Bevin, conscious of the divergence of views within the Parliamentary Labour Party and the Government on foreign policy and defence, may have deliberately wished to keep knowledge away from the left wing. Or they may have wished to evade debate because they felt peculiarly vulnerable to criticism from Mr Churchill on a subject which he had guarded so closely from them and which he considered to be so peculiarly his own. But awe and fear were common to other countries besides Britain. They were caused by an exceedingly techni-cal project which perhaps no British minister and few civil servants really understood, a project of vast and horrifying potentialities which went to the heart of national security and relationships with other countries and which might one day, have great industrial importance as well. Therefore the atomic project seemed to demand very special treatment within the British machinery of government and very special secrecy.

Following her junior partnership in the war-time Manhattan Pro-ject, Britain was uniquely well-placed to become the second nuclear power, and nuclear weapons appeared to offer the promise of 'great power' status – the Bomb would guarantee Britain a place at the 'top table'; it would allow Britain to retain her pre-war eminence in the post-war inter-state system. This erroneous strategic belief was the main rationale for building the British Bomb. In addition, the Truman administration's approach to world affairs, and Truman's elevation of America's nuclear arsenal to the realms of a 'sacred trust', gave cause for concern and a fillip to an independent British deterrent. At the vital meeting of Gen 163, Bevin had argued that 'We could not afford to acquiesce in an American monopoly of this new development' and Clement Attlee, in his autobiography (1954, p. 162) recalls that he 'was anxious for full cooperation with the United States, but was not prepared to leave Britain fully dependent in this sphere on our friends across the Atlantic'. Although not the cause, America's intransigent attitude, the tragic disintegration of the Alliance into Cold-War frigidity, and Bevin's growing distrust of Soviet intentions, formed the background against which the decision to develop the British Bomb was taken. During this period, opposi-tion to Bevin's foreign policy was spasmodically but ineffectually voiced by some sections of the left of the Labour Party; kept in complete ignorance, the left were not in a position to take issue with the secret atomic project.[40]

In the six years of the Attlee Governments then, all of the major features and characteristics of the modern British state were put in place. On the domestic front, active state intervention in the economy, nationalisation of many key industries and the expansion and consolidation of welfare provisions were firmly established. On the international front, the Anglo-American alliance was forged, NATO emerged as the solution to the perceived Russian threat, and nuclear weapons took their place in the British arsenal. The popula-rity of the domestic measures, and the acceptability of Bevin's foreign policy, ensured that when the Conservatives were returned to office in 1951, they did not mount any fundamental attacks upon Attlee's achievements. Indeed, Professor Gowing tells us (1974, p. 406) that:

When Mr Churchill returned to Downing Street, he was surprised by the size of the atomic energy project built up by the Labour Government. He found with a mixture of admiration, envy and the shock of a good parliamentarian that his predecessors had spent nearly 100 million pounds on it without informing Parliament. He felt that he would have been branded as a war-monger for a similar feat and one of his early minutes on his return to office was to ask the Permanent Secretary of the Treasury how this very large sum had been hidden away in the accounts.

Recent academic analyses have acknowledged that, in Martin Shaw's words (1987, p. 144), all states are 'Janus-faced, looking both "in" to their national societies and "out" to the world of states and determined by the interaction of the two . . .' Nevertheless, as Shaw points out (1987, p. 144), 'Although often trenchantly put, the arguments have not universally been incorporated into either Marxist or "post-Marxist" thinking about the state . . .' This recognition, that states are 'Janus-faced', is particularly important when considering the modern British experience because, as hindsight reveals, the Attlee administration had married radical, progressive domestic policies with a conservative, traditional foreign stance. Kenneth O'Morgan (1984, p. 49) reasons that 'What fused together the radical domestic programme and the strong belligerent foreign policy which Bevin was allowed to conduct was a general conviction in the Labour movement that Britain was still unquestionably a great power.' This conviction, this perception of the British state, served as the initial rationale for the British Bomb; it remained unchallenged until it was put to the test in the 1956 Suez debacle.

There is, however, a further refinement which can be made when distinguishing between the two component spheres of the British state. As I have remarked, Attlee's welfare state, although not constructed in accord with a fully-prepared blueprint, can be seen as the child of already present historical trends and structural forces, built using existing political and ideological resources, and built in public with widespread support from the British people. This was not the case for the Attlee administration's foreign policy which emerged largely as an *ad hoc* response to unforeseen international dilemmas. Turning to the specific development of Britain's nuclear arsenal, the contrast is even more stark: Labour had no prepared plans for nuclear weaponry, Labour's leaders were in ignorance of Britain's collaboration in the Manhattan Project (Churchill had deliberately kept Attlee, then deputy Prime Minister, in the dark), and they had little appreciation of the nature of atomic physics or the effects of nuclear fall-out. Labour faced a unique, unforseen challenge. Following Churchill's precedent, Attlee inaugurated the British nuclear programme in secrecy without any democratic debate, spurred on by a conception of international politics wherein armaments could be utilised as state weapons in a world divided into 'great' and 'lesser' powers.

The British Bomb programme was a new opportunity afforded by our collaboration in the Manhattan Project, although this was never an *intended* purpose of the Project. Similarly, Britain's participation in the Second World War was not predicated upon the wish to forge a military alliance with America, and few observers could have predicted in 1939 the eventual polarisation of the post-war world. Yet, these *unforeseen* realities, in combination with equally unpredictable international factors, formed the back-drop to the decisions of Gen 75 and Gen 163. Moreover, the *inherent and unique* characteristics of atomic weaponry posed *new* problems, again unplanned for and unforeseen. The British Bomb was, then, in Sir Karl Popper's phrase (1983, p. 350), 'the indirect, the unintended, and often the unwanted byproduct' of particular historical conjunctures and the actual decision was taken by individuals who had their fair share of human failings. Once begun, the nuclear arming of states generated further, nightmarish, unintended threats and problems.

The fact that British nuclear weapons are state weapons, and the fact that their genesis was an unforseen political step, provokes special theoretical and analytical problems. In particular, neo-Marxist analyses, which are so fruitful for an understanding of Britain's domestic welfare state, falter when confronted by the phenomenon. In a penetrating article entitled 'Understanding Militarism', Dr Donald Mackenzie draws attention to the fact that modern weapons and weapons-related systems are produced by corporations whose sole customer is their nation state and that 'at only one stage is there typically competition between firms involved in weapons production . . . Once the first development contract is sealed, competition effectively ceases . . .' (1983, p. 37).

These features of weapons production, acute features of nuclear weapons production, militate against any plausible Marxian economic analysis of the arms race. Mackenzie convincingly argues that neither Kidron's 'permanent arms economy' nor Leninist 'imperialist' explanations square with the reality of the present situation. Neither approach encompasses a recognition of the ways in which 'Militarism is directly and immediately tied up with the system of states. War is typically war between sovereign states . . .' (1983, p. 61). In the same article, Mackenzie also argues that explanations for the arms race in terms of an 'internal logic' overestimates the power of the weapons producers: 'My own guess is that . . . their power is real but exists in interacting with wider structures, particularly . . . the state and the international system of states' (1983, p. 46). Although nuclear weapons are produced within capitalist economies (and, of course, socialist economies), their production as state commodities under state control bypasses the competitive market-place and places them outside the valorisation processes that form the usual parameters of a Marxist analysis. The sovereign state's perception of its place in the world order, rather than the drive for capital accumulation, has been the more important sponsor of nuclear weapons programmes.

Let us face the future?

Since its revival in 1979, CND has proved a highly successful social movement: hundreds of thousand of individuals have protested against nuclear weapons in peaceful and imaginative ways and the nuclear issue has been brought firmly to the public's attention. Furthermore, CND has strongly influenced Labour Party defence policy without sacrificing the Campaign's own sovereignty. The effects of this campaigning are hard to assess for they may well bear fruit in the future and it would be foolish to underestimate the potential for change which CND has helped to foster.

As a protest movement, and as an influence upon public and political opinion, the revived CND has a record of substantial achievements. These achievements are, however, no greater than those which were made by the original Campaign of the late Fifties and early Sixties and there are now clear indications that the present CND is losing members and momentum. Crucially, as the data in Appendix C shows, CND has been unable to attract ordinary working people for its cause. A comparison of the data collected by

Peter Nias in 1982 and Paul Byrne in 1985 reveals that, despite the significant increase in the membership, the social profile of the Campaign remains static and socially unrepresentative. This failure to attract working-class support is a major campaigning weakness, for its prevents CNDers realising their chosen role of an irresistible mass pressure group. Moreover, the savage dismantling of the welfare state by Mrs Thatcher's Governments seem likely to erode CND's natural social basis of support. Indeed, there is good reason to think that by destroying the welfare state, both the institutions and the political ethos, Mrs Thatcher is silencing an important source of progressive criticism to her eighteenth-century political vision. This is a deeply disturbing trend in modern British society.

But there is a further, profound structural obstacle which impedes nuclear disarmers. Nuclear weapons are employed in the political service of countries in relation to their position in the international state system – a sphere of politics which falls outside of normal political life. In Britain, politics and political parties have a decidedly domestic bias; international political questions, questions of foreign policy (and concomitant defence policy), are rarely on the British political agenda except in times of crisis. The modern concept of democratic citizenship does not yet extend outside of the nation's territory, there is no general expectation of active, democratic participation in foreign and defence matters. Instead, these matters are left to shadowy individuals and secret committees, whose decisions, especially regarding nuclear defence policy, are usually presented to the public as *faits accomplis*. It is this exclusive area of politics which CND attempts to penetrate and influence. In their quest for disarmament, CND is attempting to weld together the two political spheres of the state by placing them both under democratic control.

This is a daunting task. British defence policy has never been subject to anything other than nominal democratic influence. British political parties, including the Labour Party, have not been willing to submit to an international authority (the dream of Beveridge), nor have they shown any enthusiasm for a policy of neutralism. Rather, they have opted for a place in the armed, nuclear-armed, international state system, an option which generates the élite, undemocratic control of defence matters. This élite manages, as best it can; an irrational, unexpected danger which threatens all our lives.[41]

One of the major legacies of the Second World War is this political cleavage, both the welfare and warfare state, both Beveridge and the Bomb. Although the development of the British Bomb did not *cause* this rent in the state, the inherent horrific nature of nuclear weaponry has served to accentuate greatly its importance and possible consequences. It is to the CNDers' credit that they have not accepted the inevitability of this petrifying danger and that they have not accepted the bifurcation of democracy. By protesting and campaigning against nuclear weapons, by resisting the lunacy of 'deterrence', CND keeps alive the search for an alternative to Armageddon. Perhaps this partly accounts for the moral flavour of their campaign; morality can provide a basis of hope which our present, restricted politics are unable to offer us.

Notes

1 CND did not become a national membership campaign until January 1967 and thus all accounts of the numbers of members before this date are only estimates. In addition, a large number of supporters are not formal members of National CND and it is easy to underestimate the measure of support which the Campaign enjoys (a point often made by CND spokespersons). Nevertheless, the following figures illustrate the dramatic revival from 1979/80 onwards.

Date	Source	Membership
31 January 1967	National Executive Minutes	1,500[a]
End of 1968	Report on Membership	3,037
23 August 1969	Acting Treasurer's Report	2,173
1970	'The CND Story'	2,120
1971	'The CND Story'	2,047
1972	'The CND Story'	2,389
1973	'The CND Story'	2,367
1974	'The CND Story'	2,350
1975	'The CND Story'	2,536
1976	'The CND Story'	3,220
1977	'The CND Story'	2,618
1978	'The CND Story'	3,220
1979	'The CND Story'	4,287
1980[b]	'The CND Story'	9,000
1981[b]	'The CND Story'	20,000
1982[b]	'The CND Story'	50,000

Notes: [a] Note this was only three months after the controversial membership scheme came into operation.
[b] Figures are 'approximate'. From 1979 onwards, an estimate of 'local members', derived from forms returned by group secretaries, were included in the figures.
Sources: For 1979 to 1982: Minnion and Bolsover, 1983, p. 150. Others from 'The Left in Britain: Part 5', The Archives of CND (Section 1: Reels 1–16).
Differences in the ways in which these figures were compiled mean that they are not strictly comparable.

2   For the distinctive contribution of conversational analysts to a sociological appreciation of context, see: Atkinson and Heritage, 1984. This
excellent collection includes a 'Transcript Notation' and is a valuable source
book and introduction to the esoteric world of sequential understanding.

3   I have in mind Davidson's arguments concerning the legitimate phrasing of reasons as causes of action. Crudely, Davidson argues that in order to
achieve an acceptable separation of cause and effect, one should consider
causal reasons in terms of desired future states (Davidson, 1963).

4   Parkin's approach is caputred by Karl Popper's concept of 'methodological essentialism'. However, as will become clear, my objection to this
approach stems from an adherence to the philosophical therapy of the 'later'
Wittgenstein which, in my opinion, suggests a profounder and more viable
alternative than the 'methodological nominalism' advocated by Popper (cf.
Popper, 1972, especially pp. 26–34).

5   Of course, the growing 'professionalisation' of these fields of
employment means that this is truer today than in the mid-Sixties when
Parkin conducted his research. Nonetheless, the objection is still valid; as
Parkin only chose to list the category of teacher training in his questionnaire,
we do not know how many of his respondents had undergone other forms of
professional training.

6   This thesis is, to my knowledge, the most comprehensive and
thorough political study of the first Movement, containing a wealth of
material on the history and development of the original CND. A work of
political and historical analysis, the thesis traces the origins and development of the Campaign and its component ideologies. Taylor argues that,
whilst the New Left represented the only viable political strategy for the
attainment of disarmament objectives, the middle-class, moralistic character
of New Left politics meant that this political faction was not adequate for the
task at the time. This, in essence, remains Taylor's position (see Chapter
Eight).

7   This article is a fine example of what Taylor means by a moral stimulus
underpinning the rise of CND. The flavour of the article is captured in the
following quote:

There may be other chain-reactions besides those leading to destruction; and we might
start one. The British of these times so frequently hiding their decent, kind faces
behind masks of sullen apathy or sour, cheap cynicism, often seem to be waiting for
something better than party squabbles or appeals to their narrowest self-interest,
something great and noble in its intention that would make them feel good again. And
this might well be a declaration to the world that after a certain date one power, able to
engage in nuclear warfare, will reject the evil thing, for ever. (Priestley, 1957, pp.
554–6)

Taylor discusses the historical background and importance of this article in
Taylor and Pritchard, 1980.

8   This self-explanatory theoretical distinction is taken from Dray, 1957,
especially Chapter 6.

9   Obviously, this is only a summary of Taylor's arguments which are
grounded in scholarly research and which, in my opinion, usefully and

correctly relate the moral nature of the movement to wider historical factors; in particular, the nation state position of Britain in the post-war world and the British wish to remain a superpower by the ownership of an independent nuclear deterrent.

10 For Wittgenstein's influence upon modern sociological thinking, see: Heritage, 1984, especially Chapter 5.

11 Wittgenstein, 1983, Sections 66 and 67. The only substantial comparisons between Wittgenstein's mature writings and the work of the 'founding fathers' of sociology are not surprisingly, with the social theory of Marx: see Easton, 1983; Rubinstein 1981; Manser, 1981; Lamb, 1980. Interesting, and markedly different biographical material is given in Malcolm, 1958 and Bartley III, 1974.

12 I am grateful to my father, a native German speaker, for bringing this to my attention. *Harrap's Standard German and English Dictionary* defines *lebensform* as a 'pattern of existence (of a tribe etc)', and *lebensformen* as 'aspects, traits of personality'. However, I use *lebensformen* as a plural, as meaning 'forms of life', as do other writers on Wittgenstein. For the origins of this phrase, see: Janik and Toulmin 1973, pp. 231–4.

13 The film referred to is *March to Aldermaston*, made in 1958 by Lindsay Anderson and shown on British television in 1984.

14 A couple of months after this interview, Brian reappeared in my office to practise his salesman interviewing techniques. Such a reversal of roles seemed poetic justice.

15 This is certainly true of the Scots City University CND group which dwindles in size and vigour as the academic year progresses. By the time the student members are sitting their exams, the group is almost annually defunct – only to be temporarily revived again the following year by a new intake of 'freshers'.

16 I am thinking here particularly of the involvement of the New Left teachers and lecturers in the first Campaign who were drawn predominantly from arts and social science disciplines. For a history of the New Left and their involvement in CND and other radical groupings, see Young, especially Chapter Eight.

17 Consider, for example, the involvement of scientists via Russell's international Pugwash group in the first Campaign and the establishment of groups such as Scientists Against Nuclear Arms in the recent revival of the Movement.

18 This ingenious portrayal of Wittgenstein's 'family resemblance' theory was given by Dr John Heritage, University of Warwick, Autumn Lectures, 1981.

19 For an interesting account of how archetypes are constructed from culturally predominant facets of a category, see: Rosch, 1977. For an insight into the anthropological basis of a category, see Bulmer, 1973.

20 Priestley, 1950, p. 311; see Chapter 1, Note 7 for Priestley's moral 'call to arms' which acted as a rallying cry for the formation of the first Campaign.

21 Dr Macman's remarks on the concept of the 'other' as a projection of our own failings echo the arguments advanced by E. P. Thompson to explain

162 222222222222

our present Cold War mentality. I do not know whether Dr Macman had read any of Thompson's work; I have no reason to believe he had, cf. Thompson, 1982.

22 Founded in July 1942 by the then Liberal MP, Sir Richard Acland, the Common Wealth Party grew out of a merger between J. B. Priestley's '1941 Committee' and Acland's 'Forward March' movement. The Party campaigned on the platform of egalitarianism and an early end to the Second World War. These aims were to be achieved by the British demanding a new moral order, a common ownership of the means and fruits of production and an immediate end to colonialism. Acland had been working with other disenchanted intellectuals and religious leaders (including J. B. Priestley and Richard Calder) since the late thirties, and Penguin published several of his short books which propagated the new moral view. See especially, Acland, 1940, p. 31, which tells the reader that 'We have failed because of our selfishness and we need a new standard or morality' and Acland 1941. Following the post-War demise of the Common Wealth Party, Acland joined the Labour Party in 1947. In 1955, he resigned from the Labour Party over the nuclear issue. Some discussion of Acland and the Common Wealth Party can be found in Angus Calder's excellent book *The People's War* (1971).

23 See, for example, Taylor and Pritchard, 1978.

24 Parkin 1968, p. 3.

25 The allusion is to a remark of Wittgenstein's: 'The will is a sort of taking up of a position to the world. Only within the framework of this taking up of a position do things in the world get their meaning.' (*Notebook 1914–16* quoted in Gerd, 1979, p. 157).

26 Shown on British television in 1983, *The Day After* was an American-made and controversial film powerfully depicting the effects of a nuclear counter-strike upon a mid-western American town.

27 For the sake of brevity, I have omitted three more interviews which were included in the original thesis. The omitted interviewees all comfortably, and idiosyncratically, fall within the pattern of the majority of non-welfare-state CNDers.

28 This was an autonomous initiative predating the formation of national CND. In March 1958, the group affiliated to the fledgling national Campaign.

29 The Suez Crisis is one of the historical events identified by Taylor and Pritchard, and other analysts, that acted as a spur to the growth of the original CND. (See Chapters 1 and 9 of this study for further discussion of this process.)

30 This now defunct national group published a monthly newsletter and tried to encourage women's involvement in the nuclear disarmament movement: 'The monthly newsletter of the Liaison Committee for Women's Peace Groups written for those women who, regardless of party political beliefs, are united in the conviction that they have a special responsibility for safeguarding children, and society, from war'. (*Call to Women*, London, Mid-October, 1964.)

31 Unfortunately, through ill-luck, I was unable to interview Derek's girlfriend. Although they act as a team in their jointly-held office, it was my

impression that at their group's meetings Derek was the vocal and dominant partner.

32 Useful accounts and analyses of the Greenham Common peace camps can be found in Harford and Hopkins, 1984, Blackwood, 1984; Davenport 1982; Thomas, 1985; *Women's Peace Camp*, 1983; Arrowsmith, 1983.

33 An enormous number of books and articles have accompanied the revival of the peace movement. For short histories and discussions of the past and present campaigning, see Byrd, 1985; Widgery, 1976; Driver, 1964; Boulton, 1964; Clark, 1963; Greer, 1964; Minnion and Bolsover, 1983; Vernon, 1981; Overy, 1982; Mattausch, 1988; Byrne, 1988.

34 See, for instance Thompson and Smith, 1980; Cox, 1981; Rogers and Dungen, 1981; Webber *et al.*, 1983.

35 Day and Robbins's article was originally a paper presented at the 1985 British Sociological Assocation; this first quotation is taken from that paper. The paper was subsequently published in Creighton and Shaw, 1987. All other quotations are referenced to this book. Sadly, David Robbins died in a climbing accident in 1986.

36 Professor Cotgrove and Dr Duff's interesting research (Cotgrove and Duff, 1980; Duff and Cotgrove, 1982; Cotgrove, 1982) explores the correlations between social values, degree subject and occupational choice. Their research builds upon earlier studies (e.g. Rosenberg, 1957; Flacks, 1971; Cherry, 1975) and, in contrast to my findings, largely concurs with Parkin's contention that occupational choice is influenced strongly by pre-formed, adolescent values and attitudes. Cotgrove and Duff's studies are, however, informed by the methodological approach which underpinned Parkin's analysis of early CND activists and are, thus, open to the same basic criticisms which I advanced against Parkin's work in Chapter One. Moreover, this body of research does not address adequately the significance of the state in contemporary British society. Consequently, explanations for the distinctiveness of the respondents' social grouping are couched only in terms of their relation to the *market* and/or in respect to their support for industrial enterprise. Naturally, this analytical omission is reflected in the selection and characterisation of the respondents' values which are presented as 'pro' or 'anti' industrialism, economic individualism, and materialism. Whilst this approach may be appropriate for North American research, it cannot be considered adequate for British sociological analysis: the empirical data in my research clearly shows that the British welfare state is an important source of values which are, in diverse ways, conducive to support for CND and an important context for changing, flexible general social attitudes.

37 I discuss the history of the original CND, and the British nuclear programme, in 'CND, the first phase, 1958 to 1965' in Klandermans, 1989. This article contains a bibliography for these issues.

38 The character and origin of the modern state is the subject of a long-running debate in sociology and political science which is complex and often, nowadays, arcane. In this discussion, I am only concerned with the 'dual character' of the *contemporary British* state and I have not considered

it profitable to engage in the wider dispute regarding the state's pedigree. For a decent overview of the main classic themes in the dispute, see David Held's clear and succinct introductory essay (Held, 1983).

Stimulating discussions on the wider political and sociological implications of the 'dual state' are given by Martin Shaw, 'The rise and fall of the military – democratic state: Britain 1940–85', in Creighton and Shaw, 1987, pp. 143–59, and Michael Mann, 'War and social theory: into battle with classes, nations and states', in Creighton and Shaw, 1987, pp. 54–73. See also the valuable set of essays in Shaw, 1984, particularly Mann and Shaw's contributions to this collection.

39 As junior partners in the Manhattan Project, British scientists had not been given full access to the plutonium technology. Right from the start, Britain's civil nuclear project was designed to meet military needs, although this was always denied by Government and nuclear industry spokesmen. However, this linkage has now been acknowledged by Lord Marshall, the Chairman of the Central Electricity Generating Board (speaking on the BBC 2 television programme 'Brass Tacks', broadcast on 16 October 1987, reported in *the Guardian* of 15 October, p. 4). For further discussion of this unholy alliance, see Durrie and Edward's excellent *Fuelling The Nuclear Arms Race* (1982). In my brief discussion of the British nuclear project, I am drawing heavily upon Prof Gowing's comprehensive and detailed study. As the official UKAEA historian, Prof Gowing was granted access to classified documents and her study remains the standard and authorative work. Prof Gowing gives a summary of her conclusions and views in Dilks, 1981.

40 Labour opposition to Bevin's policies was voiced mainly by the 'Keep Left' grouping of MPs, a voice 'silenced less than a year after its formation by the Soviet blockade of West Berlin' (Morgan, 1984, p. 239). A useful collection of essays on Bevin's foreign policies can be found in: Ovendale, 1984.

41 In *Nuclear Weapons: who's in charge?*, Hugh Miall (1987) clearly explores the élite labyrinth of nuclear decision-making. As Miall concludes, in order for these decisions to be open to democratic influence, the present intense secrecy must be changed and the public must be provided with adequate, reliable information. Uninformed democracy is of little real value.

Appendix A

Letter sent to the sample of New Town and Scots City CND members

No. ----

Dear ------- CND member,

I am writing to ask for your help. I am carrying out a study of CND and I would like to talk to you as part of a sample of CND members. I am interested in your views and opinions and your reasons for being a member of the peace movement. Your name was randomly selected for me by your group's Secretaries.

I am writing to ask if you would be prepared to help me with my research by being interviewed. In the interview I would like to ask you some informal questions on your views on CND, disarmament matters and general questions. I would like to interview you sometime between the ------; the interview could take place either at your own home, at your place of work, or at my office. Naturally, I would treat any information you give me as being strictly confidential and my research will be written in such a way as to make it impossible for you to be identified individually.

My research is being carried out with the permission and full knowledge of ---- CND's officers who have drawn up a random sample of members for me. If you would like to help me with my research by being interviewed, please would you fill in Section A overleaf and return this in the enclosed pre-paid envelope. If you decide that you do not wish to be interviewed, please would you score out Section A and return the form blank.

I should perhaps add that I personally support the peace movement and would hope that the findings from my research will be of use to CND and other peace campaigns. It is only by discovering the views of the membership that I can given an accurate portrayal of CND; without the members' co-operation my research will be impossible. If you would like any information about my research, or about the interview, please ring me at the above number or on ------ after 6.00 p.m.

I know that in all likelihood you are a very busy person, but I would be very grateful indeed if you would spare me just a little of your time to ensure that my study of CND is as good and representative as possible,

Yours sincerely,

John Mattausch

Form accompanying letter sent to CND samples of CND members

No. ------

If you would like to be interviewed please fill in Section A and return it in the enclosed pre-paid envelope. If you do not wish to participate in this study, just cross out Section A and return the form blank. If you agree to help me, I will be in touch with you soon to arrange the time and place for your interview.

Name:
Address:
Tel. No.:

Which day of the week, and at what time of day, would be most convenient for the interview?

Would you prefer the interview to be conducted at your own home, at your place of work, or at my office?

Appendix B

Semi-structured interview schedule

Preliminaries

No.:   Name: Age: Sex: M/F
Marital status:

CND and disarmament questions

Do you just belong to ------ CND, or are you a member of National CND as well?

Do you read *Sanity*?

Do you belong to any other organisation which is against nuclear weapons, or any organisation which is against nuclear energy?

When did you first become interested in the peace movement?

What was it, do you think, that made you become interested at that time:

When did you first join -----CND?

How did you find out about -----CND?

(If applicable) Does your wife/husband support the peace movement?

Do you have close friends who also support the peace movement?

(If subject is old enough) Were you a member of the original CND Movement? (If yes) Do you think it was different in any way from the present Movement? (If no) Why was it, do you think, that you didn't join?

What sort of activities have you taken part in, in support of the peace movement (e.g. leafleting, national and local demos. etc.)?

What's the best way that people can protest against nuclear weapons?

Have you been to any of ----- CND's meetings? What do you think of them?

Have you ever held any office, like secretary or treasurer, in CND?
Have you ever taken part in any peace protests where you broke any law? (If yes) How did you feel about taking part in this?
(If no) Would you feel happy about taking part in peace protesting if it meant breaking the law?
Do you think that peace protesting should always be non-violent? Why?
As you may know, CND's official policy is not to be aligned to any political party. Do you think that this is a good policy?
Would you call yourself a pacifist?
Are you interested in, or do you support, campaigns on issues such as poverty in the Third World, or local politics or charities? Do you see any links between these issues and nuclear disarmament?
Why do you think it is that we have a nuclear arms race?
Why do you think it is that the majority of the British public don't belong to the peace movement?
Some people argue that matters of defence are best left to the government. What would you say to this?
Would you say that since joining CND you have become more interested in politics in general?
I don't know whether you've got any opinions on this, but why do you think it was that the original CND movement failed to bring about nuclear disarmament?
Do you think that ----- CND's members are drawn from all walks of life? How about the national Campaign? (Probe)
Some supporters of CND, for example some of the women at Greenham Common, believe that there is a link between nuclear weapons and male attitudes. Do you think there's any truth in this?
Do you believe we will achieve nuclear disarmament?

Employment

Have you got a full-time job? (Probe for details on present employment and work history.)
Are you/were you employed by local government?
If you were completely free to choose, what sort of job would you like? Why?
Would you say that you're happy with the way you have to do (the job), or are there any changes you'd like to see brought about?
Do you/did you feel personally involved with your work?

Can I ask what your parents do/did for a living?
And can I ask what your husband's/wife's job is?

Education

Non-Student
Can I ask what exams you've passed? What subjects were they in?
Did you study for any of these qualifications because you thought
they would help you to get a particular job?

Student
Are you an under/post-graduate?
What are you studying?
Did you choose (subject) because you think it will help you get a
particular job when you leave college/university?
What sort of job do you hope to get when you leave college? Is this
the job you'd want if you were completely free to choose?
(Probe for any work history.)
Would you say that being a student has changed your views in any
way? (Probe for experiences at university.)

Politics and miscellaneous

If a General Election were called tomorrow, which party would you
want to vote for?
Have you ever belonged to a trade-union or a political party? (Probe
for details of activism.)
Can I ask you what you call yourself in political terms?
What about your parents, what would you call them/have called
them in political terms?
Apart from her Government's defence policies, are there any other of
Mrs Thatcher's Government's policies that you strongly agree or
disagree with?
Are your parents supporters of the peace movement? Did they
support the original CND?
And can I ask you about your parents' religious beliefs? Were you
brought up as a (religion)? What would you call yourself now?
Many members of the original Movement believed that the original
Campaign was a moral issue. Do you think that's true today?

Additional questions for office-holders

How long have you been (office)?

What made you become (office)?

Have you ever held a similar office in any other group you've belonged to?

It must mean a lot of work for you. How much of your time does it take up?

Do you think that ----- CND is a successful group? What do you think that ----- CND could do in the future to be more successful?

Thank you very much for your help.

Appendix C

CND and peace movement membership data

This appendix contains data on the membership of CND and peace movement from studies referred to in this book: Parkin (1968), Taylor and Pritchard (1980), Nias (1983), Day and Robbins (1987), from my own two samples, from a piece of research in progress by Nigel West (1985), and from Paul Byrne (1988). The data in this Appendix *cannot* be simply compared; each study employed different methodologies and sampled different groups. The purpose of the Appendix is only to show, where possible, the high profile of those whom Parkin classified as 'welfare/creative' employees. In addition, where possible, the secondary analyses show the educational attainments of the members. As the data is non-comparable, I have concentrated on highlighting 'welfare/creative' occupations, rather than trying to utilise Parkin's somewhat idiosyncratic three-fold classification (which he only applied to male respondents in Social Classes 1–4). This focus highlights the overrepresentation of what I have termed the 'state class' in the membership basis of CND and the peace movement. Further details on the secondary analysis of the data is given in my Doctoral thesis (1986).

I should like to thank Peter Nias, G. Day and R. Robbins for kindly lending me their data for secondary analysis, and the Bradford School of Peace Studies for permitting me to visit their department in order to reanalyse Nias's National Demonstration data. Unfortunately, Parkin's and Taylor and Pritchard's data has been destroyed; in Parkin's case owing to the passage of time, in Taylor and Pritchard's case in order to preserve the confidentiality of their sample. I should also like to thank Richard Taylor for his kind comments on my work and for discussing his research with me; to Nigel West for making his data available to me, and to Paul Byrne for generously providing me with his data prior to the publication of his book.

F. Parkin, (1968), *Middle-Class Radicalism: The Social Bases of CND* (p. 18)

Occupational breakdown of middle-class males

Commercial		Welfare & creative		Other	
Office managers & supervisors	8	Schoolteachers	40	Engineers & draughtsmen	10
Adveristing & sales	8	Clergymen	11	Civil servants & LGOs	9
Accounting & banking	4	Physicians	10	TU & Co-op	7
Company directors	3	Scientists	10	Mature students	2
Self-employed	8	Architects	9		
		Univ. & college lecturers	8		
		Social workers	5		
		Journalists	5		
		Artists/Novelists	3		
		MPs	2		
		Librarians	1		
Total	31		104		28

Note

These are male respondents in Social Classes 1–4 only; the 163 respondents in this group constitute approximately 80% of the male sample: 'Because so many of the female respondents classified themselves as part-time workers it was decided not to include them in the table. However, amongst those who were employed a pattern similar to the male respondents was found – with teaching again being by far the commonest occupation' (Parkin, 1966, p. 421, n. 39).

F. Parkin (1968), *Middle Class Radicalism* (p. 189)

Commercial and non-commercial employment (male respondents)

	Respondents' social class[1]		
	1 + 2	3 + 4	5 + 6 + 7
Commercial, profit-making organisations	19	32	67
Non-commercial, non-profit making organisations and freelance	79	61	31
No response	2	7	2
total	100	100	100
	(N = 53)	(N = 110)	(N = 39)

Note: 1 Hall-Jones scale.

R. Taylor and C. Pritchard (1980), *The Protest Makers: The British Nuclear Disarmament Movement of 1958–1965 Twenty Years On* (p. 149)

N: Committee of 100 (C.100) = 206 (51%), of which 68% male, 32% female
The rest = 197 (49%), of which 62% male, 38% female
Total N = 403

Would you please state your occupation (please be as detailed as you can):

(a) At the time of your involvement with the disarmament movement between 1958 and 1965:							
Social class[1]	1	2	3	4	5	6	7	8
C. 100	5	11	50	24	8	1	1	1
Rest	11	22	46	16	6	0	0	0
(b) Now:								
C.100	24	27	26	7	5	1	1	8
Rest	22	29	24	6	3	0	0	16

Note: 1 Registrar General classifications.

R. Taylor and C. Pritchard (1980), *The Protest Makers* (pp. 149–50)

At what age did you complete full time education?

	13+	15+	16+	18+
C.100	4	16	22	58
Rest	6	12	21	62

Please give details of your educational qualifications (e.g. GCE, Diplomas, Degrees):

	None	'O'Levels	'A'Levels	Diploma & professional	Degree
C.100	12	5	9	22	52
Rest	10	9	9	23	49

P. Nias, (1983), *The Poverty Of Peace Protest: An Analysis of the Recent Rise of the Nuclear Disarmament Movement in Britain.*

CND national membership survey: summer 1982
Method: 'A two-page postal questionnaire and a covering letter were sent to a random sample of the national CND membership in late August 1982. From the 413 sent out, 299, or 72%, replied. This is a good response from a postal survey (which included a s.a.e.). It is a statistically representative sample of just over 1% of the national membership (the sample error on the whole sample is plus or minus 6%). This means that the results can be applied to the national membership as a whole within that safety margin' (Nias, p. 1 of *Survey Report*.)

Mattausch: secondary analysis
Total analysable = 282 (148 male and 134 female)

	Welfare/Creative	Rest	Student/Pupils
Men	64 (43%)	53 (36%)	31 (21%)
Women	70 (52%)	32 (24%)	32 (24%)
Men & women	134 (48%)	85 (30%)	63 (22%)
Men & women: welfare/creative + students/pupils = 70%			

P. Nias, (1983), *The Poverty of Peace Protest*

CND national demonstration survey: London, 6 June 1982
Method: 'A statistically representative random sample of 768 marchers was interviewed by students from Bradford University. Each interviewee wore a CND identification badge signed by Bruce Kent. The three legs of the march were surveyed equally while the march was in progress. There were very few refusals (under 10). The statistical error on the whole sample is plus or minus four per cent which means that the results can be applied to the march as a whole within that safety margin' (Nias, p. 1 of *Survey Report*).

Mattausch: secondary analysis
Total number of questionnaires available for analysis = 755 (387 male, 360 female, 8 unspecified).

	Male (%)	*+ Female (%)*	*= Total (%)*[4]
No occupation given[1]	60	70	130
Analysable	327 (53%)	290 (47%)	617
Welfare & creative	129 (39%)	141 (49%)	270 (44%)
Students[2]	43 (13%)	63 (22%)	106 (17%)
School pupils	20 (6%)	24 (8%)	44 (7%)
Rest[3]	135 (41%)	62 (21%)	197 (32%)

Notes:
1   Questionnaires where no past or present occupations were given. 'Analysable' refers to questionnaires giving past or present jobs; note that the person interviewed may have been unemployed (approximately 13% of total sample) but has given a previous occupation.
2   On the questionnaire this is given as one category ('school/student'). I have classified those marchers aged 16 and under as school pupils, those aged 17–24 as students (figures also include mature students).
3   'Rest' means occupations which do not clearly fall into the 'welfare and creative' category; again, this may include unemployed marchers who gave a previous occupation.
4   Percentages of total analysable questionnaires.

It should be noted that this demonstration was held whilst the Falkland War was in progress and that the demonstration may have attracted those wishing to protest against the government on this issue (88% of the total sample disagreed with 'the British policy on the Falklands issue'). Moreover, these were demonstrators and not necessarily members of national CND or any other peace movement.
Clearly, when conducting a survey of this kind it is unlikely that

those approached will give usefully specific answers regarding their
occupations. Predictably, the sample contains many 'clerks',
'administrators', etc. I have only selected those for the 'welfare and
creative' category where it is clear that they are eligible; it is likely
that more specific answers would have revealed more 'welfare and
creative' workers.

G. Day and D. Robbins, (1987) 'Activists for peace: the social basis
of a local peace movement'

Mattausch: secondary analysis
N = 47, of which 46 analysable (23 male and 23 female)

	Welfare/creative	*Rest*	*Student*
Male	15	7	1
Female	10	10	3

Higher Education/professional qualification[1]

Male	22
Female	20

Note: 1 Includes students.

J. Mattausch, (1986), *A Commitment To Campaign*

New Town sample
N = 20 (14 female, 6 male)

	Welfare/creative	Rest	Student
Male	2	4	0
Female	8	6	0

Higher education/professional qualifications

Male	1
Female	8

Scots City sample

N = 42 (19 male, 23 female)

	Welfare/ creative	Rest	Student
Male	11	7	1
Female	17	4	2

Higher education/professional qualifications[1]

Male	15
Female	18

Note: 1 Includes students.

N. West, (1985), *research in progress*

Survey of people travelling to the national CND demonstration, London, 26 October 1985
The survey was completed by people on six coaches travelling from Bradford, Leeds, Norwich, Retford/Doncaster and Sheffield.
N = 241
Female = 60%; male = 39%; nk = 1%
Occupation

Teacher/lecturer	13%
Other public sector non-manual	14%
Private sector non-manual	7%
Public sector manual	3%
Private sector manual	2%
Self-employed	4%
Student	39%
Unwaged childcare	3%
Registered unemployed	12%
Retired	2%
Other	1%

Educational Qualifications

Higher education (eg degree, Cert. Ed., CQSW)	52%
To 'A' level	14%
To 'O' level, and still studying	13%
To 'O' level	8%
To CSE	1%
None, but still studying	10%
None	2%

P. Byrne, (1988), *The Campaign for Nuclear Disarmament*

Method: '. . . a sample survey was undertaken at the end of 1985.
This comprised a postal questionnaire sent to a randomly generated
1% of the national membership, which produced a response rate of
around 65%' (p. 55).

CND Members: past or present occupations %

	All	*Men*	*Women*
Education	25	20	28
Other professional	22	27	17
Caring	13	10	15
Scientific	3	5	2
All middle class	63	62	62
Skilled manual	15	16	14
Manual	4	4	4
Unemployed/retired	4	4	4
No response	14	14	16
Total	100	100	100
N =	620	310	306

Source: Byrne, 1988, p. 60.
Bryne also found that 'In 1985, 57% of respondents held either a degree or
diploma; only 15% completed their education at or before the age of 16' (p.
58).

Bibliography

Acland, Sir Richard (1940), *Unser Kampf (Our Struggle)*, Penguin, Harmondsworth.

Acland, Sir Richard (1914), *The Forward March*, Allen & Unwin, London.

Addison, P. (1975), *The Road to 1945*, Jonathan Cape, London.

Ambrose, S. E. (1977), *Rise to Globalism: American Foreign Policy, 1938–1976* (The Pelican History of the United States 8), Penguin, Harmondsworth.

The Archives of CND (1981–85), 'The Left in Britain: Part 5', Harvester Microfilm, Sussex.

Arrowsmith, P. (1983), *Jericho*, Heretic Books, London.

Atkinson, M. and Heritage, J. (1984), *Structures of Social Action: Studies in Conversational Analysis*, (Studies in Emotion and Social Interaction), Cambridge University Press, Cambridge.

Attlee, the Rt. Hon. C. R. (1954), *As It Happened*, Heinemann, London.

Aya, R. and Miller, N. (1971), *The New American Revolution*, Free Press, New York.

Ayer, A. J. (1985), *Wittgenstein*, Weidenfeld & Nicolson, London.

Baker, B. (1981), *The Far Left*, Weidenfield & Nicolson, London.

Bartlett, P. (1983), 'The Nuclear Disarmament Movement', unpublished M.Sc. thesis, University of Strathclyde, Dept. of Politics.

Bartley III, W. W. (1974), *Wittgenstein*, Quartet Books, London.

Bayliss, J. (ed.) (1977), *British Defence Policy in a Changing World*, Croom Helm, London.

Becker, H. S. (1960), 'Notes on the concept of commitment', *American Journal of Sociology*, 66, pp. 32–40.

Blackwood, C. (1984), *On The Perimeter*, Flamingo, London.

Bloor, D. (1983), *Wittgenstein: A Social Theory of Knowledge*, Macmillan, London.

Bolsover, P. (1982), *Civil Defence: The Cruellest Confidence Trick*, CND Pamphlet, London.

Boulton, D. (1964), *Voices From The Crowd Against The H-Bomb*, Peter Owen, London.

Bradshaw, R., Gould, D., and Jones, C. (eds.) (1981), *From Protest to Resistance*, Mushroom/Peace News, London.

Brand, G. (1979), *The Central Texts of Wittgenstein*, Basil Blackwell, Oxford.

Brockway, F. (1963), *Outside The Right*, Allen & Unwin, London.

Bulmer, R. (1973), 'Why the cassowary is not a bird', in Douglas, M. (ed.), *Rules and Meanings*, Penguin, Harmondsworth.

Byrd, P. (1985), 'The development of the peace movement in Britain', in Kaltefleiter, W. and Pfaltzgraft, R. L. (eds.), *The Peace Movement in Europe and the United States*, Croom Helm, London.

Byrne, P. (1988), *The Campaign for Nuclear Disarmament*, Croom Helm, London.

Calder, A. (1969), *The People's War*, Jonathan Cape, London.

Call to Women (Newsletter) (mid-October 1964), *Call To Women*, London.

Cameron, J. (1969), *Point Of Departure*, Panther Books, London.

Capitanchk, D. and Eichenberg, R. C. (1983), *Defence and Public Opinion* (Chatham House Papers 20), Routledge & Kegan Paul, London.

Chalmers, M. (1985), *Paying For Defence: Military Spending and British Decline*, Pluto Press, London.

Chappell, V. C. (1964), *Ordinary Language: Essays in Philosophical Method* (Contemporary Perspectives In Philosophy Series), Prentice-Hall, New York.

Chappell, V. C. (ed.) (1962), *The Philosophy of Mind*, Prentice-Hall, New York.

Chatfield, C. (ed.) (1973), *Peace Movements In America*, Schocken Books, New York.

Cherry, N. (1975), 'Occupation values and employment', *Higher Education* 4, pp. 357.

Churchill, Sir Winston S. (1948 and 1954), *The Second World War*, Vol. 1 *The Gathering Storm* and Vol. VI *Triumph And Tragedy*, Cassell & Co. Ltd, London.

Clark, C. (1963), *Second Wind: A History of CND*, Campaign Caravan Workshop (CND Pamphlet), London.

Clarke, M. and Mowlem, M. (eds.) (1982), *Debate on Disarmament*, Routledge & Kegan Paul, London.

Coates, D. (1984), *The Context of British Politics*, Hutchinson, London.

Collins, Rev. Canon L. J. (1966), *Faith Under Fire*, Leslie Frewin, London.

The Committee For The Compilation Of Materials On Damage Caused By The Atomic Bombs In Hiroshima And Nagasaki (1981), *Hiroshima And Nagasaki*, Hutchinson, London.

Cotgrove, S. (1982), *Catastrophe or Cornucopia*, John Wiley & Sons, Chichester.

Cotgrove, S. and Duff, A., 1980, 'Environmentalism, middle class radicalism and politics', *Sociological Review*, XXCIII, pp. 240–56.

Cox, J. (1981), *Overkill*, Penguin, Harmondsworth.

Creighton, C. and Shaw, M. (eds.) (1987), *The Sociology of War and Peace*, Macmillan, London.

Dando, M. R. and Newman, B. R. (eds.) (1982), *Nuclear Deterrence: Implications and Policy Options for the 1980s*, Castle House Publications Ltd, London.

Davenport, H. (1982), 'Women at the wire', *Observer*, 12 December, pp. 10–13.

Davidson, D. (1963), 'Actions, reasons and causes', *Journal of Philosophy*, 60, LX, No. 23, pp. 685–700.

Day, G. and Robbins, R., 'Activists for peace: the social basis of a local peace movement', in C. Creighton and M. Shaw (eds.) (1987), *The Sociology of War and Peace*, Macmillan, London.

Defence without the Bomb: The Report of the Alternative Defence Commission (1982), Taylor & Francis, London.

Dilks, D. (ed.) (1981), *Retreat from Power: Studies in Britain's Foreign Policy of the Twentieth Century*, 2, After 1939, Macmillan, London.

Douglas, M. (ed.) (1973), *Rules and Meanings*, Penguin, Harmondsworth.

Downs, A. (1972), 'Up and down with the ecology; the issue-attention cycle', *The Public Interest*, 28.

Dray, W. R. (1957), *Laws and Explanations in History*, Oxford University Press, Oxford.

Driver, C. (1964), *The Disarmers: A Study in Protest*, Hodder & Stoughton, London.

Duff, A. and Cotgrove, S. (1982), 'Social values and the choice of careers', *Journal of Occupational Psychology*, 55, pp. 97–107.

Duff, P. (1971), *Left Left Left*, Allison& Busby, London.

Durrie, E. and Edwards, R. (1982), *Fuelling the Nuclear Arms Race*, Pluto Press, London.

Easton, S. M. (1983), *Humanistic Marxism and Wittgensteinian Social Philosophy*, Manchester University Press, Manchester.

Edwards, D. V. (1962), 'The Movement For Unilateral Nuclear Disarmament in Britain', unpublished B.A. thesis, Swathmore College, USA.

Fay, B. (1980), *Social Theory and Political Practice*, (Controversies in Sociology), Allen & Unwin, London.

Freedman, L. (1980), *Britain and Nuclear Weapons*, Macmillan, London.

Freedman, L. (1983), *The Evolution of Nuclear Strategy*, Macmillan (published in association with The International Institute for Strategic Studies), London.

'General Secretary's Report to the 1980 Annual Conference' (1981–5), *The Archives of CND*, Harvester Microfilm, 'The Left in Britain; Part 5', reel 19, C19/68 – 276/7.

Gerd, B. (1979), *The Central Texts of Wittgenstein*, Basil Blackwell, Oxford.

Gowing, Prof. M. (1964), *Britain and Atomic Energy 1939–1945*, Macmillan, London.

Gowing, Prof. M. (1974), *Independence and Deterrence: Britain and Atomic Energy, 1945–1952 – Volume 1: Policy Making; Volume 2: Policy Execution*, Macmillan, London.

Graham, A., (1982), *It's not your Duty to Die: Nuclear Disarmament and the Birth of Protest*, Independent Labour Publications, London.

Greene, O. (1983), *Europe's Folly: The Facts and Arguments about Cruise*, CND Publications, London.

Greer, H. (1964), *Mud Pie: The CND Story*, Max Parrish, London.

Groom, A. J. R. (1974), *British Thinking about Nuclear Weapons*, Frances Pinter, London.

Harford, B. and Hopkins, S. (1984), *Greenham Common: Women at the Wire*, The Women's Press Ltd, London.

Held, D. *et al.* (1983), *States and Societies*, Martin Robertson in association with The Open University, Oxford.

Heritage, J. (1984a), *Garfinkel and Ethnomethodology*, Polity Press, Cambridge.

Heritage, J. (1984b), *Recent Developments in Conversations Analysis*, Warwick Working Papers in Sociology, Warwick University.

Hersey, J. (1946), *Hiroshima*, Penguin, Harmondsworth.

Horrie, C. (1983), 'Win some, lose some', *Sanity*, No. 7, pp. 5–6.

Janik, A. and Toumlin, S. (1973), *Wittgenstein's Vienna*, Simon & Schuster, New York.

Jenkins, M. (1979), *Bevanism: Labour's High Tide*, Spokesman, London.

Jenkins, R. (1967), 'Who are these marchers?', *Journal Of Peace Research*, 4, pp. 46–59.

Johnson-Laird, P. N. and Watson, P. C. (1977), *Thinking*, Cambridge University Press, Cambridge.

Jones, L. (1984), 'Changing ideas of authority', *New Statesman*, 30 November, pp. 8–9.

Jungk, R. (1958), *Brighter than a Thousand Suns*: A Personal History of the Atomic Scientists, Harcourt, Brace & World, New York.

Kaldor, M. (1982), *The Baroque Arsenal*, André Deutsch, London.

Kaldor, M. and Smith, D. (eds.) (1982), *Disarming Europe*, Merlin Press, London.

Kaltefleiter, W. and Pfaltzgraff, R. L. (eds.) (1985), *The Peace Movements in Europe and the United States*, Croom Helm, London.

Keane, J. (1984), 'Civil society and the peace movement in Britain', *Thesis II*, VIII, pp. 5–22.

Kelvin, R. P. (1963), (readers' questionnaire survey), *New Society*, 9 May, pp. 8–14; 16 May, pp. 11–15; 23 May, pp. 9–13.

Kent, B., Williams, F. and Gray, R. (1977), *Christians and Nuclear Disarmament*, CND Pamphlet, London.

King-Hall, Sir Stephen (1958), *Defence in the Nuclear Age*, Victor Gollancz, London.

Klandermans, B. (ed.) (1989), *Peace Movements in an International Perspective*, JAI Press, Amsterdam.

Lamb, D. (1980), 'The philosophy of praxis in Marx and Wittgenstein', *The Philosophical Forum*, XI, pp. 273–98.

Leahy, W. D. (1950), *I Was There*, Victor Gollancz, London.

London Edinburgh Weekend Return Group (1979), *In and against the State*, Conference of Socialist Economists, pamphlet, London.

Luckhardt, C. G. (ed.) (1979), *Wittgenstein: Sources and Perspectives*, Harvester Press, Sussex.

McFarlane, L. J. (1966), 'Disobedience and the Bomb', *Political quarterly* October/December, pp. 366–77.

Mackenzie, D. (1983), 'Understanding militarism', *Capital and Class*, 19, Spring 1983, pp. 33–73.

Magee, B. (1975), *Popper*, (Modern Masters), Fontana, Glasgow.

Malcolm, N. (1958), *Ludwig Wittgenstein, a Memoir*, Oxford University Press, Oxford.

Malcolm, N. (1967), *Dreaming*, (Studies in Philosophical Psychology), Routledge & Kegan Paul, London.

Mallaliev, J. P. W. (1958), 'The dogs of peace', *New Statesman*, LV, No. 1406, p. 220.

Mandel, E. (1983) 'The threat of war and the struggle for Socialism', *New Left Review*, No. 141, September/October, pp. 23–50.

Mann, M. (1987), 'War and social theory: into battle with classes, nations and states', in Creighton, C. and Shaw, M. (eds.) (1987), *The Sociology of War and Peace*, Macmillan, London.

Manser, A. R. (1981), *The End of Philosophy*, University of Southampton, pamphlet.

Martin, K. (1963), 'Where to from Aldermaston?', *New Statesman*, 63, pp. 588–90.

Marwick, A. (1968), *Britain in the Century of Total War*, Penguin, Harmondsworth.

Mattausch, J. (1985), 'The Peace Phoenix: will the revived CND fail again?', *Natur och Somhalle*, Sweden, II, No. 33.

Mattausch, J. 'The sociology of CND', in Creighton, C. and Shaw, M. (eds.) (1987), *The Sociology of War and Peace*, Macmillan, London.

Mattausch, J., CND: the first wave, 1958–65' and Byrne, P., 'CND: the second wave', both in: B. Klandermans, (1989), *Peace Movements in an International Perspective*, JAI Press, Holland.

Maxwell Atkinson, J. and Heritage, J. (eds.) (1984), *Structures of Social Action: Studies in Conversation Analysis*, Cambridge University Press, Cambridge.

Miall, H. (1987), *Nuclear Weapons: Who's in Charge?* Macmillan, London.

Minnion, J. and Bolsover, P. (eds.) (1983), *The CND Story*, Allison

& Busby, London.

Moncrieff, A. (1967), 'The rise and fall of CND', *The Listener*, 77, pp. 385–7.

Morgan, K. O. (1984), *Labour in Power, 1945–1951*, Clarendon Press, Oxford.

Morgan, K. O. (1985), 'How good was the Attlee Government?', *New Society*, Vol. 67, No. 1109, pp. 286–8.

Myers, F. E. (1965), 'British peace politics: the Campaign for Nuclear Disarmament and the Committee of 100, 1957–1962', unpublished B. Phil. thesis, Columbia University.

Nias, P. (1982), *END Supporters' Survey Report: CND National Membership Survey 1982; London Demo. 6 June 1982 Survey Report*, Research Surveys, Telford.

Nias, P. (1983), 'The poverty of peace protest', unpublished M.A. thesis, Bradford University Postgraduate School in Peace Studies.

Nias, P. (1985), 'The poverty of peace protest', unpublished paper presented at the British Sociological Association Annual Conference, Hull University, April.

'Nuclear weapons' (1958) (Letter from the Paddington Council for the Abolition of Nuclear Weapons Tests), *New Statesman*, LV, No. 1401, p. 73.

Nuttall, J. (1970), *Bomb Culture*, Paladin, London.

Ovendale, R. (ed.) (1984), *The Foreign Policy of the Labour Governments 1945–51*, Leicester University Press.

Overy, B. (1982), *How Effective are Peace Movements?*, Housemans, London.

Parkin, F., (1966), 'A study of the campaign for Nuclear Disarmament: the social bases of a political mass movement', Ph.D. thesis, Faculty of Arts, University of London.

Parkin, F. (1968), *Middle-Class Radicalism: The Social Bases of CND*, Manchester University Press, Manchester.

Pears, D., (1971), *Wittgenstein*, Fontana, Glasgow.

Pierre, A. J. (1972), *Nuclear Politics: The British Experience with an Independent Strategic Force 1939–1970*, Oxford University Press, Oxford.

Popper, Sir K., 'The autonomy of sociology', in D. Miller (ed.), (1983), *A Pocket Popper*, Fontana, Oxford.

Popper, Sir K. (1972), *The Poverty of Historicism*, Routledge & Kegan Paul, London.

Priestley, J. B. (1950), *The Plays of J. B. Priestley, Vol. 3*,

Heinemann, London.

Priestley, J. B. (1957), 'Britain and the nuclear bombs', *New Statesman*, LIV, pp. 554–6.

The Report of the Alternative Defence Commission (1982), *Defence without the Bomb*, Taylor & Francis, London.

The Report of a working party under the chairmanship of the Bishop of Salisbury (1983), *The Church and the Bomb: Nuclear Weapons and Christian Conscience*, Hodder & Stoughton, London.

Rex, J. (1963), 'The sociology of CND', *Encounter*, 1, pp. 47–55.

Richards, V. (1981), *Protest without illusions*, Freedom Press, London.

Rigby, A. (1968), 'The British Peace Movement and its members', unpublished M.A. dissertation, University of Essex.

Rogers, Dr P., Dando, Dr M. and Dungen, Dr P. van den (eds.) (1981), *As Lambs to the Slaughter: The Facts about Nuclear War*, Arrow Books in association with ECOROPA, London.

Rosch, E. (1977), 'Linguistic relativity', in Johnson-Laird and Watson, P., *Thinking*, Cambridge University Press, Cambridge.

Rosenberg, M., (1957), *Occupations and Values*, Glencoe, The Free Press, III.

Rubinstein, D. (1981), *Marx and Wittgenstein: Social Praxis and Social Explanation*, Routledge & Kegan Paul, London.

Ruddock, J. (1983), 'CND and the General Election: the obscured choice', *Sanity*, No. 7, July, p. 3.

Russell, B. (1969), *The Autobiography of Bertrand Russell: Vol. 3, 1944–1967*, Allen & Unwin, London.

Ryle, M. H. (1981), *The Politics of Nuclear Disarmament*, Pluto Press, London.

Rootes, C., 1984, 'Protest, social movements, revolution?', *Social Alternatives*, 14, p. 5.

Shaw, M. (ed.) (1984), *War, State and Society*, Macmillan, London.

Shaw, M. (1987), 'The rise and fall of the military-democratic state: Britain 1940–85', in Creighton, C. and Shaw, M. (eds.) (1987), *The Sociology of War and Peace*, Macmillan, London.

Sked, A. and Cook, C. (1983), *Post-War Britain, A Political History*, Pelican, Harmondsworth.

Skelhorn, A. (1986), 'The emergence of protest: British opposition to nuclear weapons in the 1950s', unpublished paper given at the Conflict Research Society Conference on Peace Movements, London, 17 May 1986.

Snow, C. P. (1971), *The New Men*, Penguin, Harmondsworth.

'Social protest' (Special Report) (1984), *Social Alternatives*, 4, No. 1.

'Social workers and nuclear weapons', letter (1959), *New Statesman* (57), LVII, No. 1476, p. 895.

Southall, T. and Atkinson, J. (undated, *c*. 1981), *CND 1958–65: Lessons of the First Wave*, 'A Socialist Challenge Pamphlet'.

Spiller, R., (1983), 'CND and the General Election: making disarmament the issue', *Sanity*, No. 6, June, pp. 10–11.

Taylor, A. J. P. (1983), 'CND the first 25 years', *Observer*, 29 February, pp. 13–14.

Taylor, R. (1983a), 'The British Nuclear Disarmament Movement of 1958/65 and its legacy to the Left', unpublished Ph.D., Dept. of Politics, University of Leeds, March.

Taylor, R. (1983b), 'The British Peace Movement and Socialist change', *The Socialist Register*, Merlin Press, London.

Taylor, R. (1984), 'The British Peace Movement and the New Left, 1950–1980', *Social Alternatives* (Australia), IV.

Taylor, R. (1986), 'The British Peace Movement and radical change: problems of agency', unpublished paper presented at the Conflict Research Society Conference on Peace Movements, London, 17 May.

Taylor, R. (1988), *Against the Bomb: the British Peace Movement, 1958–65*, Oxford University Press, Oxford.

Taylor, R. and Pritchard, C. (1978), *Social Work, Reform or Revolution?*, Routledge & Kegan Paul (Library of Social Work), London.

Taylor, R. and Pritchard, C. (1980), *The Protest Makers: the British Disarmament Movement of 1958–1965 Twenty Years on*, Pergamon Press, Oxford.

Taylor, R. and Young, N. (eds.) (1988), *The British Peace Movement*, Manchester University Press, Manchester.

Thomas, S. (1985), 'Why they break the law in order to keep the peace', *Guardian*, 26 January, p. 5.

Thompson, D. (1983), *Over our Dead Bodies*, Virago, London.

Thompson, E. P. (1982), *Beyond the Cold War*, Merlin Press with END, London.

Thompson, E. P. (1983), *The Defence of Britain*, CND and END pamphlet, London.

Thompson, E. P. and Smith, D. (eds.) (1980), *Protest and Survive*, (a Penguin Special) Penguin, Harmondsworth.

Upward, E. (1979), *No Home but the Struggle*, Quartet Books, London.

Vernon, R. (1981), *Protest without illusions*, Freedom Press, London.

Walker, I. (1980), 'With the peace protestors', *New Society*, 53, No. 920, pp. 12–14.

Warnock, G. J. (1958), *English Philosophy since 1900*, Oxford University Press, Oxford.

Webber, R. *et al.* (1983), *Crisis over Cruise*, (a Penguin Special) Penguin, Harmondsworth.

Widgery, D. (1976), *The Left in Britain*, Penguin, Harmondsworth.

Wilkinson, P. (1971), *Social Movement*, Macmillan, London.

Williams, F. (1961), *A Prime Minister Remembers*, Heinemann, London.

Williams, P. (1984), *The Nuclear Debate: Issues and Politics*, (Chatham House Special Paper), Routledge & Kegan Paul, London.

Wilson, A. (1983), *The Disarmers' Handbook*, Penguin, Harmondsworth.

Wittgenstein, L. (1979), *On Certainty*, Basil Blackwell, Oxford.

Wittgenstein, L. (1980), *The Blue and Brown Books*, Basil Blackwell, Oxford.

Wittgenstein, L. (1983), *Philosophical Investigations*, Basil Blackwell, Oxford.

Women's Peace Camp (Newsletter) (1983), publisher unknown, pamphlet produced by Greenham Common Women, February.

Yergin, D. (1978), *Shattered Peace*, André Deutsch, London.

Young, N. (1977), *An Infantile Disorder? The Crisis and Decline of the New Left*, Routledge & Kegan Paul, London.

Index